THE TABULA OF CEBES

Society of Biblical Literature

TEXTS AND TRANSLATIONS
GRAECO-ROMAN RELIGION SERIES

edited by
Hans Dieter Betz
Edward N. O'Neil

Texts and Translations 24
Graeco-Roman Religion Series 7

THE TABULA OF CEBES

by
John T. Fitzgerald
and
L. Michael White

THE TABULA OF CEBES

by John T. Fitzgerald
and L. Michael White

Scholars Press
Chico, California

THE TABULA OF CEBES

by
John T. Fitzgerald
and
L. Michael White

PA
3948
.C2
A24
1983

Copyright 1983

The Society of Biblical Literature

Library of Congress Cataloging in Publication Data

Kebētos Thēbaiou pinax.
  The Tabula of Cebes.

  (Graeco-Roman religion series ; 7) (Texts and transla-
tions ; 24)
  English and Greek.
  Bibliography: p.
  Includes index.
  1.Cebes, of Thebes. II. Fitzgerald, John T., 1948–
III. White, L. Michael. IV. Title. V. Series. VI. Series:
Texts and translations ; no. 24.
PA3948.C2A24   1983   883'.01   82–19118
ISBN 0–89130–601–3

In keeping with the spirit of the *Tabula*,
this work is dedicated to the Personification of

'Εγκράτεια   and   Καρτερία:

to

Karol   and   Gloria

and to their daughters,
Kirstin, Kimberly, and Jessica.

JOHN T. FITZGERALD is a member of the Department of Religion at the University of Miami in Coral Gables, Florida. He came to the University of Miami from Yale University where he was a graduate student in the Department of Religious Studies and instructor in Greek at Yale Divinity School. His dissertation is an investigation of the *peristasis* catalogues in Paul's Corinthian correspondence. In addition to his expertise in the field of New Testament studies, he is interested in pre-Talmudic Judaism and Hellenistic philosophy.

L. MICHAEL WHITE is Assistant Professor of Religion at Oberlin College in the fields of Biblical Studies and Early Christianity. He has also taught at Yale University and Indiana University. He holds a B.A. in Greek and Latin and an M.A. in Ancient Church History from Abilene Christian University, and graduated magna cum laude from Yale Divinity School with the degree of Master of Divinity. He earned his Ph.D from Yale; his primary area of research is in the social world of early Christianity, including studies in Diaspora Judaism and Graeco-Roman religion and culture.

TABLE OF CONTENTS

PLATE I: Depiction of the *Tabula*. Drawing of a relief fragment.

The old man in the center is the Daimon. He is giving
instructions to those on his left. These are identified
by the inscription below the Daimon's feet as "those
entering into Life." On the Daimon's right sits Deceit,
who is giving her potion of ignorance and error to the
young man as he enters into Life. Above Deceit is Tychē
standing on a ball. Those on Tychē's left are begging
for her gifts, while those on her right have already
received them. The identity of the figure standing
above the wall, at the place where BIOC (Life) is written,
is debated. C. Robert identifies the figure as a male
personification of Life. K. K. Müller understands it as
a female personification of Paideia, with a socle between
her legs. The identity of the other figures is likewise
disputed. A full discussion by Müller and Robert is
available in the *Archäologische Zeitung* 42 (1884) 115-30,
from which this drawing of a relief fragment is taken.
The drawing itself is preserved in the Kupfertischkabinet
of Berlin.

This project began innocently enough as an exercise
for two new graduate students at Yale under the direction
of Abraham J. Malherbe of the Divinity School and Heinrich
von Staden of the Classics Department. It was intended to
provide primary sources for the comparison of early Christian ethical language and literature with that of the
Hellenistic moral philosophers. After those initial, crude
and unassuming forays into the text we began to recognize
the broader value of the *Tabula of Cebes* for current study.
It became increasingly apparent to us that only a few
scholars today know the *Tabula* firsthand, and there is no
modern English translation whatsoever. In part, it seems
that the *Tabula* has been perceived as a "common" and therefore uninteresting example of the moralist tradition. Yet
it is precisely this feature that makes it interesting to
us. Because it consciously employs so many of the commonplaces of the moralist tradition, it is a veritable compen-
dium of popular philosophical morals and ethical terminology from the first century C.E.

We wish to express our appreciation to several people
who assisted us in the course of this project, especially
Professors Von Staden and Malherbe who started us on the
way. Professor Malherbe especially acted as our very own
Daimon guiding us at every turn along the way. We also
wish to thank those who had a hand in reading the translation at various stages along the way: Wayne A. Meeks, Carl
R. Holladay, and Everett Ferguson. A special thanks goes
to Miss Cora E. Lutz, who has been working on this literature for a number of years and most recently on the manuscript tradition of the *Tabula*, for her reading of the
translation. For the careful editorial work in reading and
providing constructive criticism for the final version of
the manuscript, we offer our appreciation to Professors
Betz and O'Neil. This project has grown and blossomed over

the years (at times it seems that it followed us around like personified Vices out of the *Tabula* itself) thanks to the care and direction of these individuals. Finally, we wish to give special attention to two people whose assistance in putting the manuscript into production has been indispensable: Ms. Maureen Frances Cunningham of the Religious Studies Department at Yale University and Ms. Joann Burnich of Scholars Press.

John T. Fitzgerald
University of Miami
Coral Gables, FL

L. Michael White
Oberlin College
Oberlin, OH

October 1, 1982

INTRODUCTION

The *Tabula* was once an immensely popular work. In 1522, less than thirty years after the appearance of the *editio princeps*, the *Tabula* was already popular enough for a woodcut illustrating it to be used for the title page of the third edition of Erasmus' New Testament.[1] In the course of the following centuries its popularity continued to grow as the work was translated into at least ten modern languages.[2] It attracted the attention of authors such as Milton[3] and Leibnitz[4] and of artists such as Holbein the Younger[5] and Bosch.[6] The *Tabula* may even have served as one of the sources of Bunyan's *Pilgrim's Progress*.[7] Indeed, the *Tabula* itself has often been referred to as a "proto-*Pilgrim's Progress*."[8]

In the 20th century, however, interest in the *Tabula* has dwindled considerably. The work is no longer well-known (except by secondary allusion)[9] and important treatments of it are often inaccessible. For these reasons it will be useful to review briefly some of the major issues that have emerged in the history of the modern study of the *Tabula*.

Authorship and Date of Composition

The *Tabula* traditionally has been attributed to Cebes of Thebes. This Cebes had studied with the Pythagorean philosopher Philolaus before coming to Athens and becoming a member of the Socratic circle (Plato, *Phaedo* 61DE). A man of some wealth (*Phaedo* 78A), he is said to have purchased the slave Phaedo and given him the opportunity to study philosophy (Aulus Gellius, *Noctes Atticae* II.18.4). He was prepared, moreover, to use his funds to help Socrates escape from prison (Plato, *Criton* 45B). He is characterized in the *Phaedo* as an astute person who is not easily convinced by arguments (63A). Indeed, as "the most obstinately

1

incredulous of mortals" (77A)[10] Cebes forces Socrates to
argue more persuasively for the immortality of the soul.
Cebes' own arguments are so incisive that he raises consid-
erable doubt concerning the soundness of Socrates' position
(88C). When Cebes is finally convinced by Socrates, the
veracity of the latter's thesis is thereby established.

    Later antiquity thus remembered him above all as the
noble and devoted disciple of Socrates (Xenophon, *Memora-*
bilia I.2.48) with whom he had discussed the soul's immortality (Pseudo-Plato, *Ep.* 13 [363A]; Pseudo-Socratic *Ep.*
14.7). His additional distinction as the author of the
Tabula was firmly established by the first half of the
third century C.E. (Diogenes Laertius II.125).[11] This tradition was reaffirmed in the medieval period by the *Suda*[12]
and in the Renaissance by numerous scholars, editors, and
scribes.[13]

    While generally defended until the end of the 18th
century, the authenticity of the document was increasingly
called into doubt, first by Hieronymous Wolf in 1561,[14] and
then by a series of scholars whose views were summarized
and evaluated by Christoph Meiners in 1782.[15]

    In the 19th century the debate concerning authenticity
continued. The traditional view was reaffirmed in the
first edition of Pauly's *Real-Encyclopaedie* by C. F. Baehr.[1]
Others who continued to maintain this position included F.
Lécluse and A. Frigell.[17] Two variations of the traditional
view were also presented. First, Klopfer argued that our
present *Tabula* not only contains interpolations but is, in
fact, a revision of an older work. This revision, moreover,
was accomplished from a Socratic and Platonic perspective.[18]
A second variation of the traditional view was the position
that the description of the tablet in chapters 1-32 stems
from Theban Cebes but that the concluding dialogue (especially chapters 36-41) is by a later hand.[19]

    The admission of interpolations and the recourse to
theories of revision and addition indicate the difficulty
of maintaining the view that Cebes is the author of the

Tabula in its present form. The more important objections to this view are as follows.

(1) The mention of the Peripatetics in 13.2 is an obvious anachronism and cannot derive from a period earlier than Aristotle and his school.

(2) Neither of the two known teachers of Cebes--Philolaus nor Socrates--is cited as an authority in the document. It is only Cebes' fellow-student Plato who is so cited (33.3) and the source of this quotation is apparently *Leges* 808DE. But this work comes from the latest period of Plato's literary activity and it is most dubious that Cebes would have been alive at this time.

(3) The earliest *possible* citation of the *Tabula* that we possess occurs in the orations of Dio Chrysostom in the first century C.E. The earliest *certain* reference to the *Tabula* is made by Lucian of Samosata in the second century. That is, more than four centuries separate Cebes of Thebes from the first allusions to the *Tabula*. It is extremely improbable that such a document would have remained uncited for so long a time if it had been in existence during this period.

These objections and others[20] could, however, only make it unlikely that the *Tabula* is the work of Theban Cebes and indicate that the present work contains interpolations. The convincing demonstration that the work as a whole derives from a time subsequent to Cebes had yet to be given. Such a proof was begun by F. Drosihn, established by K. Praechter, and confirmed by R. Joly. To his 1871 edition of the *Tabula* Drosihn appended a list of nearly seventy words and phrases found in the *Tabula*, with the earliest known instance of their use by an ancient author. His intention in so doing was to call attention to a number of late words and classical words used with nonclassical meanings. This lexical evidence would then point to a period later than the classical for the composition of the *Tabula*.[21]

Karl Praechter in his 1885 dissertation continued this
line of investigation, correcting a number of Drosihn's er-
rors and expanding the list of late words and usages. On
the basis of the nonclassical vocabulary employed in the
Tabula Praechter argued that the most likely date of composition was the first century C.E. According to Praechter'
analysis, for example, twenty-three words in the *Tabula* occur for the first time after Polybius (second century B.C.E.
and half of these in either the first century B.C.E. or the
first century C.E.[22]

Robert Joly has now confirmed Praechter's overall analysis of the language of the *Tabula*. He corrects Praechter
at only a few points and supplements Praechter's evidence.
On the basis of the vocabulary, syntax, use of the perfect
tense, optative mood and particles, Joly shows that the
Tabula is a good specimen of Koine Greek.[23]

There is then every reason to believe that the *Tabula*
is a Hellenistic work and on this point there is virtual
unanimity among contemporary scholars. Differences emerge
only when a more precise dating is attempted. Praechter,
as already noted, preferred the first century C.E. and this
is the date most frequently given in the secondary literature.[24] Some scholars, however, prefer an earlier date
while others assign it to the second century C.E. Franz
Susemihl, for example, considers the linguistic results of
Praechter's analysis to be inconclusive owing to the paucity of prose works from the period of Polybius. He assigns the *Tabula* to the third century B.C.E. and appeals to
the points of contact with other pseudo-Socratic dialogues
of this period.[25] Drosihn and Th. Sinko, on the other hand,
prefer a date closer to the *terminus ante quem* of Lucian.[26]

In summary, then, the vast majority of scholars would
prefer to assign the work to the period of the early Empire,
that is, sometime in the period from Augustus to Domitian.
That the author was a disciple of Musonius Rufus or at
least contemporary with him is a possibility suggested by
several scholars.[27]

Attribution to Cebes of Thebes

If the *Tabula* is a composition of the Hellenistic period,[28] then how is the uncontested attribution to Cebes of Thebes to be explained? At least three theories have been advanced to answer this question. The first and simplest explanation is that the work was intentionally pseudonymous.[29] The *Tabula* would then be one of the numerous compositions written in the name of the various disciples of Socrates. The twentieth pseudo-Socratic epistle, for example, probably depicts Cebes and Simmias writing to Antisthenes in Athens and praising the latter for his perseverance. They are represented as handing on to the Theban youths the words they heard from Socrates. In the twenty-second pseudo-Socratic epistle they are depicted as recipients of a letter of Xenophon. This theory can, therefore, appeal to the pseudo-Socratic writings in general and the pseudo-Cebes correspondence in particular.

The difficulty with this explanation is that there is nothing in the *Tabula* itself that would serve to establish this fiction.[30] The characters are all anonymous, the setting is left unspecified, and no explicit attempt is made to connect the teaching of the *Tabula* with that expounded by Socrates.

For these reasons several scholars reject the theory of intentional or primary pseudonymity and offer an explanation in terms of homonymy. According to this theory the *Tabula* would have been composed originally by a person named Cebes but in the course of time was falsely attributed to Cebes of Thebes.[31] In this connection Cebes of Cyzikos, a second century C.E. philosopher mentioned by Athenaeus (IV.156D), has sometimes been advanced as the most likely candidate. Garnier, for example, made this suggestion and supported it with the conjecture that Lucian's reference to ὁ Κέβης ἐκεῖνος is a corruption of an original Κυζικηνός. Lucian would then originally have been referring to his contemporary and not to Cebes of Thebes.[32]

Garnier's suggestion is ingenious but even most advocates
of the homonymous theory reject it.[33] A second but unlikely candidate is a Cebes who is called a friend of
Virgil by later writers. According to at least one interpreter, Tertullian considered this Cebes to be the author
of the *Tabula*.[34]

A weakness of this explanation is that homonymy does
not seem to do justice to the features in the *Tabula* that
are used to give the work the appearance of greater antiquity. These features include the dedication of the
tablet to Cronus, the mention of Parmenides, and the imitation of Socratic dialectic in the final chapters.[35] The
work bears the stamp of antiquity too strongly to be explained by simple homonymy.

A third possible explanation is that the work was
originally anonymous but later attributed to Cebes of
Thebes.[36] Upon examination the *Tabula* can be seen as
filled with Socratic ideas and written in a Socratic spirit. The concluding chapters in particular can be seen as
Socratic not only in form but also in content. Chapter two
of the *Tabula* identifies the dedicator of the tablet as a
person who followed a Pythagorean life-style. The riddle
of the Sphinx in chapter three has Theban connections in
the tradition. As just mentioned, there are several features in the text which seem to suggest that the *Tabula*
derives from a period earlier than the Hellenistic age.
These considerations, it can be argued, were recognized in
antiquity, and an ancient Socratic was sought as the author. Of the possible candidates the most likely was Cebes
of Thebes, who had been a disciple of both the Pythagorean
Philolaus and Socrates. The ethical concern of the *Tabula*
is certainly consistent with the tradition that Cebes followed Socrates in restricting philosophy to ethics and not
extending it to include subjects such as arithmetic, astronomy, and music (cf. *Cebetis Tabula* 13.2).[37] On the
basis then of the internal evidence of the *Tabula* and the

tradition about Cebes, it can be argued that an originally
anonymous *Tabula* was attributed to the Theban and that
this attribution soon became firmly established.

A fourth possibility seems worthy of consideration.
It may well be that the "Pythagorean" who erected the temple and dedicated the tablet to Cronus (cf. *C.T.* 2.2) was
either intended as or understood to be Cebes of Thebes.
The original meaning of "*Tabula* of Cebes" would then be
that Cebes was the originator of the story on the tablet,
not the author of the present literary composition. The
Tabula bore his name, not because he composed the dialogue,
but because the basic content of it was understood as deriving from him. The suggestion made here is similar to
one sometimes made in connection with the fourth gospel.[38]
That is, it is sometimes suggested that the latter was
originally called the "Gospel of John," not because the
apostle John composed the work, but because he was, or was
believed to be, the originator of the tradition enshrined
in this gospel. Only later was he seen as the actual author of the work. Whether the *Gospel of John* or the *Tabula*
of Cebes actually derive from their traditional authors is
not the point of the analogy. The point is rather that
such a process seems possible in both instances. If this
is the case with the *Tabula*, then the understanding of
Cebes as the literary author of the *Tabula* would be a later
development.

The Influence of the *Tabula* in Antiquity

Once written, the *Tabula* was clearly an influential
work. In the second century C.E. Lucian and Tertullian
know the work and it is likely that Julius Pollux does as
well.[39] In other instances there is uncertainty whether
authors are borrowing ideas and images from the *Tabula* or
are drawing upon the same *topoi* and genres as "Cebes" had.
A case in point is Dio Chrysostom. At least four positions
have been taken on the question of their relationship.

Gronovius and Joly argue that Dio knows the *Tabula* and borrows from it.[40]   Capelle suggests that Dio is indirectly dependent upon the *Tabula*.   Dio himself does not know the *Tabula* but is dependent upon an intermediary who knows it.[41] Praechter and von Albrecht suggest that "Cebes" and Dio are both drawing upon a common source.[42]   Finally, Drosihn argues that "Cebes" is imitating Dio.[43]   This same question of relationship has also been raised in regard to Favorinus and the *Tabula*.   The conclusion of Carlini is that both authors are independently elaborating traditional motifs and themes.[44]   The issue becomes more complicated when it is remembered that Favorinus is usually said to be the author of two orations attributed to Dio (Nos. 37 and 64) and may have heard Dio speak in Rome.[45]

Other ancient authors who may know the *Tabula* include the Christian Hermas at Rome in the second century,[46] the author of the pseudo-Plutarchian *Consolatio ad Apollonium*, and the pseudo-Philonian *De mercede meretricis*.[47]   The fifth century Christian writer C(h)alcidius, however, clearly knows the *Tabula* and paraphrases material from chapter 13 in his commentary on Plato's *Timaeus*.[48]

The Literary Character of the *Tabula*

The title and one of the major keys to understanding the document derives from the literary fiction which serves as the base for the composition.   The setting and cause for the dialogue is presented as a chance observation of an enigmatic votive tablet bearing a picture (*C.T.* 1.1-2.1). The discussion regarding the contents and meaning of the painted scene, then, provides the occasion for the moralizing dialogue.[49]   Recognition of this literary characteristic is important in reading the text since much of the peculiar language and phrasing is in service to the fiction of describing a picture.   So, for example, the frequent use of directional adverbs (*C.T.* 4.3, 9.1, 15.1,4, 17.1, 21.2) and prepositions of place (*C.T.* 5.1, 6.1, 8.1, 17.2, 18.1,

20.1) should be understood in light of the fact that the "picture" is being described and explained by an old man who points to each component as he discusses it (*C.T.* 4.2, 30.3). In this vein, too, it should be recognized that the almost annoying use of demonstrative (οὖτος; ἐκεῖνος) and indefinite (τις, τι) pronouns and of interrogatives (τίς, τί) is intentional; it produces the sense of one observing and only slowly comprehending the details of content and meaning of the picture.[50] Our translation has highlighted a number of these features so as to carry the fiction of discussing the "picture" in English as in the Greek.[51] Given this tone and setting for the *Tabula* its contents can be summarized in the following outline.

A. Introduction: The Setting (chaps. 1-3)
1. Finding the tablet in the temple (chap. 1)
2. Confusion regarding its meaning and the intro-duction of the venerable old man, the Senex (chap. 2)
3. The Senex agrees to explain the picture (chap. 3)
   a. The explanation carries a warning
   b. The riddle of the Sphinx

B. The Description and Explanation of the Picture (chaps. 4-32)
1. The outer enclosure, the entry into Life, and the Daimon who points the way (chap. 4)
2. The entrance to Life is guarded by Deceit, whose potion (ignorance and error) causes all who pass through to wander after Opinion and Desire (chaps. 5-6)
3. Tychē, standing on an orb, gives and takes what she will from all who pass by (chaps. 7-8)
4. Vices (personified as courtesans) lead those whom Tychē has blessed into the next enclosure (chap. 9)
   a. Here is the abode of Pleasure
   b. (later, in 28.1 and 35.2, it is called the First Enclosure)
5. After Pleasure has reaped its effects the indi-vidual is turned over to Punishment and Unhappi-ness (10.1-4a)
6. A way of escape is opened by encountering Repentance (10.4b)
7. Repentance reorients the traveller by introducing him to new Opinions which in turn lead him either to true Paideia or Pseudopaideia (11)

8. Pseudopaideia and her Enclosure (12-14)
   a. Pseudopaideia described (12)
   b. The deluded lovers of Pseudopaideia (13)
      [They are inside the enclosure which is later
      (35.2) called the Second Enclosure]
   c. The companions of Pseudopaideia (14)
9. The Path to true Paideia and Happiness (14)
   a. The path through the trackless waste and
      beginning the ascent (15.1-4)
   b. Scaling the precipitous boulder to reach
      Self-Control and Perseverance (15.5-16.4)
   c. After a rest, these two women lead him to
      the easy path which leads finally to Paideia
      (16.5)
   d. The hidden enclosure [called the Third En-
      closure in 35.2] is pointed out and identi-
      fied as the dwelling place of Happiness and
      all the Virtues (17)
   e. At the entrance to the enclosure Paideia
      stands on a secure square rock flanked by
      her daughters Truth and Persuasion (18.1-2)
      - The rock is a sign that her gifts (Courage
        and Knowledge) are safe and secure (18.3-4)
      - She stands outside the gate in order to
        purge the one arriving of his Vices (19)
        [The medical *topos* (19.2)]
   f. Having thus purified the person, she sends
      him inside to Knowledge and her sisters,
      the Virtues (20)
   g. The Virtues then lead him to their mother,
      Happiness, who sits enthroned at the vestibule
      of the Citadel (21)
   h. When the individual reaches Happiness, she
      crowns him as a victor in the contest [*agōn
      topos*] (22-23)
10. After receiving the reward of Happiness, the
    Virtues take him back to the First Enclosure to
    show him the miserable state (in which he used
    to be) of those who do not seek Paideia and that
    the cause is ignorance of things good and evil
    (24-25) [shipwreck metaphor (24.2)]
11. After gaining this insight the educated, virtuous
    person can go anywhere he wishes; for he is safe
    from evil and suffering and himself becomes the
    doctor of others (26) [Corycian Cavern metaphor
    (26.1); doctor *topos* (26.1); snake-bite metaphor
    (26.3)]
12. Observation of those who do not persevere to
    reach Paideia as they are turned back from the
    mountain (27-28)
13. Observation of Opinions and how they lead one to
    Paideia but themselves do not enter into the
    precinct of Happiness (29) [cargo-ship metaphor
    (29.4)]

14. Conclusion: Discourse on the command of the
    Daimon (30-32)
    a. Exhortation to have confidence (30)
    b. The commands of the Daimon for the journey
       to Paideia. The essential element is the
       injunction against putting one's faith in
       the gifts of Tychē (31) [Banker *topos* (31.4)]
    c. Instead one is to flee to the gift of Paideia,
       i.e., the secure knowledge of what is advan-
       tageous in Life (32)
       [Final warning against disobeying or mis-
       understanding the command (32.5)]

C. Concluding discussions on the meaning of the Picture
   (33-34)

   1. A question of clarification on the command of
      the Daimon regarding the value of disciplines
      learned from Pseudopaideia (33-35)
      a. They are not necessary, but they are useful
         in the matter of becoming better (33)
      b. The scholars who spend their time in the
         Second Enclosure are not really superior if
         they are hindered by their intellectual pur-
         suits (34-35) [warning directed to the inter-
         locutors as well (35.5)]
   2. A reprise on the gifts of Tychē: why are they
      not to be considered good? (36-39) [shift to
      Socratic style]
      a. the question of life (36-38)
      b. the question of wealth (39)
   3. The Conclusion of the argument (40-43)
      a. The correct attitude toward things good and
         evil (40-41.4)
      b. The longer ending [Latin only]: continuation
         of the conclusion in 41.4 and final exhorta-
         tion (42-43)

It will already be quite clear from the outline that a
number of literary conventions have been combined to produce the final form of this work. There are, in fact, at
least three genres to be observed. First, in keeping with
the attribution to the Theban Cebes and because of the form
of the dialogue in chapters 36-41, some have classified the
work as a Socratic dialogue.[52] Dialogical forms, of course,
dominate the body of the work, but for most of it they are
not in the Socratic vein. On the basis of the setting
given in *C.T.* 1.1, R. Hirzel has classified the *Tabula* as a
"temple dialogue." He sees this type of dialogue as

typically incorporating elements of information and instruction given in the temple setting.[53]

Second, the fiction of describing a work of art (as
already mentioned) places the *Tabula* in the category of
ekphrasis. As a literary device, *ekphrasis* originated in
the earliest Greek literature, as in the epic description
of Achilles' shield (*Ilias* 18.467f). By the Hellenistic
period the motif was widespread, and it was in no way confined to describing in verse works of art.[54] It had been
adapted for didactic purposes by Plato (cf. *Criton* 110D,
114E; *Leges* 745B). In this regard *ekphrasis* comes very
close to personal description (*eikonismos* and *charaktēris-
mos*) as practiced by the likes of Theophrastus, especially
as it began to employ personification and allegory. By the
early imperial period *ekphrasis* had evolved into a standard
literary device and even into a unique prose genre. The
consummate technician of the style was Lucian of Samosata.
Three works of Lucian bear special mention in this regard,
especially since Lucian has been cited as knowing the
Tabula.[55] One is Lucian's *Toxaris* which gives a description of a temple plaque. Another is *Navigium*, which uses
description in the context of a dialogue to produce an allegory on human wishes. The last (and perhaps the most
intriguing) is Lucian's *Eikones*. This work is a dialogue
between two men in which each sets out to describe a woman
(both in personal appearance and in character) on the basis
of known works of art. The *Tabula* of Cebes, in like manner, can be seen to employ *ekphrasis* not only in the literary fiction in which the work is set but also in the descriptive techniques used in personifying and allegorizing
the vices and virtues.[56] Given this literary milieu, the
formal genre of the *Tabula* should probably be seen as a
dialogical *ekphrasis*. These formal elements, then, are in
service of the moral paraenesis that is the major concern
of the content.

A third literary genre helps to complete this combination of form and function. It has already been noted that

the dialogue of the *Tabula* approaches Socratic style only in chapters 36-41. The dialogue in the first portion is dominated by the explanations of the Senex while the inter- locutor only serves to propel the dialogue through leading questions and short responses. The interlocutor, in this section, does not develop an independent argument; instead, he poses questions of the picture's contents that provide the Senex with an opportunity to give more detailed descrip- tion and explanation and, thereby, more moral exhortation. As such the style of the dialogue is characterized by a number of elliptical and paratactic constructions.[57] One often feels that there is no need for the interlocutor at all except for fleshing out the fiction of the *ekphrasis*. This type of dialogue (as found in chaps. 2-35) fits gener- ally into the genre known as *erotapokriseis*. The name (literally, "questions and answers") denotes a dialogical exchange in the form of question and response in which one of the conversants is usually given an inferior role (as opposed to the Socratic setting which is more or less be- tween equals). The form developed originally in the con- text of school discussions, especially in the explication of texts.[58] So, for example, in Aristotle (*Frag.* 70) or Plutarch (*Platonicae quaestiones*) the form might begin, "What does *so and so* (Homer, Plato, etc.) mean by the word....?" A more highly developed form of the same ap- proach might take a single topic systematically (thence to serve as *eisagogē*, cf. Epictetus II.19). From the Jewish- Christian side, the best examples of the genre are Philo's works of *Quaestiones et Solutiones* (on Genesis and Exodus) where the initial question of the text serves as the start- ing point for extended allegorical interpretations. Another kind of *erotapokriseis* may be seen in so-called revelation literature where a suppliant poses a question to the deity (e.g., in the Hermetic oracles).[59] The point of interest for understanding the *Tabula* of Cebes is this: the question- answer form of the dialogue in chapters 2-35 is very much

like that of the classical *erotapokriseis* on a text. In
this case, as in the revelation literature, the picture
(or vision) serves as the text; it is explicated point by
point with the questions of the interlocutor and the descriptions of the Senex leading the discussion. Another
point of contact between the *Tabula* and the "gnostic revelation discourse" occurs in the enigmatic warnings given
concerning the explanation (*C.T.* 2-3).[60] In the *Tabula*
these warnings serve primarily to emphasize the need for a
guarded moral decision in regard to one's chosen path in
life.

As to the document's contents, it seems at times as
if the author has made concerted efforts to accommodate
almost all of the standard *topoi* (or commonplaces) of moral
literature into what is otherwise a relatively short document. Closer analysis, however, reveals that the underly-
ing structure of the contents is really nothing more than
an expanded form of the Prodicus myth. This myth takes its
name from the story of Heracles attributed by Xenophon
(*Memorabilia* II.1.21-34) to the sage Prodicus.[61] Several
points of Xenophon's version may be repeated here to illustrate the basic storyline of the myth: (a) the fable is explicitly presented as a paradigmatic study on virtue (21);
(b) the setting of the story included the fact that Heracles
was passing into adolescence, "wherein the young, now becoming their own masters, show whether they will approach
life by the path of virtue or vice" (21); (c) Heracles was
in a quiet place pondering this choice when he was approache
by two women who are described in detail (22); (d) the two
women are identified as Vice, whom some call Happiness (26),
and Virtue (30); (e) Vice promises an easy road to pleasure
(24) while Virtue warns of a rough road and a toilsome journey leading to good and noble deeds (27); (f) finally, the
reward of following the path of Vice is pictured as transien
pleasure to be followed by hardship in old age (31), while
the path of Virtue leads to ultimate happiness (εὐδαιμονία,
32f).

These components form the basic outline of the story. It enjoyed wide circulation in the moralist literature and was known well enough to be capsuled in rather brief, formulaic allusions.[62] The literary features that one finds most pronounced in all the versions are the choice between easy and hard roads, the personifications in the form of women, and the moral interpretation (by means of metaphor or allegory). It is significant too, that the moral import of the fable is derived largely from the characterization of the women (in physical attributes, actions, and speech) and in the description of the paths (often an *ekphrasis* of the topography and the destination). The content of the picture relies quite heavily on these same literary features.

Each of the basic units of the story could be expanded by the addition of other similar *topoi* from the moralist tradition. For example, the personification of virtue and vice already had a long tradition. It could be elaborated on any particular vice or virtue, or it could treat them in groups in connection with one of the standard procedures for listing or cataloguing vices and virtues.[63] Then, too, Vice is already portrayed in the Prodicus tradition as something of a wanton, so that the more explicit inclusion of elements from the courtesan literature was a natural way of elaborating and dramatizing the characterization.[64] Or again, the characteristic stress on the smooth and rough roads is understandably augmented by the hardship and victory motifs of the *agōn topos*.[65] One further comment should be made on the structural integration of these *topoi* into the basic narrative of the *Tabula*. In almost every case the text moves first through a description of the "picture" to some indication of its moral implication. Then, a *topos* is introduced in keeping with the appropriate symbolism at that point of the narrative in order to illustrate or clarify (for the inquisitive interlocutor) the moral point. So, for example, the "wicked bankers" (*C.T.* 31.4f) serve as a metaphor to reinforce the point already made from the extensive

description of the attributes of Tychē, namely that her
gifts are transient and one should, therefore, consider
them as nothing more than a temporary trust. Similarly,
the medical *topos* (*C.T.* 19.2) follows at that point in the
journey to Paideia when she begins to purge the traveller
of his noxious vices.[66]

The middle section of the *Tabula* (4-32) forms the core
of the work which itself is nothing more than an expanded
and elaborated form of the Prodicus myth (but without the
figure of Heracles).[67] The basic components of the paths,
the women, the choice, and the rewards/punishments remain
the same. The entire work is composed so as to emphasize
one major point. In this case the major point seems to be
injunctions for youth (who are about to enter life) on the
proper path to happiness through education and the proper
perspective on matters good and evil.[68] The details of the
description (especially what is added to the basic storyline) serve to heighten this point by the use of metaphor.[69]
The final, "Socratic" dialogue, then, recapitulates the
paraenesis. Specifically, the issue is the proper attitude
to hold with respect to wealth and those other things which
the masses call good and how the proper kind of education
(i.e., in philosophy) inculcates this attitude.

The Literary Milieu of the *Tabula*

Both in form and in content the *Tabula* fits well into
the general framework of the philosophical moral tradition.
The existence of so many common stylistic features and il-
lustrative *topoi* accounts for the variety of literary connections that have been claimed for the work.[70] Its relations with Dio Chrysostom and Lucian of Samosata have already been discussed, but there are other such claimed
relationships which deserve some attention here as well.
Since the climax of Cebes-studies in the late 19th century
the most heated discussions have taken place over the relationship of the *Tabula* to *The Shepherd* of Hermas.

Recognition of the *Tabula* as a product of the first century
opened up the possibility that its religious and moral tone
might have points of contact with early Christian literature. Some of these possibilities had already been suggested regarding the *Tabula* and Philo; however, Praechter
had argued that the similarities were based primarily on a
common use of the Prodicus myth.[71]

Apparently the first claims for a connection of the
Tabula with Hermas came from a statement (made in 1885) by
J. M. Cotterill: "To anyone who makes a thorough study of
the subject it is plain that there are few passages in
Hermas in which the *Tabula* is not in his mind to a greater
or less degree."[72] On the basis of the initial observation
by Cotterill, C. Taylor set out to prove the literary dependence of Hermas on the *Tabula*.[73] Taylor's hypothesis
was predicated on the notions of literary "similarity" and
word-borrowing.[74] It must be admitted that anyone who
knows the *Shepherd* will likely be caused to think of its
imagery and style when reading the *Tabula*. Taylor's method,
however, was not well received because he tried to see
something from the *Tabula* behind almost every word of Hermas. He admits at points to looking for things in the
Tabula that "Hermas would have noticed and used." The in-
debtedness of Hermas, for Taylor, extends to single words
or isolated phrases (often taken apart from their context),
and he argues that Hermas intentionally "disguised" many of
these elements in order to Christianize them.[75] Among those
who questioned Taylor both on his conclusion and his method
was St. George Stock.[76] Taylor responded by revising the
arguments to include Plutarch, but his basic stance remained
the same.[77] With the decline of interest in the *Tabula*
among classical scholars, the continuing discussion of
"Cebes" and Hermas was left to those interested in the
early Christian writers.[78]

It should be noted that a number of the similarities
pointed out by Taylor are striking and have continued to be

the focus of attention in studies of Hermas. In contrast
to Taylor's contention that the *Tabula* lurks behind every
turn, the more convincing comparisons are largely to be
found at three points in the *Shepherd*, i.e., in *Vis*. iii,
Sim. vi, and *Sim*. ix.[79] Among the more recent scholars
who have dealt with the issue we may consider the divergent
conclusions of R. Joly and R. van Deemter. Joly, in his
study of the religious and philosophical milieu of the
Tabula,[80] basically adopts a cautious version of Taylor's
dependence theory. Thus, he sees the most profound similarities in *Sim*. vi and ix, where the personifications of
Repentance and the Vices and Virtues are most pronounced.
By way of contrast, van Deemter sees points of agreement
(*Übereinstimmung*) but of such a sort that one can in no way
conclude a direct literary dependence.[81] He would rather
understand the existence of a common background or a mutual
source behind these similarities. He cites, for example,
the hypothesis of H. Schultz, according to which both
"Cebes" and Hermas borrow from an unknown source related
to Galen's *Protrepticus*.[82]

If there is a relation between Hermas and our "Cebes"
it may well be in the use of common literary genres and
motifs, especially since moral *topoi* and *ekphrasis* were
used so widely. But there are further points to consider
in the issue of "Cebes" and Hermas. One of the main pre-
suppositions of Taylor's thesis was that the *Shepherd* represented a literary unity, a point which has come into
serious question in more recent Hermas-studies.[83] Almost
no one, it seems, has brought this structural consideration
to bear on the question of how the *Shepherd* (in its final
form) might be so thoroughly dependent on the *Tabula*.[84]
Again, the possibility of a common literary milieu would
seem to be the best explanation.[85] In this vein, too, we
should recognize the points of similarity of the *Tabula* with
both Philo and Plutarch.

As already noted, similarities with Philo had been suggested by Praechter's time; Praechter had dismissed any

direct connections on the grounds of the common usage of
the Prodicus myth.[86] But one element of the Prodicus myth
in the *Tabula* bears a striking resemblance to a peculiarity
in Philo's use of the same motif. In *C.T.* 27.3 the *Tabula*
contains a reversal of the normal typology of the rough and
smooth paths. Thus, in the general terms of the myth, after reaching a certain point the smooth path to vice becomes
rough and the hard road to virtue becomes smooth and easy.[87]
This reversal is not unique as the perils of the road to
vice are pictured both in Dio Chrysostom and in the Cynic
epistles.[88] But the use of the word ἀνοδία (*C.T.* 15.2,
27.3) as a technical term is somewhat surprising. The word
is rarely used in this connection, and yet it is one of the
more common features of the Prodicus myth as adapted by
Philo. Interestingly enough, the word also appears in
Hermas. Similarly, in Philo repentance plays a major role
in his allusions to the road to virtue.[89]

There are parallels of this same type in works usually
attributed to Plutarch. It is thought by some that *C.T.*
31.3-4 (the metaphor of the "wicked bankers") is virtually
a direct quotation from ps-Plutarch, *Consolatio ad Apollonium* 28.[90] Indeed, much of the *Moralia* would have provided a common medium for discussing the same ethical issues.[91] Two other works bear special mention. The curious
role of the Daimon in the *Tabula* may be explained in part
by two converging traditions. The first is the appearance
in some versions of the Prodicus myth of a "divine guide"
who shows Heracles the two paths and helps him make the
proper decision. Thus, in Dio Chrysostom, *Or.* 1.66 Hermes
is sent by Zeus to assist in the young Heracles' education.[92] The other tradition comes from the common use of
the term δαίμων/δαιμόνιον in the traditions about Socrates,
perhaps as represented best by Plato's *Phaedo* and Plutarch's *De genio Socratis* (Mor. 575A-598F). The discussion
of the δαιμόνιον functions in Plutarch's dialogue as a symbol for the struggle toward virtue and excellence (ἀρετή)

as a way to be free of blind Fate (τύχη).[93] It is interesting, too, that the journey and *tabula* of Trophonius
occur in this same treatise.[94]

Finally, with the exception of the *Shepherd*, the relation of the *Tabula* to early Christian literature has
hardly been explored. References are usually confined to
the shipwreck imagery shared by 2 Tim 1:19 and *C.T.* 24.2
and the two ways motif of Matt 7:13-14 and the *Tabula*.[95]
Occasionally a comparison of the banker *topos* of *C.T.* 31.5
with the agraphon of Jesus γίνεσθε τραπεζῖται δόκιμοι has
been attempted.[96] J. van Wageningen has called attention
to the contrasts of the ἀπολλύμενοι and σῳζόμενοι in Paul
and the *Tabula* and to the role of repentance in each.[97]
W. Jaeger has observed a formal similarity between Acts 17
and the *Tabula*. In the former an inscription provides the
occasion for the sermon that follows. In the latter the
tablet gives rise to the dialogue.[98]

The Philosophical and Religious Milieu of the *Tabula*

A primary issue in Cebes-research has concerned the
philosophical standpoint of the work. Although it has
sometimes been argued that the author of the *Tabula* was
only a philosophically inclined rhetorician,[99] most scholars have claimed him as a representative of one or more of
the various philosophical schools. He has been identified
as a Socratic, a Platonist, a Stoic, a Cynic, and a Pythagorean. Very frequently a combination of these designa-
tions is employed in order to indicate that he is indebted
to several philosophical movements. Given this eclecticism,
the issue of his basic orientation still remains.

The Socratic Interpretation
The presence of Socratic ideas, sentiments, and style
in the *Tabula* is an uncontested fact. Even some of those
who reject the Theban as the author still treat the *Tabula*
as an essentially Socratic work.[100] Over against this
stress on the Socratic elements, however, Praechter

correctly emphasizes that these had become commonplaces in Hellenistic philosophy and thus can not be used to establish the author's philosophical orientation.[101]

But it does not follow from Praechter's observation that the Socratic elements can now be dismissed. Rather the issue must now be raised in a new manner. As to content, it must be asked whether the author employs Socratic ideas in order to foster the impression that the work stemmed from the Socratic circle. Again, the issue becomes a key question in regard to the dialectic style of chapters 36-41. It remains debated whether the author is here employing an older Socratic source or consciously imitating the Socratic method.[102] In either case, it must be asked what this suggests about "Cebes'" purpose in so doing. Or, if the view is correct that these chapters are a late addition to the *Tabula*,[103] the basis and purpose of this addition needs to be clarified. Thus the presence of Socratic lineaments in the *Tabula* remains an issue worthy of investigation.

The Platonic Interpretation

Plato is the only philosopher explicitly cited as an authority in the *Tabula*. Thus there is an *a priori* basis for assuming that the author was at least sympathetic to certain Platonic ideas as well as to more specifically Socratic ones. The most recent advocate of the Platonic inspiration of the *Tabula* is Thaddaeus Sinko. But whereas earlier scholars appealed to Platonic parallels in order to argue for an early date for the *Tabula*, Sinko places it as late as possible, viz., in the second century C.E.[104] This dating would then coincide with the renaissance of Platonism at that time.

The Stoic Interpretation

The standard interpretation of the *Tabula* remains the Stoic-Cynic one. This designation is somewhat unfortunate, for it not only obscures the differences between the two but also fails to allow adequately for the diversity present in

each. Some scholars have sought to be more specific and
have expressed themselves in favor of one part of the hy-
phen. Thus it is possible to distinguish the Stoic and
the Cynic interpretations.

The Stoic elements in the *Tabula* were recognized as
early as H. Wolf, who pointed to them in support of the
doubts he raised in regard to the attribution of the *Tabula*
to Cebes. In this he was followed by critics such as
Meiners and Domedden.[105] Gradually in the nineteenth
century this Stoic (-Cynic) interpretation became the viewpoint of most of those who rejected the old Socratic interpretation.[106]

The major scholar to argue that the basic orientation
of the *Tabula* is Stoic rather than Cynic was K. Praechter.
His procedure was to minimize the Socratic elements in the
Tabula and emphasize the Stoic ones. For Praechter these
decidedly Stoic elements included the following theses:
(1) external things do not belong to the category of things
good; (2) the happiness of the sage is purely internal; (3)
happiness depends on the knowledge of good and evil; (4)
good can not derive from evil. The conception of δόξα and
the lists of virtues and vices were also regarded by
Praechter as Stoic.[107] His reasons for regarding the
Tabula as Stoic as opposed to Cynic were primarily two.
First, the author advises people to accept the gifts of
Tychē (31.6). Second, while Pseudopaideia is attacked, the
arts and sciences themselves are not rejected. These are
given a qualified endorsement and some time is to be spent
in the acquisition of them (32.4). Therefore, the author
views the arts and sciences in the same way as the gifts of
Tychē. They are not goods but belong to the Stoic category
of preferred, indifferent things. Cynicism, in Praechter's
opinion, was more hostile in its attitude toward both these
matters, extolling poverty and rejecting the academic disciplines. Therefore, although the author avoids technical
terminology, his basic orientation was more Stoic than
Cynic.[108]

The Cynic Interpretation

Karl Joël rejected Praechter's distinctions between Stoics and Cynics in regard to their attitudes toward external things and the arts and sciences. He sought to prove that Cynics such as Antisthenes and Diogenes did not reject the gifts of Tychē but acted precisely as the *Tabula* recommends. Similarly the Cynics are said to have rejected the arts and sciences only to the extent that they are not concerned with ethics and making people better. For Joël the sharp distinction between Pseudopaideia and true Paideia is most natural in Cynicism's critique of the arts and sciences.[109]

Joël then proceeded to cite an impressive number of Cynic parallels for the ideas and vocabulary of the *Tabula*. This evidence was adduced as part of Joël's larger thesis that the Cynic Antisthenes was the real author of the Prodicus myth about Heracles. It is this myth which clearly provides the basic construct for the *Tabula*. In Joël's view the variations to this myth found in the *Tabula* are all Cynic. Moreover, Joël even derives the treatment of Paideia in a tablet format from Antisthenes.[110]

A more reserved appeal to the Cynic features of the *Tabula* was made by von Arnim.[111] He pointed to features such as the dispensability of the arts and sciences for the attainment of true Paideia, the use of the Cynic term σύντομος, the comparison of the successful struggle against the vices to the conquest over wild beasts, the return of the crowned victor to men as a physician, and the ideal of ἐλευθερία. At the same time he did not discount Stoic, Socratic and Pythagorean elements entirely. Indeed, von Arnim argued that the author of the *Tabula* not only portrayed his work as Pythagorean but believed himself to be writing as a Pythagorean in recommending abstinence over sensuality, emphasizing the need for ἐγκράτεια and καρτερία, and calling for μετάνοια and κάθαρσις.

The Neo-Pythagorean Interpretation

In chapter two of the *Tabula* the founder of the temple and dedicator of the tablet is described as one who had "emulated in word and deed a Pythagorean and Parmenidean way of life." The *Tabula* is then ostensibly Pythagorean. But is it actually Pythagorean in content? On this question scholarly opinion has been divided. Among the first to defend the Pythagorean character of the work were Brucker and Sevin.[112] Twentieth century interpreters to treat the *Tabula* as a Neo-Pythagorean work include Werner Jaeger and Robert Joly.

In a very detailed review of Eduard Norden's *Agnostos Theos*, Jaeger discussed the *Tabula* in connection with Norden's treatment of μετάνοια. Norden had suggested that μετάνοια as an ethical rather than a noetic change was a concept deriving from oriental, specifically Jewish, religion. Jaeger responded by invoking the *Tabula* as evidence that this new notion of μετάνοια was not the result of oriental influence but of an indigenous Greek development. For Jaeger the *Tabula*'s positive concept of μετάνοια reflects its use in Pythagorean moral preaching. The *Tabula* is then a product of the Pythagorean morality-movement and its preaching of the two ways. These two ways are those of ἀρετή and ἀπάτη. The choice between them coincides with the decision made at the crossroad of life, symbolized by the letter Y. The *Tabula* is therefore not Stoic, but Neo-Pythagorean. In fact, the Stoic polemic against μετάνοια is directed against the sort of popular understanding of the term found in the *Tabula*.[113]

Robert Joly has presented the most extensive case for understanding the *Tabula* as a Neo-Pythagorean work.[114] He moves beyond Jaeger to argue for the Neo-Pythagorean origin of this popular understanding of μετάνοια. Not only this but also the concepts of ἀπάτη, κάθαρσις, τιμωρία, the two ways, and πόνος are all viewed from a Neo-Pythagorean perspective. Yet this is a Pythagoreanism that has been greatly influenced by the mystery religions. The *Tabula*, as a product of this circle of thought, is really an eschatological work. It presents a picture of the hereafter in terms of this earthly life. But only the Neo-Pythagorean would recognize it as such. The noninitiate would see only the Stoic and Cynic banalities that are undeniably present in the work. The initiate, however, given his clue already in the mention of Cronus (the god of the underworld) and told that he must treat the old man's explanation of the tablet as a riddle to be interpreted, would see the true meaning of what is unfolded in the *Tabula*.

An initiate in the mystery religions could not, of course, reveal the content of the mystery. Similarly, the author of the *Tabula* does not reveal openly and directly the content of the Neo-Pythagorean mystery. But he does give the revelation in an allusive and enigmatic manner. Joly does for us what the author of the *Tabula* could not, viz., he gives us the revelation in a clear way. Joly's interpretation will be treated in some detail in the notes. It will suffice here to note that there is some evidence that may suggest that the *Tabula* was interpreted in antiquity in the manner Joly proposes. The note of the *Suda* apparently refers to the *Tabula* when it is stated that ἔστι δὲ τῶν ἐν ᾅδου διήγησις.[115] A relief fragment may also reflect this understanding of the *Tabula*.[116]

Thus, even when interpreters view the *Tabula* as a product of the Neo-Pythagorean movement, the nature of the document remains disputed. Jaeger follows most interpreters in seeing it as a popular work and adds the nuance that it contains Pythagorean popular preaching. Joly, on the other hand, views it as an esoteric work that can be correctly understood only by the initiate.

Interpretations Emphasizing Two or More Philosophical Traditions

Few modern interpreters, including those just mentioned, would deny that the author of the *Tabula* was

somewhat eclectic. The five interpretations just discussed
would hardly have been possible if this were not the case.
In view of the presence of various philosophical traditions
in the *Tabula*, several scholars have preferred to emphasize
this combination. The most common example of this tendency
is the Stoic-Cynic interpretation mentioned above. Even
Praechter, when pressed about his Stoic interpretation,
would concede that the author was neither Stoic nor Cynic
but stood on the border between them.[117] But our interest
here lies in combinations that we would not anticipate
except in a syncretistic period.

Croiset treated the *Tabula* as a Pythagorean-Stoic
work.[118] It is said to be Stoic in its conception of life
and in its imitation of a composition of Cleanthes. Its
Pythagoreanism surfaces in its use of allegory and its desire to summarize and present in one image the axioms necessary for living well. In contrast to Joly, the *Tabula*
is not seen as a religious work. The religious idea is
absent because the author is making his appeal to out-
siders.

Hirzel argued that the author intended to make visible
the joining of two philosophical streams. The first is the
Parmenidean-Pythagorean stream and the second is the Cynic-
Socratic one. In support of this combination of Socratic
Cynicism and Pythagoreanism, Hirzel pointed to Varro, the
Cynic in Athenaeus IV.157D who knew Pythagorean principles,
and Sextius.[119]

Summary and Conclusions

In view of the eclecticism of the author and the diversity of scholarly opinion concerning him, a dogmatic conclusion concerning the basic orientation(s) of the *Tabula* is
unwarranted. "Cebes" does not fit easily into any of the
usual categories. Indeed, the old categories themselves
are presently under discussion and it is premature to say
what the new landscape of Hellenistic philosophy will be.
Each of the proposed interpretations has its strengths as

well as its weaknesses. We should acknowledge, however,
that we have been especially impressed by the Cynic features of the *Tabula*. The author, however he may have understood himself and however we choose to label him, certainly was influenced by Cynic thought.

That he was, in this regard, a person somewhat like
Seneca or Epictetus does not seem unlikely. Seneca had
been exposed early to various viewpoints, including those
of two Sextian eclectics. Later, as a Stoic, he was greatly influenced by the thought of his intimate friend Demetrius the Cynic. Seneca was then a "Cynicized Stoic," that
is, a Stoic enamored of certain Cynic ideals. Likewise
Epictetus seems to represent a number of strong Cynic tendencies, even giving a treatise on the ideal Cynic (III.22),
but he himself was more of a Stoic. He taught in his own
school and regularly took in young students for philosophic
and moral instruction. The author of the *Tabula* may have
been such a person, influenced by Cynics but not personally
a Cynic. This question cannot be answered, however, until
we have a clearer idea as to the varieties of Cynic life,
thought, and self-understanding. At the present time we
would emphasize only the fact that "Cebes" was influenced
by the Cynics and leave open the issue of his self-
understanding.[120]

Manuscripts, Versions, and the Edition of Praechter

The standard edition of the *Tabula* and the one reprinted in this volume is that of Karl Praechter.[121] The
text of Praechter's edition is based primarily on twelve
Greek manuscripts and two Latin versions (those of Odaxius
and Elichmann).[122] In the preparation of his edition,
Praechter benefited from the prior work of two men in particular, Hermann Sauppe[123] and K. K. Müller.[124] Reaping
the harvest of their labors, Praechter sought to base the
text of the *Tabula* as far as possible on the witness of a
small number of good manuscripts. This meant that from

1.1.1-23.2.3 Praechter accorded codex A a preferred position in the construction of the text.[125] From 23.2.3 to the ending of the Greek text at 41.4.1 a similar preference was given to the readings of codex V.[126] The concluding section is extant only in an Arabic paraphrase made from a Greek manuscript and a literal translation of this Arabic paraphrase. For this section Praechter printed, with a few minor changes, this Latin translation (made by J. Elichmann and published posthumously in 1640).[127] Praechter's prudence as an editor, his reluctance to emend the text, and his growing reputation as a scholar, won for his edition the renown of being the standard.[128]

While Praechter's edition is justifiably considered the standard one, there is also a pressing need for a new edition of the *Tabula*. New Greek manuscripts and Latin translations unknown to Praechter have been discovered and instances of incorrect citation by him have been published, especially by C. E. Finch.[129] Praechter himself later expressed a preference for alternate readings.[130] Until a new edition is forthcoming, however, it seems expedient to use Praechter's text. But, in the interim, we have sought to be of service to textual critics by supplementing and correcting the critical apparatus where new information has been brought to light or older, pertinent information has been omitted. [An asterisk (*) beside a line of the apparatus indicates that such information has been provided in the supplementary notes. By so doing we disavow any intention of re-editing the text or of constructing a new apparatus. Our desire is merely to make available the information published by others.]

The accompanying translation is thus that of Praechter' text. In only a few instances have we departed from this text, and these exceptions are indicated in the "Notes to the Translation." A complete listing of all the witnesses used by Praechter is given under "Sigla."[131] To this is added a list of Greek manuscripts and Latin versions either not known to Praechter or not utilized by him.

NOTES TO THE INTRODUCTION

[1]S. C. Chew, *The Pilgrimmage of Life* (New Haven, 1962) 206; cf. also note 5 below.

[2]For listings of individual titles, cf. S.F.W. Hoffmann, *Bibliographisches Lexicon der gesammten Literatur der Griechen* (Amsterdam, 1961, a reprint of the second [1838] Leipzig edition) I, 445-48; and the *British Museum General Catalogue of Printed Books*, Vol. 35 (1965) cols. 914-18. For facsimilies of the Greek text and various translations, cf. Sandra Sider, *Cebes' Tablet: Facsimiles of the Greek Text, and of Selected Latin, French, English, Spanish, Italian, German, Dutch, and Polish Translations* (Renaissance Text Series; New York, 1979).

[3]Milton recommends the *Tabula* in his 1644 tractate *Of Education*. Cf. O. M. Ainsworth (ed.), *Milton on Education* (Cornell Studies in English XII; New Haven, 1928) 55-56.

[4]Cf. Madeleine David, "Leibniz et le 'Tableau de Cébès' (*Nouveaux Essais*, 1.IV, chap. III, §20) ou le problème du langage par images," *Revue philosophique* CLI (1961) 39-50.

[5]It was a woodcut by Holbein that Johann Froben used for the title page of the third edition of Erasmus' New Testament. For a reproduction and detailed discussion of the cut, cf. H. Knackfuss, *Holbein*, trans. by C. Dodgson (Bielefeld/Leipzig, 1899) 50, 71-73.

[6]Cf. Sider, 2. For a collection and discussion of numerous woodcuts, paintings, and frescos illustrating the *Tabula*, cf. Reinhart Schleier, *Tabula Cebetis; oder Spiegel des menschlichen Lebens, darin Tugent und Untugent abgemalet ist. Studien zur Rezeption einer antiken Bildbeschreibung im 16. und 17. Jahrhundert* (Berlin, 1974).

[7]This is asserted without qualification by Richard Parsons, *Cebes' Tablet* (Boston, 1887) 5, and J. G. Phillips, "The Garden of False Learning," *Bulletin: The Metropolitan Museum of Art*, N.S. 1 (1942/1943) 243-47. W. C. Hazlitt, *Offspring of Thought in Solitude* (London, 1884) 215, is more cautious. Hazlitt gives the *Tabula* as one of six works from which Bunyan "may, with greater or less probability, be supposed to have been a borrower." In the view of J. B. Wharey, however, it is "extremely improbable" that Bunyan had even heard of, much less used, the *Tabula*. Cf. his *A Study of the Sources of Bunyan's Allegories* (Baltimore, 1904) 99-102.

[8]C. E. Lutz, "Aesticampianus' Edition of the *Tabula* Attributed to Cebes," *The Yale University Library Gazette* 45 (1971) 110-17, esp. 111. This perception has been incorporated in the titles of several works. Cf., for example, Addison Hogue, "A Greek 'Pilgrim's Progress,'" *Union Seminary Magazine*, Richmond, VA, Feb.-March, 1902, pp. 211-24, and K. S. Guthrie, *The Greek Pilgrim's Progress, Generally Known as the Picture by Kebes, a disciple of Sokrates?* (London/Philadelphia, 1910).

[9]Cf., for instance, the brief discussion by A. D. Nock in *Conversion* (Oxford, 1933) 180-81.

[10]The translation is that of H. N. Fowler in the Loeb edition.

[11]Cf. also Lucian, *De merc. cond.* 42; *Rhet. praec.* 6; Tertullian, *De praescr. adv. haeret.* 39; and Julius Pollux, *Onomasticon* III.95.

[12]Cf. Robert Joly, *Le Tableau de Cébès et la philosophie religieuse* (Collection Latomus, Vol. LXI; Bruxelles-Berchem, 1963) 67.

[13]Codex Parisinus graec. 1774 (designated as C in the Praechter edition) of the 16th century and Codex Vaticanus Latinus 4037 both state in the titles to the *Tabula* that Cebes the Theban is the author. It is likely that this tradition already stood in the title of the archetype of the CK(P) family. Cf. C. E. Finch, "The Translation of Cebes' *Tabula* in Codex Vaticanus Latinus 4037," *Transactions and Proceedings of the American Philological Association* 85 (1954) 79-87, esp. 83.

[14]H. Wolf, *Epicteti Enchiridion...*, *Cebetis Thebani tabula...* (Basileae, 1561-63).

[15]C. Meiners, "Iudicium de quibusdam Socraticorum reliquiis, inprimis de Aeschinis dialogis, de Platonis eiusque condiscipulorum epistolis, nec non de Cebetis tabula," in *Commentatt. reg. Soc. Scient. Gottingensis hist. et philog. Class.* (1782) Vol. V, pp. 45ff. For the history of the investigation to 1798, cf. J. Schweighaeuser *Epicteti Manuale et Cebetis Tabula, Graece...* (Lipsiae, 1798) *in loc.* 13.2 and 33.3. For a summary of Schweighaeuser and the history of the investigation to 1813, cf. J. D. Büchling and G.F.W. Grosse, *Des Cebes Gemälde* (Meissen, 1813) v-xlii.

[16]C. F. Baehr, "Cebes," in A. Pauly (ed.), *Real-Encyclopaedie der classischen Alterthumswissenschaft* (Stuttgart, 1842) II, 232-33.

[17]F. Lécluse, *Tableau de Cébès lê Thebain* (Paris,
1877), and A. Frigell, *Kebes' Tafla* (Uppsala, 1878). Both
these editions of the text we know only by the review of
K. K. Müller in *Philologische Rundschau* IV (1884) 1423-24.

[18]F. G. Klopfer, *De Cebetis tabula dissertat. III.4*
(Zwickau, 1818, 1820, 1822). The distinctiveness of
Klopfer's proposal makes it difficult to classify him. We
follow Franz Susemihl, *Geschichte der griechischen Literatur in der Alexanderinzeit* (Hildesheim, 1965, a reprint of
the Leipzig edition of 1891-92) I, 25 n. 66, in viewing
him essentially as a defender of the genuineness of the
work. Hoffmann, however, classifies him with those who
deny the authenticity of the work (cf. Hoffmann, 448).

[19]This position is adopted by David Smith, "Had Our
Lord Read the 'Tablet' of Kebes?," *The Expositor*, Sixth
Series, 3 (1901) 387-97, esp. 391, and Guthrie (cf. his
"Introduction").

[20]Another important objection raised early against the
traditional attribution was that it contains Stoic ideas
and principles (so already Wolf, followed by Meiners and
many others). Since Smith and Guthrie (cf. n. 19 above)
saw these influences only in the concluding dialogue, they
considered only the dialogue to be spurious. Additional
objections concern matters such as the use of allegory as
a vehicle of instruction, the language of the *Tabula*, and
the presence of anachronisms in the text.

[21]Friedrich Drosihn, *Cebetis Tabula* (Lipsiae, 1871)
37-39. Drosihn intended to discuss this lexical evidence
in part four of an article dealing with the date of the
Tabula's composition. Unfortunately, Drosihn died before
completing this part of the article. The first three
parts were published posthumously by Dietlein under the
title "Die Zeit des ΠΙΝΑΞ ΚΕΒΗΤΟΣ. Aus den Papieren des
verstorbenen Oberlehrer Drosihn vom Prorector Dietlein,"
in *Programm des fürstlich hedwigschen Gymnasiums zu Neustettin* (Neustettin, 1873) 3-15. In undertaking this lexical investigation Drosihn was pursuing observations that
had been made earlier in regard to the presence of late
words in the *Tabula*. Büchling and Grosse (p. xl) had, for
example, pointed to βουνός.

[22]Karl Praechter, *Cebetis Tabula quanam aetate conscripta esse videatur* (Marburgi, 1885). His results are
summarized in a chart on pp. 129-30.

[23]Joly, 13-21.

[24]Cf., for example, H. von Arnim, "Kebes," in Pauly-
Wissowa-Kroll, *Pauly's Real-Encyclopädie der classischen
Alterthumswissenschaft* XI.1 (1921) 102-5, esp. 103;

Glanville Downey, "The Pilgrim's Progress of the Byzantine Emperor," *Church History* 9 (1940) 207-17, esp. 210-11; W. D. Ross, "Cebes," *The Oxford Classical Dictionary* (2nd ed. by N.G.L. Hammond and H. H. Scullard; Oxford, 1970) 218; Lutz, 110; Sider, 1; cf. also H. Dörrie, "Kebes," *Der Kleine Pauly* (Stuttgart, 1969) III, 173.

[25] Susemihl, I, 26 n. 66; II, 657-58. C. S. Jerram, *Cebetis Tabula* (Oxford, 1878) xiii, xxxiii, xxxix, would apparently assign it to either the fourth or the third century B.C.E. Since he considers the *Tabula* to be "classical in style and diction, and a good imitation of the best specimens of Attic prose," he wants to remain as close to the traditional dating as possible. H. Usener also wished to date the *Tabula* early. According to K. K. Müller in *Phil. Rund.* IV (1884) 1423, Usener had for a long time assigned the *Tabula* to the third century B.C.E. In his *Epicurea* (Lipsiae, 1887) lxxi n. 1, Usener claims that the *Tabula* is an imitation of Cleanthes' allegorical tablet. Since Cleanthes was head of the Stoic school from 263-232, Usener probably preferred a date during this period or shortly thereafter.

[26] Drosihn, "Die Zeit," argues that the author of the *Tabula* imitated the fourth oration of Dio Chrysostom and therefore had to be dated subsequent to that oration. It would fall at the earliest in the second half of the first century. Even if this imitation of Dio is denied, Drosihn contends that the work must be assigned to a date no earlier than the first half of the first century C.E. Thaddaeus Sinko, "De lineamentis Platonicis in Cebetis q.v. tabula," *Eos* 45 (1951) 3-31, places it in the second century C.E.

[27] A. T. Phloros, "'Ο Κέβητος Πίναξ," *Platon* 7 (1955) 287-95, suggests that the *Tabula* is written by a disciple of Musonius Rufus. Earlier, Rudolf Hirzel, *Der Dialog* (Leipzig, 1895) II, 258, had suggested that the author of the *Tabula* was a contemporary of Musonius and went on to suggest that in Musonius one finds the same combination of Cynicism and Pythagoreanism that he claimed for the *Tabula*.

[28] We are using the term "Hellenistic" broadly, so that it includes both the Hellenistic period proper and the early imperial period that followed (the "Hellenistic-Roman" period).

[29] This is the position of Drosihn; cf. "Die Zeit," 15.

[30] The criticism of von Arnim (102-3) is particularly incisive on this point.

[31] Those who favor an explanation involving homonymy include von Arnim (102-3) and Joly (8 n. 2).

[32] J. J. Garnier, "Dissertation sur le tableau de Cebes. I: Conformité de doctrine de l'auteur du tableau avec celle des Stoiciens. II: Examen des raisons, qui ont fait attribuer cet ouvrage à Cebes le Thebain; Conjectures sur le véritable auteur," in *Mém. de l'Acad. des Inscr.* T.48, p. 455. This is the listing given in Hoffmann, 448. Büchling and Grosse (xxix) give tome 47 and date it to 1808. Joly (8) dates it to 1786. We have not been able to locate a copy to clarify this confusion and are dependent on these secondary discussions.

[33] Von Arnim (103) mentions this theory only to reject it. He is not even prepared to say that this Cebes of Cyzikos is a historical person.

[34] This is the position taken by Stein in his article "Kebes," in Pauly-Wissowa-Kroll, XI.1 (1921) 101-2. He cites Donatus, *Vita Verg.* 9 and Servius, *Verg. Buc.* II.15 as indicating that this Cebes was also a poet. It should be noted, however, that this interpretation of the statement in Tertullian, *De praescr. haeret.* 39 is not uncontested. The standard interpretation is that Tertullian is referring to a relative of his who turned the *Tabula* "into a cento of Virgilian verses" (so T. D. Barnes, *Tertullian* [Oxford, 1971] 195). Cf. also the statement by Jean-Claude Fredouille, *Tertullien et la conversion de la culture antique* (Paris, 1972) 60, that Tertullian knew our *Tabula* since "un ses parents l'avait interprétée en composant un centon virgilien." Tertullian in chapters 38 and 39 is arguing that the corruption of Sacred Scripture by heretics should not be astonishing since one can witness the same phenomenon transpiring in secular literature. Scripture, just like Virgil and Homer, serves as the source for new literary productions. Virgil has been the source for the production of a *Medea* by Hosidius Geta and of a *Tabula of Cebes* by one of Tertullian's relatives. Homer is the source for numerous "Homerocentons." It seems most likely then that Tertullian is referring to his relative producing out of Virgil a new, poetic version of the *Tabula of Cebes*, just as Hosidius Geta had produced a new version of Euripides' *Medea*. A Latin *Medea* is extant in which the characters speak Virgilian hexameters that have been patchworked together, but it is debated whether it is the version produced by Hosidius Geta.

[35] Cf. the "Notes to the Text and Translation" for details.

[36] G. Downey, "Ekphrasis," in T. Klauser (hrsg.), *Reallexikon für Antike und Christentum* IV (1959) 923, refers to the *Tabula* as an "anonyme Traktat" but does not elaborate on this point. Dörrie's position (273) is not completely clear. He explicitly rejects the view that the author wrote under the name of Cebes of Thebes, but he fails to provide an alternate explanation.

34 The *Tabula* of Cebes

[37]Themistius, *Orat.* 34 (447-48). This is said in contrast to Plato, who is said to have made this extension. H. Schneider argues that Themistius is following Sotion's *Diadochoi* in his selection of Socrates' students who held themselves back from foreign influences. If this is correct, then the mention of Cebes in this context is based on a tradition that antedates the writing of the *Tabula*. That is, Themistius is not including Cebes in this list because of his knowledge of the *Tabula*, as Drosihn, "Die Zeit," 5, suggests. Rather, it may be that this tradition is in part responsible for the attribution of the *Tabula* to Cebes. For the text of Themistius' *Orat.* 34 with translation and commentary, cf. H. Schneider, *Die 34. Rede des Themistios* (Winterthur, 1966).

[38]Cf. the collection of views in Robert Kysar, *The Fourth Evangelist and His Gospel* (Minneapolis, 1975) 92-96.

[39]Cf. nn. 11 and 34 above.

[40]J. Gronovius, Κέβητος Θηβαίου πίναξ. *Cebetis Thebani tabula, Graece et Latine...* (Amstelaedami, 1689) 105-8; and Joly, 54, 83-85.

[41]G. Capelle, *De cynicorum epistulis* (Gottingae, 1896) 32 n. 2.

[42]Praechter, 96-102; and Michael von Albrecht, Review of *Le Tableau* by Robert Joly, in *Gnomon* 36 (1964) 755-79.

[43]Drosihn, "Die Zeit," 14-15.

[44]Antonio Carlini, "Appunti di lettura," *Maia* 21 (1969) 273-79, esp. 277-79.

[45]Cf. H. S. Long, "Favorinus," in *The Oxford Classical Dictionary*[2], 432-33.

[46]Cf. the discussion below.

[47]For discussions of these, see Praechter, 48, 94-96, and Joly, 79-80, 85. Some have thought that the *Tabula* mentioned by Zosimus, the fourth century alchemist, is that attributed to Cebes. But this interpretation involves an emendation of the text from τὸν πίνακα ὂν καὶ Βίτος to either ὂν Κέβητος γράψας (Ruelle in his text) or Κέβης τε ἔγραψε (Ruelle in his apparatus) or τὸν Κέβητος (Ferguson). Since this *Tabula* is said to deal with the *Urmensch*, however, it is extremely unlikely that the *Tabula* of Cebes is intended. For this and other reasons, A. D. Nock correctly rejected such emendations. Cf. A. D. Nock and A. J. Festugière, *Corpus Hermeticum* (Les Belles Lettres; Paris, 1954) IV, frag. 21, pp. 119-21, and also Walter Scott and A. J. Ferguson, *Hermetica* (Oxford, 1936) IV, 129 n. 1.

[48]Cf. Joly, 79, and Sinko, 11-12.

[49]Some have suggested that the votive tablet actually existed and that it was the source for the literary composition. Schilling, for example, assumed the existence of an actual tablet and conjectured that one of the difficulties in the interpretation of the *Tabula* stems from the artist and the author having divergent understandings of the meaning of the work (see Büchling and Grosse, xxxviii). More recently E. H. Gombrich has asked "whether the claims of the dialogue to describe a real painting have not been somewhat too lightly dismissed by classical scholars" (cf. his "A Classical 'Rake's Progress,'" *Journal of the Warburg and Courtauld Institutes* 15 (1952) 254-56, esp. 256 n. 5). The composition clearly gave rise to artistic attempts at rendering the work pictorially. See Plate I for an example of this and also the discussion by K. K. Müller and C. Robert in the *Archäologische Zeitung* 42 (1884) 115-30. In the present form, at least, the composition is clearly predicated on the fiction of describing the picture by literary means where the fiction serves to propel the dialogue toward its moralizing conclusions.

[50]Note especially *C.T.* 9.1. Here the literary fiction is used not only to create the sense of progressing through the analysis of the painting, but it also begins to draw the observer into the fictional scene. So, for example, the use of παρέλθης tends to push the interlocutor (and the reader) into the role of the characters in the painted scene.

[51]It may be that failure to give sufficient weight to the literary fiction of describing and examining the picture has added to a number of confusions regarding the text. For example, as far as we can tell very few scholars (except perhaps Praechter) have given any real attention to the fact that there are actually four walled enclosures identified in the description, of which the *last* three are enumerated in the text as first, second and third (cf. 35.2 and n. 57 in the "Notes to the Translation"). A general discussion of the grammar and syntax of the *Tabula* as an example of Koine Greek may be found in Joly, *Le Tableau*, chap. 1.

[52]Cf. Jerram, xxxiv, and Richard Parsons, *Cebes' Tablet, with Introduction, Notes, Vocabulary, and Grammatical Questions* (Boston, 1887) 18.

[53]Hirzel, II, 258; cf. I, 558 n. 3. Hirzel also classes among this type of dialogue Plutarch's *De E apud Delphos* (cf. II, 198). W. Jaeger in discussing this same aspect points also to Acts 17 (Paul's "sermon" on the Areopagus) as deriving from the same sort of formal setting; see Jaeger's review of E. Norden's *Agnostos Theos* now reprinted in the collection of his *Scripta Minora* I, 120-21, 140-41.

[54]For a general discussion with further bibliography see the article on "Ekphrasis" by Glanville Downey cited in n. 36. Cf. also E. Norden, *Antike Kunstprosa* (reprint; Leiden, 1958) sv. index and esp. 285, 441.

[55]Cf. n. 11 above. For a general discussion of the ethical features of Lucian's work see H. D. Betz, *Lukan von Samosata und das Neue Testament* (TU 76; Berlin, 1961) esp. 205ff.

[56]See Downey in *RAC* IV, 924, and his "The Pilgrim's Progress of the Byzantine Emperor," 22-34. Downey points out further that Jewish and Christian literature made relatively little use of *ekphrasis* with one fairly consistent exception, i.e., in apocalyptic literature. This point is of further interest when one begins to consider the relationship of the *Tabula* with the *Shepherd* of Hermas.

[57]Cf. especially *C.T.* 10.1, 15.1-2, 17.1, 19.2, 35.3 and note 104 in the "Notes to the Translation."

[58]See the article "Erotapokriseis" by H. Dörrie and H. Dörries in *RAC* VI, 342-70.

[59]There are few parallels in the Jewish-Christian tradition except in apocalyptic and in the so-called "Gnostic Gospels" or "Gnostic Dialogues." Later Christian writers (from the fourth century onwards) would finally begin to develop the more classical forms of *erotapokriseis* both in dogmatic debates and in catechesis, cf. *RAC* VI, 349ff. It is not insignificant that in both classical apocalyptic and the gnostic literature much of the *erotapokriseis* that does occur relies on detailed and vivid visionary description (*ekphrasis*) to provide the content for the questions and answers.

[60]The appeals to antiquity, the transmission of knowledge by venerable elders, and the promises/warnings issued to the hearer (cf. *C.T.* 20.2; 35.5) are similar to the devices used to signify and protect the esoteric gnosis in the *Apocryphon of John* and other such documents. Note especially the first and last paragraphs of the *Apocryphon of John* (cf. the translation by F. Wisse in *The Nag Hammadi Library*, ed. J. M. Robinson [New York, 1977] 98-116). Given this kind of similarity, it is not altogether surprising that one could see hints of esoteric religious/philosophical phenomena in the *Tabula*. Cf. the discussion of Joly's Neo-Pythagorean interpretation of the *Tabula* on pp. 24-25.

[61]This line of dependence for our author has long been recognized and was considered in some detail by Praechter in his dissertation, *Quanam aetate*, 99ff. See also Parsons, 15f. The major studies of the tradition are to be found in

K. Joël, *Der echte und xenophontische Sokrates* II.1 (Berlin, 1901), 294ff. and J. Alpers, *Hercules in bivio* (Göt-
tingen, 1912), *passim*. See also the article on "ὅδος" by
W. Michaelis in *TDNT* V, 43-48.

[62]Among the ancient authors who explicitly use the
storyline or abbreviated allusions to it are the following:
Dio Chrysostom, *Or.* 1.66-81 (cf. 4.113); Maximus of Tyre,
Diss. XIV (p. 17d, Hobein), XXXIX (p. 454, Hobein); ps.-
Diogenes, *Epp.* 12, 30, 37 (Hercher/Malherbe); Persius III.
56; Cicero, *De officiis* I.32.118f; Lucian, *Hermotimus* 22f;
Gall. 6ff; *Bis accusat.* 19f; Quintillian IX.2, 36; Silius
Italicus, *Pun.* XV.18f, 96ff; Philo, *De sacr. Cain et Abel*
20ff; *Vita Mosis* 2.138f; Clement of Alexandria, *Paed.*
II.10.110.

[63]For description of the Vices in the *Tabula* see *C.T.*
5.1; 9.1; 10.1, 3; 12.2; 29.1; for the Virtues see *C.T.*
16.1; 18.1; 20.2; 21.3. It should be noted that the char-
acteristics of the Virtues are naturally set in direct opposition to those of the Vices. This device of the *ekphrasis* applies equally to physical appearance and to character and actions. For general discussions, see A. Vögtle,
Die Tugend- und Lasterkataloge im Neuen Testament (Neutestamentliche Abhandlungen XVI; Münster, 1936), and S.
Wibbing, *Die Tugend- und Lasterkataloge im Neuen Testament*
(BZNW 25; Berlin, 1959) *passim*. Their personification in
Dio, *Or.* 4.113f, said by some to be borrowed from the
Tabula (cf. n. 66 below), may represent such an independent
tradition. The figure of Deceit might have constituted an
existing tradition involving the personification of one
Vice which the *Tabula* had incorporated into an expanded
outline of the Prodicus myth with its multiple "leading
ladies."

[64]Cf. especially *C.T.* 9.1-10.3 and our n. 33 in the
"Notes to the Translation."

[65]*C.T.* 15-16; 22-23. This connection had already been
well established in the use of the Prodicus myth, especially in Cynic circles. Compare, for example, Ps-Diogenes,
Epp. 30 and 37 (Hercher/Malherbe); cf. n. 74 in the "Notes
to the Translation." The other *topoi* to be included in the
Tabula may be found in the notes to the translation; they
include the riddle of the sphinx (*C.T.* 3), medical imagery
(19.2), the philosopher as doctor (26.2), shipwreck metaphor (24.2), and the banker *topos* (31.4). Cf. also V. C.
Pfitzner, *Paul and the Agon Motif* (Leiden, 1967).

[66]A good example of the way in which the basic storyline could be elaborated is seen in Dio Chrysostom's version of the Prodicus Myth (*Or.* 1.51ff). Here the cast of
characters, the detail of the descriptions, and the use of

an old woman (πρεσβύτερα, 53) as the "divine guide" are all
elaborations to adapt the story to Dio's own moralizing
purpose. Another point of comparison with Dio comes in his
description of personified Deceit in *Or.* 4.113ff, sometimes
claimed to be a paraphrase of the *Tabula* (cf. p. 8, above).
While the similarities may be as well explained on the basis of a common literary milieu, Dio's stated intent to use
ekphrasis for a moral intent is interesting. For a general
discussion of the Heracles traditions in Dio (though the
Tabula is never mentioned), see P. Tzaneteas, "The Symbolic
Heracles in Dio Chrysostom's Orations on Kingship," (unpublished Ph.D. thesis, Columbia University, 1972) *passim.*

[67]In this feature the *Tabula* is perhaps more reminis-
cent of the two-ways motif as found in Hesiod, *Opera et
Dies*, 287ff. There it is not a Heracles-fable at all but
a rather simple pronouncement on the smooth road of vice
and the rough road to virtue. W. Michaelis has argued
against J. Alpers that the *Tabula* is really based on the
tradition from Hesiod rather than on the Prodicus myth.
Two features of the storyline in the *Tabula* help to make
this point. First, there is the obvious absence of the
figure of Heracles as the heroic exemplar, and second,
there is the reversal of the rough and smooth roads after
one has reached the summit of Virtue, cf. *TDNT* V, 45, nn.
8 and 9. On the other hand, it may be the case that the
author of the *Tabula* has combined several "two-ways" traditions into his more elaborate storyline, a possibility suggested by Dio as well. The absence of Heracles from the
Tabula is striking, but it is interesting to note that in
three cases, all very strategically placed within the composition, the expletive ῏Ω ‘Ηράκλεις is used in place of
the more common Νὴ Δία/Πρὸς Διός (*C.T.* 4.1, 12.1, 19.1), cf.
n. 43 in the "Notes to the Translation." It may be that
Heracles has been intentionally omitted for the purpose of
drawing the interlocutor(s), and thereby the readers, into
the role of travellers on the journey depicted by the picture. That the author could have found the traditions of
Hesiod and Prodicus easily compatible is readily understood
when one notices that Xenophon recounts this portion of
Hesiod along with two verses from Epicharmus in *Mem.* II.1.20
just before he presents the Prodicus myth (beginning in 21).

[68]Thus, we see in the introduction, setting the stage
for the dialogue, and carrying throughout the text, that
there is an old-young dialectic at work. The Senex was a
νεώτερος when he received the interpretation of the picture
from its dedicator as a πολυχρονιώτατος (*C.T.* 2.3). The
Senex is called a πρεσβύτης in *C.T.* 2.1, and the interlocutor is explicitly called νεανίσκος in 23.4. Finally, the
Daimon is portrayed in the picture as a γέρων (*C.T.* 1.3).
Therefore, it is logical to consider those who "are about
to enter life" (4.2) as young men on the verge of manhood.

This parallelism is given further weight by the reference
to Plato in *C.T.* 33.3 which makes the object of education
the guidance of νέοι. This dialectic may serve to place
the reader in the position of receiving sage wisdom from
venerable age, and it reinforces our contention that the
author's primary audience was rich young men about to go
out into the world. This point is of some interest given
the more or less standard interpretation which sees the
Tabula as a popularization of philosophical paraenesis for
the lower classes, as in G. Downey, "The Pilgrim's Progress
of the Byzantine Emperor," 210f. The fact is that the entire work is concerned with those who actually receive
something from Tychē (*C.T.* 9.2), i.e., those things which
the masses call good, such as wealth, fame, honor, children, etc. (cf. 8.4, 36.1f). The final discussion comes
down to wealth and the proper attitude to have regarding it
(*C.T.* 39f). On the education of "rich young men," compare
ps-Plutarch, *De liberis educandis* (Mor. 1A-17C), esp. 5D.

[69] The characterization through *ekphrasis* of each Vice
and Virtue is intentionally done so as to create a diame-
trical opposition (compare the attributes of the Virtues in
18.1, 20.2, 21.3 with those of the Vices in 5.1, 9.1,
10.1ff). In addition, the vices and virtues are picked up
throughout the work as part of the larger discussion, e.g.,
in naming the beasts (23.1-2) vices are drawn from several
points in the work as fits the discussion.

[70] See the select bibliography for a general overview
of claimed points of contact with other authors ranging
from Plato and Thucydides to the *Shepherd* of Hermas and
Jesus himself.

[71] Praechter refers specifically to (ps-) Philo, *De
merc. meretr.* 2, cf. *Quanam aetate*, pp. 94f. In general,
W. Michaelis (*TDNT* V, 60ff) agrees with Praechter's analysis, but he goes on to suggest that (ps-)Philo does not
really use the Prodicus myth or a fully developed "two-
ways" typology. But the discussion can be carried farther,
cf. pp. 18f.

[72] The statement was from an unpublished letter from
Cotterill to Taylor and was quoted by Taylor in *J. Phil.* 27
(1901) 319, cf. 276.

[73] Taylor's article was published in three parts under
the title "Hermas and Cebes," *J. Phil.* 27 (1901) 276-319;
28 (1903) 24-38; 94-98. Despite the appearance of Praechter's text, Taylor seems to have used only the edition of
Jerram.

[74] See, for example, *J. Phil.* 27 (1901) 291-97.

[75] *J. Phil.* 28 (1903) 33-34, 37. We may cite as only
one example of his method the connection elicited by Taylor
between the riddle of the Sphinx (*C.T.* 3.2-4) and Hermas's
"disguised" use of the same imagery in the seats of the
woman. In Hermas, *Vis.* i.2; ii.1; iii.2, 10.3-5, the woman
appears three times and in different guises. She also sits
on a chair, a bench, and a stool, which fact Taylor takes
as the equivalent of the questions of legs in the Sphinx's
riddle. Taylor adds further that the reversal of the number
of legs is an attempt by Hermas to hide the use of a non-
Christian tradition, cf. *J. Phil.* 27 (1901) 288-90. Taylor
and others have generally placed great stress on the fact
that the visions of Hermas are explained by an old woman
(γυνὴ πρεσβῦτις) and the *Tabula* by an old man (πρεσβύτης).
But it would seem that Hermas could have as easily drawn
the imagery from Dio's *Or.* 1.51ff where the gender of the
revealer and the wilderness setting are more comparable.

[76] St. George Stock, "Hermas and Cebes--A Reply,"
J. Phil. 28 (1903) 87-93.

[77] J. M. Cotterill and C. Taylor, "Plutarch, Cebes, and
Hermas," *J. Phil.* 31 (1908-10) 14-41. Despite the appearance of Cotterill's name as the co-author, the article was
published some time after his death. It is possible that
Taylor is only giving credit for earlier collaboration and
advice. Most of the same conclusions reached in this article had been incorporated into Taylor's text and commentary of *The Shepherd*, cf. C. Taylor, *The Shepherd of Hermas*,
2 vols. (Early Church Classics Series; London, 1903) I, 38-
49 and notes *passim*.

[78] See, for example, S. Giet, *Hermas et les Pasteurs*
(Paris, 1963) 279ff; Roelef van Deemter, *Der Hirt des
Hermas--Apokalypse oder Allegorie?* (Delft, 1929) 104ff.
M. Dibelius, *Der Hirt des Hermas* (Tübingen, 1923) 579ff.
R. Joly, *Hermas, Le Pasteur*[2] (Sources Chrétiennes; Paris,
1968) 15ff; and H. Schultz, *Spuren heidnische Vorlagen im
Hirt des Hermas* (Dissertation; Rostock, 1913) *passim*.

[79] A few comparisons are still drawn from *Vis.* i, i.e.,
from the setting of the vision/revelation (cf. Joly, *Le
Tableau*, 82). But for the most part these seem a bit
stretched. In fact, the setting of *Vis.* i.2 is more like
that of Dio *Or.* 1.51ff.

[80] Joly, *Le Tableau*, 81ff.

[81] Van Deemter, *Der Hirt*, 106f.

[82] Ibid., 107. Schultz would also claim that both the
unknown "Cebes"/Hermas source and Galen were dependent on a
common source which may be Posidonius.

[83] A convenient summary of the issues in composition and authorship of the *Shepherd* may be found in the translation and commentary by Graydon F. Snyder in *The Apostolic Fathers*, ed. by R. M. Grant, Vol. VI (Camden, 1968) 3-18, 22-24. The basic point regarding the text is that *Vis.* i-iv are seen to be an earlier work to which *Vis.* v, the *Mand.* and the *Sim.* were added later. Some have even argued that *Sim.* ix was a later addition still.

[84] The first major proponent of multiple authorship and redaction in the *Shepherd* was Martin Dibelius in his *Der Hirt des Hermas* (1923). It should be noted that Dibelius generally denied any direct dependence of the *Shepherd* on the *Tabula*.

[85] If one wishes yet to maintain a more direct connection in the light of his redactional view of the *Shepherd* it seems that some possibility should be suggested for the author of *Sim.* ix, having recognized generic similarities (i.e., in imagery, style, etc.) between two otherwise independent works, to have drawn the relations more explicitly in his final reworking of the vision of the tower.

[86] See p. 17 and n. 71 above.

[87] See *C.T.* 15.2-16.5, 18.3, 27.1-28.3; cf. n. 85 in the "Notes to the Translation."

[88] As noted above, this reversal was already a feature of the "two-ways" motif in Hesiod, *Op. et Dies* 287ff. See also Dio Chrysostom, *Or.* 1.77 and ps-Diogenes, *Ep.* 37.6 (Hercher/Malherbe).

[89] The best example in Philo is *Vita Mosis* 2.138 (II.156, Cohn-Wendland) but see also *De Abram.* 85f and *De. Agric.*22.110. The term occurs some seventeen times in all in Philo. The first to make specific mention of this point was J. M. Cotterill as cited by Taylor in *J. Phil.* 27 (1901) 303. See also Hermas, *Man.* vi.1.3, cf. *Vis.* iii.7.1. For repentance see Philo, *De Abram.* 17-59. We may mention also Philo's *De gigantibus* 13.60-61 which classifies three types of men. The first two types, the "earth-born" who seek bodily pleasure and the "heaven-born" who are lovers of learning, correspond to the inhabitants of the first and second enclosures of the *Tabula*.

[90] See the discussion of Joly, *Le Tableau*, 79-80. The passage from Plutarch is quoted in n. 92 in the "Notes to the Translation."

[91] For a general discussion of Plutarch's ethics in relation to early Christian literature, see H. D. Betz, *Plutarch's Ethical Writings and Early Christian Literature* (Studia ad Corpus Hellenisticum Novi Testamenti 4; Leiden, 1978).

[92]Much the same role is played by the old woman who tells Dio the story of Heracles (*Or.* 1.51-58), which helps to understand the old-young motif in the passing on of tradition in the *Tabula*. Compare ps-Diogenes, *Epp.* 39.2, 37.4 (Hercher/Malherbe).

[93]See the discussion of D. A. Stoike, in H. D. Betz, *Plutarch's Theological Writings and Early Christian Literature* (Studia ad Corpus Hellenisticum Novi Testamenti 3; Leiden, 1975) 237-85.

[94]See n. 2 in the "Notes to the Translation."

[95]On the latter, cf. esp. C. F. Georg Heinrici, *Die Bergpredigt quellenkritisch und begriffsgeschichtlich untersucht* (Leipzig, 1900-05) 89f. for the history of the concept, and Hans Windisch, "Die Sprüche vom Eingehen in das Reich Gottes," *Zeitschrift für die Neutestamentliche Wissenschaft* 27 (1928) 163-92, esp. 189-92.

[96]Cf. the article by Smith cited in n. 19. For a discussion of the agraphon and a list of the places where it occurs, cf. A. Resch, *Agrapha*[2] (Leipzig, 1906) 112-28.

[97]Cf. his "Ad Cebetis tabulam," *Album gratulatorium in honorem Henrici van Herwerden* (Utrecht, 1902) 223-26, with specific reference to 1 Cor 1:18.

[98]Cf. n. 53 above. Finally, on the grammar and syntax of the *Tabula* vis-à-vis the style of the New Testament, the best survey remains that of Joly, *Le Tableau*, chap. 1. The extent to which there is a shared vocabulary with early Christian literature is indicated in the *index verborum* at the end of this volume. An asterisk designates those few words from the *Tabula* which are not listed in the lexicon of Bauer-Arndt-Gingrich-Danker.

[99]So Susemihl, *Geschichte*, 26 n. 66. The view that the author was a sophist was articulated earlier by an anonymous writer (perhaps Heyne) in the *Göttingische Gelehrte Anzeigen* of 1790, p. 799. This suggestion was also embraced by Grosse in Büchling and Grosse, xl-xlii. Against this position it has been pointed out that the rhetoricians are included among the devotees of Pseudopaideia. Cf. Alfred Croiset and M. Croiset, *Historie de la littérature grecque* (Paris, 1899) V, 416 n. 1.

[100]Jerram, xxvii-xxxiv; Parsons, 13-18; Lutz, "Aesticampianus' Edition," 111, speaks for many when she calls it "Socratic in spirit."

[101]Praechter, 24ff.

[102] Von Arnim (104-5) argues that the author is abbre-
viating a source that had a Socratic-dialogic form.
Carlini goes so far as to suggest that the author is bor-
rowing from the fourth century B.C.E. Socratic Aeschines.
Cf. A. Carlini, "Sulla composizione della *Tabula* di Cebete,"
Studi classici e orientali 12 (1963) 164-82, esp. 179-80.
Most scholars, however, seem to regard this as a conscious
imitation of Socratic style.

[103] See n. 19 above.

[104] See n. 26 above.

[105] Büchling and Grosse, xxviii n. 10, xxxvi. Cf. n.
20 above.

[106] So, for example, Drosihn in his "Die Zeit." By
1901 Karl Joël could say without qualification that no one
doubted the Cynic-Stoic character of the *Tabula*. See his
Der echte und der xenophontische Sokrates (Berlin, 1901)
II, 322.

[107] Joly (25-33) lists and criticizes each of these
points as to their specifically or exclusively Stoic character.

[108] Praechter, esp. 24-83.

[109] Joël, II, 322-32.

[110] Ibid., 327-32.

[111] See n. 24 above.

[112] J. J. Brucker, *Historia critica philosophiae* (1742)
Tom. I, p. 577sqq; and F. Sevin, "Examen si le tableau,
attribué à Cébès, est veritablement de cet auteur," in
Mém. de l'Acad. des Inscriptions, Th. III. hist. pp. 137ff;
ed. 8. Th. II. hist. p. 229. For a summary of Sevin's
views, see Büchling and Grosse, xxxii.

[113] Cf. n. 53 above.

[114] See n. 12 above. For an excellent survey of recent
scholarship on the Neo-Pythagoreans in general, see David
L. Balch, "The Neo-pythagorean Moralists and the New Testament," in H. Temporini and W. Haase (ed.), *Aufstieg und
Niedergang der roemischen Welt* (Berlin, 1983) Teil II, Band
26. To the list of translations cited by Balch in this
article, add K. S. Guthrie (trans.), *The Life of Pythagoras*
and *Pythagorean Library*, 2 vols. in 1 (Alpine, 1919). We
are indebted to Balch for this bibliographical addition to
his article.

[115]Some scholars, such as Stanley in his *hist. phil.*, have denied that this is a reference to the *Tabula* (cf. Büchling and Grosse, xxv). But it is difficult to believe that the Greek can be interpreted in any other way than as a reference to the *Tabula*. Joly (67) naturally sees this as a confirmation of his proposed interpretation, for the Pythagoreans understood Hades as this earthly life in which sins are expiated. Praechter (11-12) agrees that the *Suda* is referring to the *Tabula*, but he thinks that the *Suda* is simply mistaken. Praechter suggests that the *Suda* has interpreted the *Tabula* in light of Plato, *Republica* 614sqq. and that this is the source of the error. Whereas most scholars would supply either δώματι or πραγμάτων after ᾅδου, I. A. Meyer proposes ἱερέων. Thus the *Tabula* would then be seen by the *Suda* as containing the explanation given by priests in an oracular cave. The old man of the *Tabula* would then be seen as the mystagogue and the visiting strangers as the initiates to whom the explanation is given. See his *Eruditio veterum duplex...* (Hildesheim, 1792), cited by Büchling and Grosse, xxv-xxvi n. 9.

[116]Only a sketch of this relief fragment now survives. It is fully discussed by K. K. Müller in his article, "Relieffragment mit Darstellungen aus dem ΠΙΝΑΞ des Kebes," *Archäologische Zeitung* 42 (1884) 115-28. At the end of Müller's discussion a few dissenting remarks have been appended by C. Robert (127-30). Cf. also Joly, 67-69, and Roger Hinks, *Myth and Allegory in Ancient Art* (London, 1939) 119-21. For a reproduction of this drawing, see the beginning of this volume (Plate I).
Another bit of archaeological evidence that is frequently cited in support of a Neo-Pythagorean milieu for the composition of the *Tabula* is a tombstone from Alaschehir. It comes from the beginning of the first century C.E. and thus coincides with the most likely date for the *Tabula*. Like the *Tabula* it presents itself as Pythagorean. It contains the Pythagorean Y as well as contrasting images of the good and evil life. See Josef Keil and Anton v. Premerstein, *Bericht über eine Reise in Lydien und der südlichen Aiolis, ausgeführt 1906 im Auftrage der kaiserlichen Akademie der Wissenschaften* (Denkschriften der kaiserlichen Akademie der Wissenschaften in Wien, Philosophisch-historische Klasse; LIII, 2; Wien, 1909) Num. 55, Abb. 28, pp. 34-35; O. Kern's review of this *Bericht* in the *Deutsche Literaturzeitung* 30 (1909) 1887-88, where the connection with the *Tabula* is first suggested; A. Brinkmann, "Ein Denkmal des Neupythagoreismus," *Rheinisches Museum für Philologie*, Neue Folge, 66 (1911) 616-25; Carlini, "Sulla composizione," 165-69.

[117]K. Praechter, "Bericht über die Litteratur zu den nacharistotelischen Philosophen (mit Ausschluss der älteren Akademiker und Peripatetiker und von Lukrez, Cicero, Philon

und Plutarch) für 1889-1895," in Bursian's *Jahresbericht über die Fortschritte der classischen Altertumswissenschaft* 96 (1898) 45-47.

[118] See n. 99 above.

[119] See n. 27 above. For Praechter's critique of this analysis, see the article listed in n. 117 above.

[120] Compare the statement of J. V. Luce that "I would be content to believe of Cebes that the Cynics taught him and Plato inspired him." Cf. his review of Joly in *The Classical Review*, N.S. 14 (1964) 38-39.

[121] Karl Praechter, Κέβητος πίναξ. *Cebetis Tabula* (Lipsiae, 1893).

[122] Also, limited consideration is accorded to the text and variants of a highly debated edition by M. Meibomius. The controversy centers on the sources used for the text and the list of variant readings printed as an appendix to this edition. Some maintain that the readings found here come from a now lost "codex Meibomianus." Others, however, deny that such a codex ever existed and maintain that the readings of codex M are drawn from other manuscripts and represent the conjectures of an unknown scholar. For the circumstances that gave rise to the edition, cf. the *Biographie universelle*, vol. 28 (Paris, 1820) 142-43. For the debate over M, cf. K. K. Müller, *De arte critica Cebetis Tabulae adhibenda* (Virceburgi, 1877) 19-49, and "Zur Kritik des Kebes," *Zeitschrift für die österreichischen Gymnasien* 30 (1879) 241-52, esp. 246-47, and P. Knöll's review of Müller's work in the journal listed above, 29 (1878) 97-102, in which he defends M against the charges made by Müller.

[123] Hermann Sauppe, Review of Friedrich Drosihn's *Cebetis Tabula* in *Göttingische gelehrte Anzeigen*, 1872, 769-77, reprinted in Sauppe's *Ausgewählte Schriften* (Berlin, 1896) 651-56.

[124] Cf. n. 122 above and the select bibliography for references to Müller's work. It is tragic that Müller himself did not live to publish an edition of the *Tabula*.

[125] Codex A is the most reliable of the various manuscripts, but it breaks off at 23.2.3. Its general reliability is reflected in the fact that Praechter frequently adopts readings that are unique to A. See, for example, 1.1.5; 2.1.1; 2.1.5; 5.1.2; 8.2.5; 9.2.7; 10.1.2; 10.3.2; 12.2.3; 15.2.3; 15.4.2; 16.2.3; 19.1.5; 19.2.4; 19.2.5; 22.1.3; 23.1.4. At other times Praechter gives readings that are very close to ones found in A. See, for example, 3.3.3; 4.1.4; 4.3.5-6; 5.1.5; 8.4.6; 10.4.5-6. But

Praechter's use of A is not uncritical. Instances where
Praechter reads against A include 2.3.5; 3.1.2; 3.1.5;
7.1.2; 7.3.4; 11.1.1; 11.2.3; 12.3.5; 13.2.4; 16.1.2;
16.3.2; 18.1.4; 20.3.4; 20.4.4. Codex A may also be the
earliest manuscript, but there is, in fact a small debate
concerning the date of its transcription. Schweighaeuser
and Drosihn had dated it to the twelfth century, but Müller
in his dissertation (10) assigned it to the eleventh century. In his edition (iv, xii) Praechter followed the
eleventh century date given by Müller. It is this early
date that is commonly given by contemporary scholars. This
may well be the correct date, but it should be noted that
in an 1884 article Müller changed the date for A from the
eleventh to the fourteenth century. He explained that,
when he wrote his dissertation, he personally had not seen
codex A but had relied upon the collations of H. Dulac for
the readings of this manuscript. But having himself seen
the codex, he reached the conclusion that the part of codex
A that contains the *Tabula* was written in the fourteenth
century. This change in dating, however, did not involve
for Müller a lessening of A's reliability. Cf. the *Phil.
Rund.* IV (1884) 1419-20. It is interesting to note that
Susemihl follows Müller's fourteenth century dating in his
1891 *Geschichte der griechischen Literatur*, 26 n. 66. But
in his 1894 review of Praechter's edition he reverts without explanation to the eleventh century date given by
Praechter. Susemihl appears simply to have forgotten his
reason for assigning A to the fourteenth century in his
earlier work. Cf. the *Berliner Philologische Wochenschrift*
14 (1894) 1249-51, esp. 1249.

[126]Müller (*De arte critica*, 46-48) had attempted to
prove that Codex V is the archetype of all manuscripts of
the *Tabula* that have been preserved (with the exception of
A). While rejecting this claim and thus giving more weight
to the readings of other manuscripts than did Müller,
Praechter still accords the readings of V some preference.
Praechter's rejection of Müller's thesis and his concomi-
tant distinction of four subfamilies (VL, BR, CK(P), and
FEDW) have now been corroborated by the investigations of
C. E. Finch. Cf. especially "The Place of Codex Vat. Gr.
1823 in the Cebes Manuscript Tradition," *American Journal
of Philology* 81 (1960) 176-85. Finch, however, dissents
in part from Praechter (and Müller) as to the relationship
of manuscripts within these subfamilies.

[127]C. Salmasius in 1640 published a triglot edition of
the Arabic, Latin, and Greek, that had been prepared by
Elichmann. On this edition, cf. now the fine article by
C. E. Lutz, "The Salmasius-Elichmann Edition of the *Tabula*
of Cebes," *Harvard Library Bulletin* 27 (1979) 165-71.

[128]For a collection of Praechter's more important articles and monographs, see Karl Praechter, *Kleine Schriften*,
ed. H. Dörrie (Hildesheim/New York, 1973).

[129]Cf. the Select Bibliography for a list of Finch's articles. Already before his death, K. K. Müller had called Praechter's attention to other Greek codices and Latin versions. The 1903 edition of the *Tabula* by Jacob van Wageningen made use of a Codex Neapolitanus. Finch has uncovered even more Greek and Latin manuscripts. In regard to the value of the Latin versions for the establishment of the text, Finch differs from both Müller and Praechter. Praechter utilized only the readings of Odaxius and Elichmann in constructing the text and these only sparingly. Finch, on the other hand, accords greater value to the readings of both of these and those of Codex Vaticanus Latinus 4037. K. K. Müller had seen this manuscript (*Phil. Rund.* IV [1884] 1420) but had, in contrast to Finch, judged it to be of no value for the establishment of a critical text. Therefore, while we frequently cite readings from this Latin codex in our "Notes to the Text" the reader should know that the value of this witness is not uncontested.

[130]Cf. his review of van Wageningen's edition in the *Berliner Philologische Wochenschrift* 25 (1905) 145-56, esp. 149. Van Wageningen's text has remained inaccessible to us, despite diligent efforts to obtain a copy. Therefore we are unable to say with certainty what Praechter would have changed in regard to his edition. The places at which he might have done this, however, are 16.4, 19.2, 34.1, 37.1.

[131]This information is drawn from Praechter's review of van Wageningen in the *Berliner Philolog. Wochen.* 25 (1905) 147-48; Müller's review of Krauss in *Phil. Rund.* IV (1884) 1419-20, and Finch's articles as given in the Select Bibliography.

SELECT BIBLIOGRAPHY

I. Editions (by date)

Wolf, Hieronymous. *Epicteti enchiridion...*, *Cebetis The-bani tabula...: Graece & Latine....* 3 tom. Basileae: per Ioannem Oporinum, 1561-63.

Gronovius, Jacob. Κέβητος Θηβαίου πίναξ. *Cebetis Thebani tabula, Graece et Latine....* Amstelaedami: apud Henricum Wetstenium, 1689.

Schweighäuser, Johannes. *Epicteti Manuale et Cebetis tabula... Graeca recensuit et collata omni lectionis varietate vindicavit illustravitque; Latinam versionem....* Lipsiae: in libraria Weidmannia, 1798.

_____. *Cebetis tabula sive vitae humanae pictura. Graece....* Argentorati: apud Joh. Henr. Heitz, Acad. Typogr. et apud Societatem Bipontinam, 1806.

Büchling, Johann David, and Grosse, Georg Friedrich Wilhelm. Κέβητος πίναξ. *Des Cebes Gemälde.* Meissen: Friedrich Wilhelm Gödsche, 1813.

Thieme, Martin Heinrich. Κέβητος Θηβαίου πίναξ. *Cebes des Thebaners Gemälde.* Dritte Auflage. Berlin: In der Maurerschen Buchhandlung, 1829.

Drosihn, Friedrich. Κέβητος πίναξ. *Cebetis Tabula.* Lipsiae: in aedibus B. G. Teubneri, 1871.

Jerram, C. S. Κέβητος πίναξ. *Cebetis Tabula with Introduction and Notes.* Clarendon Press Series. Oxford: Clarendon Press, 1878.

Parsons, Richard. Κέβητος πίναξ. *Cebes' Tablet, with Introduction, Notes, Vocabulary, and Grammatical Questions.* Boston: Ginn and Company, 1887.

Praechter, Karl (= Carolus). Κέβητος πίναξ. *Cebetis Tabula.* Lipsiae: in aedibus B. G. Teubneri, 1893.

Wageningen, J. van. Κέβητος πίναξ. *Cebetis Tabula.* Bibliotheca Batava Script. Graec. et Rom. curantibus K. Kuiper, J. S. Speyer, J. van Wageningen. Groningen: Wolters, 1903.

II. Modern Translations

A. English

Guthrie, Kenneth Sylvan (trans.). *The Greek Pilgrim's
    Progress, Generally Known as the Picture by Kebes,
    a disciple of Sokrates?* London: Luzac and Company,
    and Philadelphia: Monsalvat Press, 1910.

B. French

Commelin, P. (trans.). *Pensées de Marc Aurèle Antonin
    précédées de la vie de cet empereur, suivies du
    Manuel d'Epictète et du Tableau de Cébès*. Paris:
    Librairie Garnier Frères, n.d.

Méautis, Georges (trans.). *Les pelerinages de l'ame*.
    Paris: Adyar, 1959.

Meunier, Mario (trans.). *Marc-Aurèle, Pensées pour moi-
    même, suivies du Manuel d'Epictete et du Tableau de
    Cébès*. Classiques Garnier. Paris: Garnier Frères,
    1960.

C. German

Krauss, Friedrich S. (trans.). *Das Gemälde im Kronostempel
    von Kebes*. Zweite Auflage. Wien: Carl Gerold's Sohn,
    1890.

Niederegger, A. (trans.). *Das Gemälde* (πίναξ).
    Maraschein, 1924.

III. Secondary Works

Albrecht, Michael von. Review of Robert Joly's *Le Tableau
    de Cébès et la philosophie religieuse*, in *Gnomon* 36
    (1964) 755-59.

Alpers, J. *Hercules in bivio*. Gottingae: apud Dieterich-
    ium, 1912.

Ameisenowa, Zofia. "Tabula Cebetis, nieznany rysunek z XVI
    wieku w Bibliotece Jagiellońskiej," *Biuletyn Historii
    Sztuki* 18 (1956) 476-81.

Arnim, H.F.A. von. "Kebes," *Pauly's Real-Encyclopädie der
    classischen Altertumswissenschaft*, XI.1, 101-104, ed.
    by Georg Wissowa, re-ed. by Wilhelm Kroll. Stuttgart:
    J. B. Metzler'sche Verlagsbuchhandlung, 1921.

Bähr, C. F.   "Cebes," *Real-Encyclopädie der classischen
    Alterthumswissenschaft*, ed. August Pauly, II, pp. 232-
    33. Stuttgart: J. B. Metzler'sche Buchhandlung, 1842.

Boas, M. "De Illustratie der Tabula Cebetis," *Het Boek* 9
    (1920) 1-16, 105-14.

_____. "De Nederlandsche Cebes-Literatuur," *Het Boek* 7
    (1918) 11-28.

Boll, F.   Review of Carolus Praechter's *Cebetis Tabula*, in
    Blätter für das Gymnasial-Schulwesen 31 (1895) 470-71.

Brinkman, A.   "Ein Denkmal des Neupythagoreismus,"
    Rheinisches Museum für Philologie, Neue Folge 66
    (1911) 616-25.

C., P.   Review of Carolus Praechter's *Cebetis Tabula*, in
    *Revue de philologie de littérature et d'historie
    anciennes* 19 (1895) 96.

Capelle, Guilelmus. *De cynicorum epistulis*. Gottingae:
    Jaenecke Fratres Hannoverae, 1896.

Carlini, Antonio. "Appunti di lettura," *Maia* 21 (1969)
    273-79.

_____. "Sulla composizione della *Tabula* di Cebete,"
    Studi classici e orientali 12 (1963) 164-82.

"Cebes," *Harper's Dictionary of Classical Antiquity*, ed.
    H. T. Peck. New York: Harper and Brothers, 1897.

Chew, Samuel Claggett. *The Pilgrimage of Life*. New
    Haven: Yale University, 1962.

Cotterill, J. M. (dec.) and Taylor, C.   "Plutarch, Cebes,
    and Hermas," *The Journal of Philology* 31 (1910) 14-41.

Croiset, Alfred, and Croiset, Maurice. *Historie de la
    littérature grecque*, V.   Paris: Albert Fontemoing
    Éditeur, [1899].

David, Madeleine. "Leibniz et le 'Tableau de Cébès'
    (*Nouveaux Essais*, 1, IV, chap. III, §20) ou le
    problème du langage par images," *Revue philosophique*
    151 (1961) 39-50.

Dibelius, Martin. *Der Hirt des Hermas*. Tübingen: J.C.B.
    Mohr (Paul Siebeck), 1923.

Dörrie, Heinrich. "Kebes," *Der Kleine Pauly*, ed. K.
    Ziegler and W. Sontheimer, III, col. 173. Stuttgart:
    Alfred Druckenmüller Verlag, 1969.

Dörrie, Heinrich, and H. Dörries, "Erotapokriseis," *Real-lexikon für Antike und Christentum*, VI, 342-70, ed. by T. Klauser. Stuttgart: Anton Hiersemann, 1966.

Downey, Glanville. "Ekphrasis," *Reallexikon für Antike und Christentum*, IV, 921-44, ed. by T. Klauser. Stuttgart: Anton Hiersemann, 1959.

_____. "The Pilgrim's Progress of the Byzantine Emperor," *Church History* 9 (1940) 207-17.

Drosihn, Friedrich. "Die Zeit des ΠΙΝΑΞ ΚΕΒΗΤΟΣ. Aus den Papieren des verstorbenen Oberlehrer Drosihn vom Prorector Dietlein," *Programm des fürstlich hed-wigschen Gymnasiums zu Neustettin* (Neustettin: F. E. Keilich, 1873) 3-15.

Eberhard, A. "Jahresbericht über die Erscheinungen auf dem Gebiete der späteren griechischen Prosa sowie der mittel- und neugriechischen Prosa und Poesie," *Jahres-bericht über die Fortschritte der classischen Alter-tumswissenschaft*, Erster Band, Zweiter Jahrgang, 1873, pp. 1293-1334, esp. p. 1299, ed. C. Bursian. Berlin: S. Calvary & Co., 1876.

Finch, Chauncey Edgar. "Fragment of Cebes' *Tabula* in Codex Urb. Gr. 125," *The Classical Bulletin* 34 (1957) 22.

_____. "Fragment of Cebes' *Tabula* in Codex Vaticanus Chisianus Graecus 17," *The Classical Bulletin* 35 (1958) 21.

_____. "Notes on Codex V of Cebes' *Tabula*," *Classical Philology* 53 (1958) 240-41.

_____. "The Place of Codex Vat. Gr. 1823 in the Cebes Manuscript Tradition," *American Journal of Philology* 81 (1960) 176-85.

_____. "The Translation of Cebes' *Tabula* in Codex Vaticanus Latinus 4037," *Transactions and Proceedings of the American Philological Association* 85 (1954) 79-87.

_____. "Value of Odaxius' Translation of Cebes' *Tabula*," *The Classical Bulletin* 35 (1958/1959) 27-28.

Gombrich, E. H. "A Classical 'Rake's Progress,'" *Journal of the Warburg and Courtauld Institutes* 15 (1952) 254-56.

Grübler, H. Review of Carolus Praechter's *Cebetis Tabula*, in *Revue des études grecques* 7 (1894) 98.

Hazlitt, William Carew. *Offspring of Thought in Solitude*.
    London: Reeves & Turner, 1884.

Heinrici, C. F. Georg. *Die Bergpredigt quellenkritisch
    und begriffsgeschichtlich untersucht*. Leipzig:
    Verlag der Dürr'schen Buchhandlung, 1900-1905.

Heinze, Max. "Bericht über die im Jahre 1873 erscheinenen,
    auf die nacharistotelische Philosophie bezüglichen
    Arbeiten," *Jahresbericht über die Fortschritte der
    classischen Alterthumswissenschaft*, Erster Jahrgang,
    Erster Band, 1873, pp. 187-210, esp. 201-202, ed. by
    C. Bursian. Berlin: S. Calvary & Co., 1875.

Herwerden, H. van. "Ad Cebetis Tabulam," *Mnemosyne* II:22
    (1894) 263.

Hinks, Roger. *Myth and Allegory in Ancient Art*. London:
    The Warburg Institute, 1939.

Hirzel, Rudolf. *Der Dialog*, II. Leipzig: S. Hirzel, 1895.

Höistad, Ragner. *Cynic Hero and Cynic King*. Uppsala/Lund:
    Carl Bloms Boktryckeri A.-B., 1948.

Hogue, Addison. "A Greek 'Pilgrim's Progress,'" *The Union
    Seminary Magazine*, Richmond, VA, Feb.-March, 1902,
    211-24.

Jaeger, Werner. Review of Eduard Norden's *Agnostos Theos*,
    in *Göttingische gelehrte Anzeigen* (1913) 569-610.
    Reprinted in Jaeger's *Scripta Minora*, I. Roma: Edi-
    zioni di Storia e Litteratura, 1960.

Joël, Karl. *Der echte und der xenophontische Sokrates*,
    II.1. Berlin: R. Gaertners Verlagsbuchhandlung, 1901.

Joly, Robert. *Hermas: Le Pasteur*. Second Edition.
    Sources Chretiennes 53 bis. Paris: Editions du Cerf,
    1968.

_____. *Le Tableau de Cébès et la philosophie religieuse*.
    Collection Latomus LXI. Bruxelles-Berchem: Latomus,
    1963.

Keil, Josef and Premerstein, Anton v. *Bericht über eine
    Reise in Lydien und der südlichen Aiolis, ausgeführt
    1906 im Auftrage der Kaiserlichen Akademie der Wissen-
    schaften*. Denkschriften der Kaiserlichen Akademie der
    Wissenschaften in Wien, Philosophisch-historische
    Klasse, LIII, 2. Wien: Alfred Hölder, 1909.

Kern, O. Review of Josef Keil and Anton v. Premerstein's
    *Bericht über eine Reise in Lydien und der südlichen
    Aiolis*, in *Deutsche Literaturzeitung* 30 (1909) 1887-88.

Knöll, P.   Review of K. K. Müller's *De arte critica Cebetis Tabulae adhibenda*, in *Zeitschrift für die österreichischen Gymnasien* 29 (1878) 97-102.

_____. "Zur Kritik des Kebes," *Zeitschrift für die österreichischen Gymnasien* 30 (1879) 335-36.

Kroll, W.   Review of Carolus Praechter's *Cebetis Tabula*, in *Deutsche Literaturzeitung* 15 (1894) 1513.

Lehmann, Karl.   "Ignorance and Search in the Villa of the Mysteries," *Journal of Roman Studies* 52 (1962) 62-68.

Luce, J. V.   "The Tablet of Cebes," review of Robert Joly's *Le Tableau de Cébès et la philosophie religieuse*, in *The Classical Review*, N.S. 14 (1964) 38-39.

Lutz, Cora E.   "Aesticampianus' Edition of the *Tabula* Attributed to Cebes," *The Yale University Library Gazette* 45 (1971) 110-17.

_____. "Cebes," *Catalogus Translationum et Commentariorum*. (Forthcoming)

_____. "The Salmasius-Elichmann Edition of the *Tabula* of Cebes," *Harvard Library Bulletin* 27 (1979) 165-71.

Malherbe, Abraham Johannes.   *The Cynic Epistles*. Society of Biblical Literature: Sources for Biblical Study. Missoula, MT: Scholars Press, 1977.

Moreau, Joseph.   Review of Robert Joly's *Le Tableau de Cébès et la philosophie religieuse*, in *Revue des études anciennes* 65 (1963) 432-33.

Müller, H.   Review of K. K. Müller's *De arte critica Cebetis Tabulae adhibenda*, in *Philologischer Anzeiger* 9 (1878) 266-69.

Müller, Karl Konrad.   *De arte critica Cebetis Tabulae adhibenda*. Virceburgi: C. J. Becker, 1877.

_____. "Relieffragment mit Darstellungen aus dem ΠΙΝΑΞ des Kebes," *Archäologische Zeitung* 42 (1884) 115-30.

_____. Review of F. S. Krauss' *Das Gemälde des Kebes*, in *Philologische Rundschau* 4 (1884) 1416-24.

_____. "Zu Cebes," *Philologischer Anzeiger* 9 (1878) 269-70.

_____. "Zur Kritik des Kebes," *Zeitschrift für die österreichischen Gymnasien* 30 (1879) 241-52.

Phillips, John Goldsmith. "The Garden of False Learning,"
    Bulletin: The Metropolitan Museum of Art, N.S. 1
    (1942-1943) 243-47.

Phloros, A. T. "'Ανάλυσις τοῦ Πίνακος τοῦ Κέβητος,"
    Platon 10 (1958) 69-74.

_____. "Παρατηρήσεις εἰς τὸ τὸν βιβλίον τοῦ Θουκυδίδου
    καὶ εἰς τὸν Πίνακα τοῦ Κέβητος," *Platon* 7 (1956)
    86-90.

_____. "'Ο Κέβητος Πίναξ," *Platon* 7 (1955) 287-95.

Praechter, Karl (= Carolus). "Bericht über die Literatur
    zu den nacharistotelischen Philosophen (mit Ausschluss
    der älteren Akademiker und Peripatetiker und von
    Lukrez, Cicero, Philon und Plutarch) für 1889-1895,"
    *Jahresbericht über die Fortschritte der classischen
    Altertumswissenschaft*. Sechsundzwanzigster Band,
    1898, pp. 1-106, esp. 45-47, ed. by L. Gurlitt und
    W. Knoll. Leipzig: O. R. Reisland, 1899.

_____. *Cebetis Tabula quanam aetate conscripta esse
    videatur*. Marburgi: G. Braun, 1885.

_____. *Kleine Schriften*. Ed. by Heinrich Dörrie.
    Collectanea VII. Hildesheim/New York: Georg Olms,
    1973.

_____. Review of J. van Wageningen's *Cebetis Tabula*,
    in *Berliner Philologische Wochenschrift* 25 (1905)
    145-46.

_____ (ed.). *Die Philosophie des Altertums*. Erster Teil
    of *Friedrich Ueberwegs Grundriss der Geschichte der
    Philosophie*. 12th edition. Berlin: E. S. Mittler &
    Sohn, 1926.

Radermacher, L. "Varia," *Rheinisches Museum für Philologie*
    55 (1900) 149-51.

Robert, C. Comment on K. K. Müller's "Relieffragment," in
    Archäologische Zeitung 42 (1884) 127-30.

Rossetti, Livio. "Spuren einiger *Erōtikoi Logoi* aus der
    Zeit Platons," *Eranos* 72 (1974) 185-92.

Sauppe, Hermann. Review of Friedrich Drosihn's *Cebetis
    Tabula*, in *Göttingische gelehrte Anzeigen*, 1872, 769-
    77. Reprinted in Sauppe's *Ausgewählte Schriften*.
    Berlin: Weidmannische Buchhandlung, 1896.

Schleier, Reinhart. *Tabula Cebetis; oder Spiegel des
    menschlichen Lebens, darin Tugent und Untugent ab-
    gemalet ist. Studien zur Rezeption einer antiken*

Bildbeschreibung im 16. und 17. Jahrhundert. Berlin:
Mann, 1974.

Sider, Sandra. *Cebes' Tablet: Facsimiles of the Greek Text
and of Selected Latin, French, English, Spanish, Italian, German, Dutch, and Polish Translations*. Renaissance Text Series. New York: The Renaissance Society
of America, 1979.

Sinko, Thaddaeus. "De lineamentis Platonicis in Cebetis
q.v. tabula," *Eos* 45 (1951) 3-31.

Sittl, K. *Geschichte der griechischen Literatur bis auf
Alexander den Grossen*, II. München: T. Ackermann,
1887.

Smith, David. "Had Our Lord Read the "Tablet" of Kebes?,"
The Expositor, Sixth Series, 3 (1901) 387-97.

Starnes, D. T. "The Figure Genius in the Renaissance,"
Studies in the Renaissance 11 (1964) 234-44.

Stock, St. George. "Hermas and Cebes--A Reply," *The
Journal of Philology* 23 (1903) 87-93.

Susemihl, Franz. *Geschichte der griechischen Literatur in
der Alexandrinerzeit*, 2 vols. Hildesheim: G. Olms,
1965, a reprint of the Leipzig edition of 1891-1892.

_____. Review of Carolus Praechter's *Cebetis Tabula*,
in *Berliner philologische Wochenschrift* 14 (1894)
1249-51.

Taylor, C. "Hermas and Cebes," *The Journal of Philology* 27
(1901) 276-319; 28 (1903) 24-38.

_____. "Note on 'Hermas and Cebes--A Reply,'" *The
Journal of Philology* 28 (1903) 94-98.

_____. *The Shepherd of Hermas*, I. Early Church Clas-
sics. London: Society for Promoting Christian Knowledge, 1903.

Wageningen, J. van. *Aanteekeningen op de Cebetis Tabula*.
Groningen: Wolters, 1903.

_____. "Ad Cebetis tabulam," *Album gratulatorium in
honorem Henrici van Herwerden*, pp. 223-26. Utrecht:
Kemink et Filium, 1902.

Weinreich, Otto. *Stiftung und Kultsatzungen eines Privat-
heiligtums in Philadelpheia in Lydien*. Sitzungsbericht
der Heidelberger Akademie der Wissenschaften. Stiftung
Heinrich Lanz, Philosophisch-historische Klasse, Jahrgang 1919, 16. Abhandlung. Heidelberg: Carl Winters
Universitätsbuchhandlung, 1919.

Westerink, L. G.   Review of Robert Joly's *Le Tableau de
     Cébès et la philosophie religieuse*, in *Mnemosyne*,
     Fourth Series, 18 (1965) 85-86.

Windisch, Hans.   "Die Sprüche vom Eingehen in das Reich
     Gottes," *Zeitschrift für die Neutestamentliche
     Wissenschaft* 27 (1928) 163-92, esp. 189-92.

Wharey, James Blanton.   *A Study of the Sources of Bunyan's
     Allegories*.   Baltimore: J. H. Furst Company, 1904.

Zeller, Eduard.   *Die Philosophie der Griechen*, II.1.
     Fünfte Ausgabe.   Leipzig: O. R. Reisland, 1922.

ADDENDUM

The recent book by Stephen Orgel (ed.), *Cebes in England:
English Translations of the Tablet of Cebes from Three
Centuries, with Related Material* (New York/London:
Garland, 1980), was brought to our attention too late
and has been unavailable to us for use in the present
study.   We include the reference here for the sake of
completeness.

SIGLA

Manuscripts cited in Praechter's apparatus:

Greek Manuscripts

A	Cod. Parisinus graec. 858 membr.	(XI cent? XIV?)
B	Cod. Parisinus graec. 1001 chart.	(XV cent)
C	Cod. Parisinus graec. 1774 chart.	(XVI cent)
D	Cod. Parisinus graec. 2992 chart.	(XVI cent)
E	Cod. Marc. (Venetus) graec. 391 chart.	(XV cent)
F	Cod. Marc. (Venetus) graec. 594 chart.	(XV cent)
K	Cod. Corsin. ex bibl. Nic. Rossii 292	
	(Coll. 43. D. 30)	(XV cent?)
L	Cod. Laurentianus plut. 57 cod. 45	(XV cent)
M	Cod. Meibomianus	(?)
P	Cod. Palatinus graec. 134 chart.	(XV cent)
R	Cod. Riccard. 25 chart.	(XV cent)
V	Cod. Vaticanus 112 bombyc.?	(XIV cent)
W	Cod. Vindobonensis phil. graec. 167 chart.	(XV cent?)

Latin Versions

A	Arabic version, trans. into Latin	(XI cent Arabic,
	by Elichmann	XVI cent Latin)
O	Latin version of Odaxius	(XV cent Latin)

Manuscripts not used by Praechter but cited in "Notes to Translation"

An	Cod. Vaticanus Latinus 4037	(XV-XVI cent)
Ch	Cod. Vaticanus Chisianus Graecus 17	(XVI cent)
S	Cod. Vaticanus Graecus 1823	(XV-XVI cent)
U	Cod. Vaticanus Urbinas Graecus 125	(XV cent)

Additional manuscripts not used by Praechter or cited in the "Notes to Translation"

N	Cod. Neapolitanus	(XV cent)
	Cod. Paris. suppl. gr. 1116 (Bibl. de l'école d. chartes 53,366)	
	Cod. Riccard. 766	

TEXT AND TRANSLATION

ΚΕΒΗΤΟΣ ΠΙΝΑΞ.

I. Ἐτυγχάνομεν περιπατοῦντες ἐν τῷ τοῦ Κρόνου ἱερῷ, ἐν ᾧ πολλὰ μὲν καὶ ἄλλα ἀναθήματα ἐθεωροῦμεν· ἀνέκειτο δὲ καὶ πίναξ τις ἔμπροσθεν τοῦ νεώ, ἐν ᾧ ἦν γραφὴ ξένη τις καὶ μύθους ἔχουσα ἰδίους, οὓς 5 οὐκ ἠδυνάμεθα συμβαλεῖν, τίνες καί ποτε ἦσαν. οὔτε 2 γὰρ πόλις ἐδόκει ἡμῖν εἶναι τὸ γεγραμμένον οὔτε στρατόπεδον, ἀλλὰ περίβολος ἦν ἐν αὐτῷ ἔχων ἑτέρους περιβόλους δύο, τὸν μὲν μείζω, τὸν δὲ ἐλάττω. ἦν δὲ καὶ πύλη ἐπὶ τοῦ πρώτου περιβόλου. πρὸς δὲ τῇ 10 πύλῃ ὄχλος ἐδόκει ἡμῖν πολὺς ἐφεστάναι, καὶ ἔνδον 3 δὲ ἐν τῷ περιβόλῳ πλῆθός τι γυναικῶν ἑωρᾶτο. ἐπὶ δὲ [τῆς εἰσόδου] τοῦ [πρώτου] πυλῶνος [καὶ περιβόλου] γέρων τις ἑστὼς ἔμφασιν ἐποίει ὡς προστάττων τι τῷ εἰσιόντι ὄχλῳ. 15

II. Ἀπορούντων οὖν ἡμῶν περὶ τῆς μυθολογίας πρὸς ἀλλήλους πολὺν χρόνον πρεσβύτης τις παρεστώς, Οὐδὲν δεινὸν πάσχετε, ὦ ξένοι, ἔφη, ἀπορροῦντες περὶ

---

1 titulum om A Κέβητος πίναξ Θηβαίου C Κέβητος πίναξ πάνυ ἀναγκαῖος καὶ ὠφέλιμος V ‖ 2 Κρόνου] ἡλίου C³ mg M ‖ 4 ἐνέκειτο CKP ‖ 5 ξένη τις A τις ξένη reliqui ‖ 6 ἐδυνάμεθα R² ‖ συμβαλλεῖν CP, in D alterum λ erasum | τίνες τε F | ποτ' M ‖ 8 αὐτῷ libri corr Saupp. p. 774 ‖ 11 πολὺς om P¹ add πόλις P² mg | καὶ A sscr C² om reliqui | ἔνδον in rasura V² ‖ 12 ἐν τῷ περιβόλῳ] τοῦ περιβόλου KP² mg ‖ 13 καὶ] τοῦ CM | τῆς εἰσόδου — πρώτου — καὶ περιβόλου in suspicionem adduxit Sauppeus p. 774 ad eandem portam 𝔄 ‖ 14 ἐφεστὼς M | προσ-
* τάττειν P¹ corr P² ‖ 16 οὖν A δὲ reliqui | ἡμῶν e corr V² ‖
* 17 πολὺν χρόνον πρὸς ἀλλήλους FDW

CEBETIS TABULA, ed. Praechter.   1

THE *TABULA* OF CEBES

I.   We happened to be strolling in the temple
of Cronus,[1] looking at the many different votive
offerings in it. In front of the shrine was set
up a tablet,[2] on which there was an unusual painting
with peculiar fables, and we were not able to make
out what they could possibly be. For what was
depicted seemed to us to be neither a walled city nor
a military camp; it was, rather, a circular enclosure
having within itself two other circular enclosures,
one larger and one smaller.[3] There was also a gate
in the first enclosure. It appeared to us that a
large crowd was standing nearby before the gate, and
within the enclosure quite a number of women were
visible. Standing in [the entry way of] the [first]
gate [and enclosure] an old man looked as though he
were giving orders of some sort to the entering crowd.

II.   Then, while we were questioning one another
at length as to the meaning of the fable, an old man
who was standing nearby said, "If you have questions
about this picture, O strangers, your reaction is
not unusual,

τῆς γραφῆς ταύτης. οὐδὲ γὰρ τῶν ἐπιχωρίων πολλοὶ
2 οἴδασι, τί ποτε αὕτη ἡ μυθολογία δύναται· οὐδὲ γάρ
ἐστι πολιτικὸν ἀνάθημα· ἀλλὰ ξένος τις πάλαι ποτὲ
ἀφίκετο δεῦρο, ἀνὴρ ἔμφρων καὶ δεινὸς περὶ σοφίαν,
5 λόγῳ τε καὶ ἔργῳ Πυθαγόρειόν τινα καὶ Παρμενίδειον
ἐζηλωκὼς βίον, ὃς τό τε ἱερὸν τοῦτο καὶ τὴν γραφὴν
ἀνέθηκε τῷ Κρόνῳ.
3   Πότερον οὖν, ἔφην ἐγώ, καὶ αὐτὸν τὸν ἄνδρα
γινώσκεις ἑωρακώς;
10   Καὶ ἐθαύμασά γε, ἔφη, αὐτὸν πολυχρονιώτατον
νεώτερος ὤν. πολλὰ γὰρ καὶ σπουδαῖα διελέγετο.
τότε δὴ καὶ περὶ ταύτης [δὲ] τῆς μυθολογίας πολλάκις
αὐτοῦ ἠκηκόειν διεξιόντος.
     III. Πρὸς Διὸς τοίνυν, ἔφην ἐγώ, εἰ μή τίς σοι
15 μεγάλη ἀσχολία τυγχάνει οὖσα, διήγησαι ἡμῖν· πάνυ
γὰρ ἐπιθυμοῦμεν ἀκοῦσαι, τί ποτέ ἐστιν ὁ μῦθος.
     Οὐδεὶς φθόνος, ὦ ξένοι, ἔφη. ἀλλὰ τουτὶ πρῶτον
δεῖ ὑμᾶς ἀκοῦσαι, ὅτι ἐπικίνδυνόν τι ἔχει ἡ ἐξήγησις.
Οἷον τί; ἔφην ἐγώ.

1 οὐδὲ ΑΜ οὐ reliqui | ἐγχωρίων Μ ‖ 2 ἴσασι CKP | δύνα-
ται Α δύναιτο reliqui | οὐ P¹ οὐδὲ P² reliqui ‖ 3 ante ἀνάθημα
add τὸ Μ sscr C rec man | ἀλλὰ om V¹ sscr V² ‖ 4 ἔμφρων]
ἄφρων Μ ‖ 5 τε ΑΜ δὲ reliqui ‖ 5. 6 λόγῳ . . . βίον] ex terra
peregrina regionis Lacedaemoniorum 𝔄 ‖ 7 Κρόνῳ] ἡλίῳ C³
mg Μ ‖ 8 οὖν] οὓς sed oblit P ‖ 10 γ' Β ‖ 10. 11 πολυχρονι- ✳
ωτ✳✳✳✳ών. πολλὰ γὰρ Α πολὺν χρόνον νεώτερος ὤν. πολλὰ γὰρ Μ
πολὺν χρόνον νεώτερος γὰρ ὢν πολλὰ reliqui πολυχρόνιον νεώτερος ὢν Sauppeus p. 772 ‖ 12 τότε δὴ] ἅτε δὴ ΑΜ idem sscr C
rec man, om reliqui. estne scribendum καὶ δὴ? δὲ inclusi
(om Μ) ‖ 14 Διὸς om Μ ‖ 15 μεγάλη ἀσχολία τυγχάνει οὖσα Κ
ἡ μεγάλη ἀσχολία τυγχάνει οὖσα (τυγχάνουσα P¹) P², (post τις)
εἴη μεγάλη σχολία (sic) τυγχάνουσα Μ ἢ μεγάλη ἀσχ. τυγχάνουσα
(ἢ ex εἰ corr F) reliqui ‖ 16 γὰρ ex καὶ corr Κ² | ποτ' PM |
ἐστι V¹ ἐστιν V² ‖ 17 πρῶτον ΑΜC² primum 𝔄 prius O om
reliqui ‖ 18 ὑμᾶς δεῖ VLBRF δεῖ erasum C ἡμᾶς Α

for many of the local inhabitants do not know
2   what the fable could possibly mean, since it is
not a dedication of a citizen. Rather, once long
ago, a certain foreigner[4] came here, a sensible
man and exceptional in wisdom, who was emulating
in word and deed a Pythagorean[5] and Parmenidean
way of life, and he dedicated both this temple and
the painting to Cronus."

3   "Have you, then, seen the man," I asked,
"and do you know him personally?"

    "Yes, indeed," he said, "being but a youth,
I marveled at the venerable old man,[6] for he used
to discourse about many weighty things. At that
time I often heard him expound on the meaning of
this fable as well."

III.   "By Zeus, then," I said, "unless you happen
to have some pressing business, tell us, for we
desire very much to hear what the fable is about."

    "I have no objection, strangers," he said.
"But first you must hear this--namely, that the
explanation carries with it an element of danger."

    "What sort of danger?" I asked.

Ὅτι εἰ μὲν προσέξετέ, ἔφη, καὶ συνήσετε τὰ λεγό-
μενα, φρόνιμοι καὶ εὐδαίμονες ἔσεσθε, εἰ δὲ μή, ἄφρονες
καὶ κακοδαίμονες καὶ πικροὶ καὶ ἀμαθεῖς γενόμενοι
κακῶς βιώσεσθε. ἔστι γὰρ ἡ ἐξήγησις ἐοικυῖα τῷ τῆς 2
Σφιγγὸς αἰνίγματι, ὃ ἐκείνη προεβάλλετο τοῖς ἀνθρώποις. εἰ μὲν οὖν αὐτὸ συνίει τις, ἐσώζετο, εἰ δὲ μὴ
συνίει, ἀπώλετο ὑπὸ τῆς Σφιγγός. ὡσαύτως δὲ καὶ
ἐπὶ τῆς ἐξηγήσεως ἔχει ταύτης. ἡ γὰρ ἀφροσύνη τοῖς
ἀνθρώποις Σφίγξ ἐστιν. αἰνίττεται δὲ τάδε, τί ἀγα- 3
θόν, τί κακόν, τί οὔτε ἀγαθὸν οὔτε κακόν ἐστιν ἐν 10
τῷ βίῳ. ταῦτ᾽ οὖν ἐὰν μέν τις μὴ συνιῇ, ἀπόλλυται
ὑπ᾽ αὐτῆς, οὐκ εἰσάπαξ, ὥσπερ ὁ ὑπὸ τῆς Σφιγγὸς
καταβρωθεὶς ἀπέθνησκεν, ἀλλὰ κατὰ μικρὸν ἐν ὅλῳ
τῷ βίῳ καταφθείρεται καθάπερ οἱ ἐπὶ τιμωρίᾳ παραδιδόμενοι. ἐὰν δέ τις γνῷ, ἀνάπαλιν ἡ μὲν ἀφροσύνη $^{15}_{4}$
ἀπόλλυται, αὐτὸς δὲ σώζεται καὶ μακάριος καὶ εὐδαίμων γίνεται ἐν παντὶ τῷ βίῳ. ὑμεῖς οὖν προσέχετε
καὶ μὴ παρακούετε.

IV. Ὦ Ἡράκλεις, ὡς εἰς μεγάλην τινὰ ἐπιθυμίαν
ἐμβέβληκας ἡμᾶς, εἰ ταῦθ᾽ οὕτως ἔχει.   20

Ἀλλ᾽ ἔστιν, ἔφη, οὕτως ἔχοντα.

Οὐκ ἂν φθάνοις τοίνυν διηγούμενος ὡς ἡμῶν

---

1 ἔφη om M ‖ 3 πικροὶ libri (πιαροὶ A?) μιαροὶ coni *
Sauppeus p. 775 ‖ 4 ἐοικυῖα om A ἔοικε pro ἔστι ἐοικυῖα M ‖
5 προεβάλλετο A προυβάλετο RFC¹PM προυβάλλετο C² reliqui ‖
6 συνιείς EDW sed ς in W oblit συνίη K ‖ 7 συνίη K |
ἀπώλετο A ἀπόλετο M ἀπώλλετο VL ἀπόλλυτο BCKP ἀπώλλυτο
reliqui | καὶ om L ‖ 8 ἔχει om CKP ‖ 9 ἐστι V¹ ἐστιν V² | καὶ
τάδε KP² ‖ 11 μέν om P μὴ CK alterum μὴ oblit C | συνιεῖ A
συνίη reliqui ‖ 14 διαφθείρεται sscr κατα E¹ καταδιαφθείρεται W ‖
* καθάπερ .... παραδιδόμενοι del Drosihnus ‖ 15 ἐὰν] ἂν K ‖
20 ἡμᾶς ἔφην BRFEDW | ἔχοι P ‖ 22 φθονοῖς A φθονοίης M
φθάνῃς V idem sed sscr οι L φθανοῖος B¹ φθάνοις B²

"Just this," said he. "If you pay attention
and understand what is said, you will be wise and
happy. If, on the other hand, you do not, you will
become foolish, unhappy, sullen, and stupid, and you
2   will fare badly in life. For the explanation is
similar to the riddle that the Sphinx used to pose to
men:[7] if someone understood it he was spared, but if
he did not understand, he was destroyed by the Sphinx.
It is just the same in the case of this explanation.
You see, for mankind, Foolishness is the Sphinx.[8]
3   Foolishness[9] speaks in riddles of these things: of
what is good, what is bad, and what is neither good
nor bad in life. Thus, if anyone does not understand
these things he is destroyed by her, not all at once,
as a person devoured by the Sphinx died. Rather, he
is destroyed little by little, throughout his entire
life, just like those who are handed over for retri-
4   bution. But if one does understand, Foolishness is
in turn destroyed, and he himself is saved and is
blessed and happy in his whole life. As for you,
then, pay attention; do not misunderstand."[10]

IV.   "Heracles, with what desire have you
charged us, if this is so!"
         "Well," he said, "it is indeed so."
         "Then, be quick and explain, since we

προσεξόντων οὐ παρέργως, ἐπείπερ καὶ τὸ ἐπιτίμιον
τοιοῦτόν ἐστιν.

2 Ἀναλαβὼν οὖν ῥάβδον τινὰ καὶ ἐκτείνας πρὸς τὴν
γραφήν, Ὁρᾶτε, ἔφη, τὸν περίβολον τοῦτον;
5 Ὁρῶμεν.

Τοῦτο πρῶτον δεῖ εἰδέναι ὑμᾶς, ὅτι καλεῖται οὗτος
ὁ τόπος Βίος. καὶ ὁ ὄχλος ὁ πολὺς ὁ παρὰ τὴν πύλην
ἐφεστὼς οἱ μέλλοντες εἰσπορεύεσθαι εἰς τὸν Βίον οὗτοί
3 εἰσιν. ὁ δὲ γέρων ὁ ἄνω ἑστηκὼς ἔχων χάρτην τινὰ
10 ἐν τῇ χειρὶ καὶ τῇ ἑτέρᾳ ὥσπερ δεικνύων τι, οὗτος
Δαίμων καλεῖται· προστάττει δὲ τοῖς εἰσπορευομένοις,
τί δεῖ αὐτοὺς ποιεῖν, ὡς ἂν εἰσέλθωσιν εἰς τὸν Βίον·
δεικνύει δὲ ποίαν ὁδὸν αὐτοὺς δεῖ βαδίζειν, εἰ μέλλουσι σώζεσθαι ἐν τῷ Βίῳ.

15 V. Ποίαν οὖν ὁδὸν κελεύει βαδίζειν ἢ πῶς; ἔφην ἐγώ.

Ὁρᾷς οὖν, εἶπε, παρὰ τὴν πύλην θρόνον τινὰ κεί-
μενον κατὰ τὸν τόπον, καθ᾽ ὃν εἰσπορεύεται ὁ ὄχλος,
ἐφ᾽ οὗ κάθηται γυνὴ πεπλασμένη τῷ ἤθει καὶ πιθανὴ
φαινομένη, ἢ ἐν τῇ χειρὶ ἔχει ποτήριόν τι;

20
2 Ὁρῶ. ἀλλὰ τίς ἐστιν αὕτη; ἔφην.

Ἀπάτη καλεῖται, φησίν, ἡ πάντας τοὺς ἀνθρώπους
πλανῶσα.

*   1 προσεχόντων sscr ξον M | ἐπείπερ] ἐπεὶ M ‖ 3 οὖν] γοῦν L ‖
6 οὗτος ὁ τόπος AM ὁ τόπος οὗτος reliqui ‖ 7 articulum ante
ὄχλος om V¹ add V² | παρὰ] περὶ M ‖ 8 πορεύεσθαι M ‖ 12 ἔλ-
θωσιν EW ἐσέλθωσιν K ‖ 13 δεικνύει δὲ] in A videtur scriptum *
fuisse δείκνει δὲ vel δεικνύει δὲ; καὶ δεικνύει omisso δὲ reliqui ‖
13—15 εἰ . . . βαδίζειν om M ‖ 13 μέλλωσι σώζεσθαι A σώζεσθαι
μέλλουσι reliqui ‖ 15 οὖν om P | αὐτοὺς add ante κελεύει P ‖
16 οὖν εἶπε A οὖν M εἶπε reliqui ‖ 17 τὸν τόπον AM τὸν τόπον
τοῦτον reliqui ‖ 18 τὸ ἦθος B ‖ 19 καὶ ἐν τῇ χειρὶ ἔχει AM καὶ
ἐν (ἐν om V¹ add V²) τῇ χειρὶ ἔχουσα ceteri; ἢ — ἔχει Sauppeus *
p. 775 | τι om M ‖ 20 post ἔφην add ἐγώ C rec ἔφην om K ‖
21 φησί V¹ φησίν V² | τοὺς om M

shall pay careful attention, not carelessly,
especially since the penalty is so great."

2   So, taking a staff, he pointed toward the
picture and said, "Do you see this enclosure?"

   "We do."

   "You must know, first of all, that this place
is called Life, and the large crowd standing at the

3 gate consists of those who are about to enter Life.
The old man standing up here--who has a scroll in one
hand and who appears to be pointing at something with
the other--is called Daimon.[11] To those who are entering he prescribes[12] what they must do upon entering into Life; he shows them what kind of path they
must take if they are to be saved in Life."

V. "Then, on what kind of path and in what
manner does he urge them to go?"[13] I said.[14]

   "Do you see, then, alongside the gate," he
said, "a throne situated at the spot where the crowd
enters? And sitting on it do you see a woman who is
counterfeit in character[15] and yet persuasive in her
appearance, with a cup in her hand?"

2   "Yes, I see, but who is she?" I said.

   "Deceit she is called,"[16] he said, "the one
who leads all mankind astray."

Εἶτα τί πράττει αὕτη;

Τοὺς εἰσπορευομένους εἰς τὸν Βίον ποτίζει τῇ ἑαυτῆς δυνάμει.

Τοῦτο δὲ τί ἐστι τὸ ποτόν;　　3

Πλάνος, ἔφη, καὶ ἄγνοια.　　5

Εἶτα τί;

Πιόντες τοῦτο πορεύονται εἰς τὸν Βίον.

Πότερον οὖν πάντες πίνουσι τὸν πλάνον ἢ οὔ;

VI. Πάντες πίνουσιν, ἔφη, ἀλλ' οἱ μὲν πλεῖον, οἱ δὲ ἧττον. Ἔτι δὲ οὐχ ὁρᾷς ἔνδον τῆς πύλης πλῆθός 10 τι γυναικῶν ἑτέρων παντοδαπὰς μορφὰς ἐχουσῶν; Ὁρῶ.

Αὗται τοίνυν Δόξαι καὶ Ἐπιθυμίαι καὶ Ἡδοναὶ 2 καλοῦνται.ᵒ ὅταν οὖν εἰσπορεύηται ὁ ὄχλος, ἀναπηδῶσιν αὗται καὶ πλέκονται πρὸς ἕκαστον, εἶτα ἀπ- 15 άγουσι.

Ποῦ δὲ ἀπάγουσιν αὐτούς;

Αἱ μὲν εἰς τὸ σώζεσθαι, ἔφη, αἱ δὲ εἰς τὸ ἀπόλλυσθαι διὰ τὴν ἀπάτην.

Ὦ δαιμόνιε, ὡς χαλεπὸν τὸ πόμα λέγεις.　　20

Καὶ πᾶσαί γε, ἔφη, ἐπαγγέλλονται ὡς ἐπὶ τὰ βέλ- 3

---

1 εἶτα τί] διτατὶ M ‖ 2 τῇ ἑαυτῆς (ἑαυτῇ V¹ corr V²) δυνάμει libri, τὴν — δύναμιν Drosihnus approbante Sauppeo p. 769. Cum dativo rei ποτίζειν coniungitur a Plutarcho quaest. conv. 6, 2, 5 p. 687 f. ita tamen, fateor, ut sit irrigare. Neque vero contra codicum consensum facere ausus sum ‖ 4 τουτὶ M ‖ 5 πλάνος AML πλάν sscr in ras o V² πλάνη BRFEDWCKP ‖ 6 διατί M ‖ 7 πίνοντες MW² mg ‖ 8 πότερον οὖν om M | post πίνουσι add ἔφη P¹ mg ἔφην corr P² ‖ 10 ἧττον D in ras, ἔλαττον W ‖ 11 τι *om M | ἑτέρων] ἑταιρῶν V²BRFEDWCKP mulieres diversarum ac variarum formarum 𝔄 ‖ 14 εἰσπορεύεται P ‖ 15 περιπλέκονται BM συμπλέκονται K πλέκονται reliqui προσπλέκονται coni Sauppeus p. 773 | ἕκαστον in rasura V² ‖ 17 ποῖ K ‖ 18 ἀπόλυσθαι KC¹ alterum λ sscr C² ‖ 20 πῶμα P ‖ 21 ἀπαγγέλλονται K ἐπαγγέλλονται ἔφη CP

"Well then, what does she do?"

"She causes the ones entering Life to drink of her power."[17]

3   "And what is this drink?"

"Error and ignorance," he said.

"Then what?"

"After drinking it, they enter Life."[18]

"Then do all of them drink the error, or not?"

VI.   "All drink," he said, "but some more, some less.[19] Then, don't you see, inside the gate a crowd of other women[20] with forms of every kind?"

"I see them."

2   "Now they are called Opinions, Desires, and Pleasures. When the crowd enters they jump up and embrace[21] them one by one; then they lead them away."

"Where do they lead them?"

"Some of these women lead to salvation," he said, "while others by deception lead to destruction."

"Sir, how harsh is the drink you describe!"

3   "And, indeed, all these women," he said, "promise[22] that

τιστα ἄξουσαι καὶ εἰς βίον εὐδαίμονα καὶ λυσιτελῆ.
οἱ δὲ διὰ τὴν ἄγνοιαν καὶ τὸν πλάνον, ὃν πεπώκασι
παρὰ τῆς Ἀπάτης, οὐχ εὑρίσκουσι ποία ἐστὶν ἡ ἀληθινὴ ὁδὸς ἡ ἐν τῷ Βίῳ, ἀλλὰ πλανῶνται εἰκῆ, ὥσπερ
5 ὁρᾷς καὶ τοὺς πρότερον εἰσπορευομένους ὡς περιάγον-
ται ὅποι ἂν τύχῃ.

VII. Ὁρῶ τούτους, ἔφην. ἡ δὲ γυνὴ ἐκείνη τίς
ἐστιν ἡ ὥσπερ τυφλὴ καὶ μαινομένη τις εἶναι δοκοῦσα
καὶ ἑστηκυῖα ἐπὶ λίθου τινὸς στρογγύλου;

10 Καλεῖται μέν, ἔφη, Τύχη· ἔστι δὲ οὐ μόνον τυφλὴ
καὶ μαινομένη, ἀλλὰ καὶ κωφή.

2 Αὕτη οὖν τί ἔργον ἔχει;

Περιπορεύεται πανταχοῦ, ἔφη· καὶ παρ' ὧν μὲν
ἁρπάζει τὰ ὑπάρχοντα καὶ ἑτέροις δίδωσι· παρὰ δὲ
15 τῶν αὐτῶν πάλιν ἀφαιρεῖται παραχρῆμα ἃ δέδωκε καὶ
ἄλλοις δίδωσιν εἰκῆ καὶ ἀβεβαίως. διὸ καὶ τὸ σημεῖον καλῶς μηνύει τὴν φύσιν αὐτῆς.

3 Ποῖον τοῦτο; ἔφην ἐγώ.

Ὅτι ἐπὶ λίθου στρογγύλου ἕστηκεν.

1 ἄξουσαι] ἤξουσι M αὔξουσαι FEDW | εἰς om V¹ add V²
ἐς M | ἄλλον post βίον add M ‖ 3 παρὰ τῆς Ἀπάτης] παρα-
πορεύονται P ‖ 3. 4 ἀληθινὴ ὁδὸς] ἀλήθεια M ‖ 5 τοὺς .. εἰσπο-
ρευομένους sscr οἱ .. οι K¹ | περιάγοντας omnes sed B¹ sscr αι ‖
6 ὅποι ἂν τύχοι AM ὅπη ἂν αὗται δεικνύουσιν BK ὅπη (ὅποι W
ὀπ terminatione foramine abrepta V) ἂν αὗται δεικνύωσιν re-
liqui. ὅποι ἂν τύχωσι coni Sauppeus p. 775 ‖ 7 τοῦτον KP τού-
τους reliqui (C ex corr) ‖ 8 ἡ om A | καὶ· μαινομένη del Drosih-
nus, vid. infra ad vv. 10. 11 | τις om M ‖ 10 οὐ sscr D ‖ 10. 11 τυφλὴ *
ἀλλὰ καὶ μαινομένη καὶ κωφή libri, corr Gronovius. Nescio an
καὶ μαινομένη eiciendum sit: *nec caeca tantummodo est, sed
surda etiam* Ꝁ ‖ 12 post αὕτη inser μὲν F | ἔχει] ἔφη D ‖
13 μὲν om in textu add in mg D rec ut videtur manu ‖ 14 ὑπ-
άρχοτα V¹ corr V² | δίδωσιν B | δὲ om W ‖ 15 ἔδωκε M ‖
16 βεβαίως V¹ ἀβεβαίως V² | διὸς W ‖ 19 λίθου στρογγύλου
AM στρογγύλου λίθου reliqui

they will lead them to the best things and to a
happy and profitable life. But because of the
ignorance and error which they have drunk from
Deceit, they do not discover of what kind is the
true way in Life. Instead, they wander about aimlessly, even as you see how those who have entered
previously wander about wherever they chance to go."

VII.   "I see them," I said, "but who is that woman
there who appears to be blind and mad[23] and who
stands on some sort of round rock?"

   "She is called Fortune," he said, "and not
only is she blind and mad, but deaf as well."

2   "What then is her task?"[24]

   "She makes her way around everywhere," he
said. "She both snatches possessions away from
some and gives them to others.[25] Yet from the latter
in turn she immediately takes away what she has given
and gives them to others instead in an aimless and
fickle way. Hence, even her sign aptly attests to
her nature."[26]

3   "What kind of sign is this?" I said.

   "That she stands upon a round rock."[27]

Εἶτα τί τοῦτο σημαίνει;

Οὐκ ἀσφαλὴς οὐδὲ βεβαία ἐστὶν ἡ παρ᾽ αὐτῆς δόσις. ἐκπτώσεις γὰρ μεγάλαι καὶ σκληραὶ γίνονται, ὅταν τις αὐτῇ πιστεύσῃ.

VIII. *Ὁ δὲ [τῶν ἀνθρώπων] πολὺς ὄχλος οὗτος ὁ 5 περὶ αὐτὴν ἑστηκὼς τί βούλεται καὶ τίνες καλοῦνται;*

Καλοῦνται μὲν οὗτοι ἀπροβούλευτοι· αἰτοῦσι δὲ ἕκαστος αὐτῶν ἃ ῥίπτει.

Πῶς οὖν οὐχ ὁμοίαν ἔχουσι τὴν μορφήν, ἀλλ᾽ οἱ μὲν αὐτῶν δοκοῦσι χαίρειν, οἱ δὲ ἀθυμοῦσιν ἐκτετα- 10 κότες τὰς χεῖρας;

Οἱ μὲν δοκοῦντες, ἔφη, χαίρειν καὶ γελᾶν αὐτῶν 2 οἱ εἰληφότες τι παρ᾽ αὐτῆς εἰσιν· οὗτοι δὲ καὶ ἀγαθὴν Τύχην αὐτὴν καλοῦσιν. οἱ δὲ δοκοῦντες κλαίειν [καὶ ἐκτετακότες] εἰσὶ παρ᾽ ὧν ἀφείλετο ἃ δέδωκε πρότερον 15 αὐτοῖς. οὗτοι δὲ πάλιν αὐτὴν κακὴν Τύχην καλοῦσι.

Τίνα οὖν ἐστιν ἃ δίδωσιν αὐτοῖς, ὅτι οὕτως οἱ 3 μὲν λαμβάνοντες χαίρουσιν, οἱ δὲ ἀποβάλλοντες κλαίουσι;

Ταῦτα, ἔφη, ἃ παρὰ τοῖς πολλοῖς ἀνθρώποις δοκεῖ εἶναι ἀγαθά. 20

Ταῦτα οὖν τίνα ἐστί;

---

2 ante *οὐκ* add *ὅτι* praeter AM omnes ‖ 4 *αὐτῇ* om B ǀ *πιστεύῃ* M ‖ 5 *ὁ δὲ τῶν ἀνθρώπων πολὺς ὄχλος* A *ὁ δὲ ὁ πολὺς ὄχλος* V¹ *ὁ δὲ ὄχλος ὁ πολὺς* V²LBRFEDWCKP *τῶν ἀνθρώπων* add C mg M, ignorant 𝔄 et O, del Drosihnus ǀ *ὁ* post *οὗτος* om M ‖ 7 *καλοῦνται* om W ǀ post *μὲν* add *οὖν* B ‖ 9 *οὖν* om L ‖ 10 *δοκοῦσιν αὐτῶν* F ǀ *δοκοῦντες* P ‖ 12 *μὲν*] *δὲ* K ‖ 13 *οἱ*] *εἴη* P ǀ *τι* om B ǀ *παρ᾽ αὐτῆς* A *παρ᾽ αὐτοῦ* M *παρὰ τῆς τύχης* reliqui ‖ 14 *αὐτὴν* om B ǀ *καλοῦσι* F ‖ 14—16 *οἱ — καλοῦσι* om FL add mg L ‖ 14. 15 *καὶ ἐκτετακότες* AMV¹ *καὶ τὰς χεῖρας ἐκτετακότες* V² reliqui. *καὶ — ἐκτετακότες* ignorat 𝔄 del Muellerus ‖ 15 *δέδωκεν* BP *ἔδωκε* M ‖ 16 *κακὴν Τύχην αὐτὴν* praeter A omnes ‖ 17 *οὖν* om M ‖ 18 *ἀποβαλόντες* WK ǀ *κλαίουσιν* FE DWP ‖ 19 *ταῦτα οὖν* B *ταῦτ᾽ οὖν* M ‖ 21 *ταῦτ᾽* M

"Then, what does it signify?"

"That a gift from her is neither safe nor secure.[28] For severe and bitter disappointments ensue whenever someone puts his trust in her."[29]

VIII.   "Now this large crowd [of men] standing around her, what do they want and what are they called?"

"They are called those who are without forethought, and each one is begging for what she throws out."

"Then how is it that they are not similar in appearance? Instead, some seem to be rejoicing while others stretch out their hands toward her in despair."[30]

2   "These people here, who appear to be rejoicing and laughing, are those who have received something from her. They call her Good Fortune. But these who appear to be crying [with outstretched arms], are those from whom she has taken back what she had earlier given them. These, in turn, call her Bad Fortune."

3   "What are the things, then, that she gives them, that those who receive are so happy while those who lose are sad?"

"Those things," he said, "deemed good by the majority of mankind."

"And, what are these things?"

4 Πλοῦτος δηλονότι καὶ δόξα καὶ εὐγένεια καὶ τέκνα καὶ τυραννίδες καὶ βασιλεῖαι καὶ τἆλλα ὅσα τούτοις παραπλήσια.

Ταῦτα οὖν πῶς οὐκ ἔστιν ἀγαθά;

5 Περὶ μὲν τούτων, ἔφη, καὶ αὖθις ἐκποιήσει διαλέγεσθαι, νῦν δὲ περὶ τὴν μυθολογίαν γινόμεθα.

Ἔστω οὕτως.

IX. Ὁρᾷς οὖν, ὡς ἂν παρέλθῃς τὴν πύλην ταύτην, ἀνωτέρω ἄλλον περίβολον καὶ γυναῖκας ἔξω τοῦ περι-
10 βόλου ἑστηκυίας κεκοσμημένας ὥσπερ ἑταῖραι εἰώθασι;

Καὶ μάλα.

Αὗται τοίνυν ἡ μὲν Ἀκρασία καλεῖται, ἡ δὲ Ἀσωτία, ἡ δὲ Ἀπληστία, ἡ δὲ Κολακεία.

2 Τί οὖν ὧδε ἑστήκασιν αὗται;

15 Παρατηροῦσιν, ἔφη, τοὺς εἰληφότας τι παρὰ τῆς Τύχης.

Εἶτα τί;

Ἀναπηδῶσι καὶ συμπλέκονται αὐτοῖς καὶ κολακεύουσι καὶ ἀξιοῦσι παρ' αὐταῖς μένειν λέγουσαι ὅτι βίον
20 ἕξουσιν ἡδύν τε καὶ ἄπονον καὶ κακοπάθειαν ἔχοντα
3 οὐδεμίαν. ἐὰν οὖν τις πεισθῇ ὑπ' αὐτῶν εἰσελθεῖν εἰς τὴν Ἡδυπάθειαν, μέχρι μέν τινος ἡδεῖα δοκεῖ

---

1 δηλονότι] δηλαδὴ K | καὶ ante δόξα om W ‖ 2 τὰ ἄλλα F ἄλλα M ‖ 4 ταῦτ' EDWPM ‖ 5 ἐκποιήσει διαλέγεσθαι AM διαλεξόμεθα reliqui ‖ 6 γινόμεθα A γενόμεθα D γενόμεθα reliqui ‖* 8 παρέλθῃς sscr οι B παρέλθοις RFCKP | post παρέλθῃς add ἔφη V²L | post ταύτην add ἔφη BFEDW ‖ 9 ἀνωτέρω AM ἀνώτερον reliqui | post περίβολον AM ex superiore linea repet ὡς ἂν ‖ 10 ἑταῖραι] αἱ ἑταῖραι C²KF αἱ ἕτεραι C¹?P | εἰώθασιν αἱ ἑταῖραι F ‖ 12 αὗται — καλεῖται om C¹ add C² mg | ἀσωτεία RFCKP ‖ 13 ἀπληστεία A ἀπλειστία M ‖ 15 παρατηροῦσι F | ἔφη om F ‖ 19 αὐταῖς A αὐτὰς reliqui corr Saupp. p. 774 ‖* 20 τε om omnes praeter A | ante ἔχοντα add οὐκ EDW ‖ 21 οὖν om M

4   "Wealth,[31] of course, reputation, nobility, children, monarchies, kingdoms, and all the other things like these."

        "But how can these things not be good?"

        "It will suffice," he said, "to discuss the subject later.[32] But for now, let's concern ourselves with the interpretation of the fable."

        "Fine!"

IX.   "Do you see, then, that when you pass beyond this gate, there is another enclosure higher up, and standing outside the enclosure are women adorned as courtesans usually are?"[33]

        "Certainly."

        "Now, they are as follows: one is called Incontinence, another Profligacy, another Covetousness, and the other Flattery."

2   "Why are they standing here?"

        "They are," he said, "closely watching those who have received something from Fortune."

        "What then?"

        "They jump up and embrace them, they flatter and coax them to stay with them, saying that they will have a life that is pleasant and painless, with

3 no misery at all.[34] If, then, someone is persuaded by them to enter Luxury,[35] the diversion seems pleasant up to a point,

εἶναι ἡ διατριβή, ἕως ἂν γαργαλίζῃ τὸν ἄνθρωπον,
εἶτ᾽ οὐκέτι. ὅταν γὰρ ἀνανήψῃ, αἰσθάνεται ὅτι οὐκ
ἤσθιεν, ἀλλ᾽ ὑπ᾽ αὐτῆς κατησθίετο καὶ ὑβρίζετο. διὸ 4
καὶ ὅταν ἀναλώσῃ πάντα ὅσα ἔλαβε παρὰ τῆς Τύχης,
ἀναγκάζεται ταύταις ταῖς γυναιξὶ δουλεύειν καὶ πάνθ᾽ 5
ὑπομένειν καὶ ἀσχημονεῖν καὶ ποιεῖν ἕνεκεν τούτων
πάντα ὅσα ἐστὶ βλαβερά, οἷον ἀποστερεῖν, ἱεροσυλεῖν,
ἐπιορκεῖν, προδιδόναι, λῃίζεσθαι καὶ πάνθ᾽ ὅσα τούτοις παραπλήσια. ὅταν οὖν πάντα αὐτοῖς ἐπιλίπῃ,
παραδίδονται τῇ Τιμωρίᾳ.   10

X. Ποία δέ ἐστιν αὕτη;

Ὁρᾷς ὀπίσω τι, ἔφη, αὐτῶν ἄνω ὥσπερ θυρίον
μικρὸν καὶ τόπον στενόν τινα καὶ σκοτεινόν;

⟨Καὶ μάλα.⟩

Οὐκοῦν καὶ γυναῖκες αἰσχραὶ καὶ ῥυπαραὶ καὶ ῥάκη 15
ἠμφιεσμέναι δοκοῦσι συνεῖναι;

Καὶ μάλα.   2

Αὗται τοίνυν, ἔφη, ἡ μὲν τὴν μάστιγα ἔχουσα
καλεῖται Τιμωρία, ἡ δὲ τὴν κεφαλὴν ἐν τοῖς γόνασιν
ἔχουσα Λύπη, ἡ δὲ τὰς τρίχας τίλλουσα ἑαυτῆς Ὀδύνη. 20

---

1 ἕως] ὡς F ἂν om P | γαργαρίζῃ M ‖ 2 εἶτα F | οὐκ ἔτι
AM οὐκ ἔστι V¹ οὐκ ἔστιν V² reliqui | ἀνανίψῃ AP ἀνάψῃ M |
ὅτι] ὅτ᾽ P ‖ 3 κατεσθίετο AK ‖ 5 γυναιξὶν B | 6 ἕνεκεν] ἐκ M ‖
7 πάντα A πάνθ᾽ MC rec man, om reliqui ‖ 9 ἐπιλίπῃ A ἐπι-
λείπῃ M ἀπολίπῃ reliqui ‖ 11 ἐστιν ἔφην RFED αὕτη ἔφην B ‖
*12 τι om M | ἔφη αὐτῶν ἄνω A αὐτῶν ἔφη ἄνω LBRFEDW
αὐτῶν om M ἄνω om VCKP | τι μικρὸν ἄνω ὥσπερ θυρίον M
Annon vides, inquit, ostiolum parvum in loco angusto et caligi-
noso? 𝔄 | θυρίον ABR² θύριον P θηρίον VLR¹FEDK θη-
ρίον sscr v W θυρίον corr ex θηρίον C ‖ 14 καὶ μάλα deest in
omnibus libris, inser Drosihnus, ὁρῶ B mg. Video, inquam,
eccam 𝔄 (statim v. 17 καὶ μάλα = eccas, inquam, video) ‖
15—17 οὐκοῦν — καὶ om M ‖ 16 συνεῖναι ex εἶναι corr L δο-
κοῦσιν εἶναι P ‖ 18 αὗται] τούτων M | μάστιχα E ‖ 20 ἔχουσαν W |
ante Λύπη add καλεῖται FEDW | αὐτῆς M

so long as it titillates[36] the individual, but not
beyond that. For when he comes to his senses[37] he
realizes that he was not doing the eating but was
being devoured and violated by her.[38] Therefore,
whenever he has squandered all that he has received
from Fortune, he is compelled to be a slave to these
women, to submit in everything, to act disgracefully,
and, for their sake, to commit all that is injurious,
such as fraud, desecration, perjury, treason, pillage,
and all that is like them. When, then, they have
committed all these acts, they are delivered to
Retribution."[39]

X.   "And what kind is she?"

"Do you see a bit behind them, up above,
something like a small door and some sort of dark,
narrow place?"

<"Certainly.">

"And don't ugly, filthy women dressed in rags
appear to have gathered?"

"Certainly."

"Well, these women," he said, "are the following: the one with the whip is called Retribution,
the one with her head on her knees is Grief, and the
one pulling out her own hair is Sorrow."

3 Ὁ δὲ ἄλλος οὗτος ὁ παρεστηκὼς αὐταῖς δυσειδής τις καὶ λεπτὸς καὶ γυμνός, καὶ μετ᾽ αὐτοῦ τις ἄλλη ὁμοία αὐτῷ αἰσχρὰ καὶ λεπτή, τίς ἐστιν;

Ὁ μὲν Ὀδυρμὸς καλεῖται, ἔφη, ἡ δὲ Ἀθυμία, ἀδελφὴ
⁵₄ δ᾽ ἐστὶν αὕτη αὐτοῦ. τούτοις οὖν παραδίδοται καὶ μετὰ τούτων συμβιοῖ τιμωρούμενος· εἶτα ἐνταῦθα πάλιν εἰς τὸν ἕτερον οἶκον ῥίπτεται, εἰς τὴν Κακοδαιμονίαν, καὶ ὧδε τὸν λοιπὸν βίον καταστρέφει ἐν πάσῃ κακοδαιμονίᾳ, ἂν μὴ ἡ Μετάνοια αὐτῷ ἐπιτύχῃ
10 ἐκ προαιρέσεως συναντήσασα.

XI. Εἶτα τί γίνεται, ἐὰν ἡ Μετάνοια αὐτῷ συναντήσῃ;

Ἐξαιρεῖ αὐτὸν ἐκ τῶν κακῶν καὶ συνίστησιν αὐτῷ ἑτέραν Δόξαν [καὶ Ἐπιθυμίαν] τὴν εἰς τὴν ἀληθινὴν
15 Παιδείαν ἄγουσαν, ἅμα δὲ καὶ τὴν εἰς τὴν Ψευδοπαιδείαν καλουμένην.

2 Εἶτα τί γίνεται;

Ἐὰν μέν, φησί, τὴν Δόξαν ταύτην προσδέξηται τὴν ἄξουσαν αὐτὸν εἰς τὴν ἀληθινὴν Παιδείαν, καθαρ-

1 δὲ ΑΜ δ᾽ reliqui ‖ 2 καὶ γυμνὸς καὶ λεπτὸς Μ | μετ᾽ αὐτοῦ ΑΜ μετὰ τοῦτον Β κατὰ ταῦτα W μετὰ ταῦτα reliqui | ἄλλη Α om reliqui ‖ 3. αὐτῷ om EDW | λεπτή] ῥυπαρὰ ex ῥυπαραὶ corr P | ἐστι V¹ ἐστιν V² ‖ 4. 5 Ἀθυμία — αὐτοῦ] sic Α * ἀδελφὴ αὐτοῦ ἀθυμία reliqui (αὐτοῦ ἀθυμία om M) ‖ 6 μετὰ] κατὰ W ‖ 6. 7 ἐνταῦθα πάλιν ΑΜ πάλιν ἐνταῦθα VLBRFCP πάλιν ἐντεῦθεν Κ ἐνταῦθα om EDW ‖ 7 τὸν ante ἕτερον Α (sed erasum), Μ, om reliqui ‖ 8 βίον] τοῦ βίου Β τούτου βίου Μ ‖ 9 μετάνοι V¹ corr V² | ἐπιτύχῃ] ἀπὸτύχῃ Α ἀπὸ τύχης ΚΜ ἀπὸ τῆς τύχης reliqui ἐπιτύχῃ Johnsonus approbantibus Sauppeo * p. 773 et Muellero p. 67 ‖ 10 ἐκ προαιρέσεως del Drohsinus | * συναντήσασα Α συναντήσῃ reliqui ‖ 11 εἶτα ... συναντήσῃ om * WP add W mg | ἡ om ΑΒ ‖ 13 ἐξαίρει libri ἐξαιρεῖ Sauppeus p. 775 | ἐκ] ἀπὸ ΒL | συνίστησι VEDK ‖ 14 καὶ Ἐπιθυμίαν del Drosihnus ‖ 15 „τὴν deest" (in M) Meibomius ‖ 18 φησί] φῆ W ‖ 19 αὔξουσαν CP | αὐτὴν P | ἀλήθειαν P

3   "And this other man who is standing by them,
some deformed, emaciated, and naked man, and with him
some other woman resembling him, ugly and emaciated,
who is he?"

           "He is called Lamentation," he said, "and
4   she Despondency, and she is his sister. So, he is
being delivered over to them and is living with them
while being punished. Next, from there he is once
again being thrown into another house here, into
Unhappiness, and here he spends the rest of his life
in total unhappiness, unless from her own choice
Repentance[40] happens to encounter him."

XI.   "Then what happens if Repentance encounters
him?"

           "She releases him from his ills and introduces
to him another Opinion [and Desire], who leads him to
true Education, and at the same time to yet another
who leads to the one called False Education."[41]

2   "Then, what happens?"

           "If," he said, "he welcomes this Opinion, the
one who is to lead him to true Education, then once
he is

θεὶς ὑπ' αὐτῆς σώζεται καὶ μακάριος καὶ εὐδαίμων γίνεται ἐν τῷ βίῳ· εἰ δὲ μή, πάλιν πλανᾶται ὑπὸ τῆς Ψευδοδοξίας.

XII. Ὦ Ἡράκλεις, ὡς μέγας ὁ κίνδυνος ἄλλος οὗτος. ἡ δὲ Ψευδοπαιδεία ποία ἐστίν; ἔφην ἐγώ. 5

Οὐχ ὁρᾷς τὸν ἕτερον περίβολον ἐκεῖνον;

Καὶ μάλα, ἔφην ἐγώ. 2

Οὐκοῦν ἔξω τοῦ περιβόλου παρὰ τὴν εἴσοδον γυνή τις ἕστηκεν, ἣ δοκεῖ πάνυ καθάριος καὶ εὔτακτος εἶναι;

Καὶ μάλα. 10

Ταύτην τοίνυν οἱ πολλοὶ καὶ εἰκαῖοι τῶν ἀνδρῶν 3 Παιδείαν καλοῦσιν· οὐκ ἔστι δέ, ἀλλὰ Ψευδοπαιδεία, ἔφη. οἱ μέν τοι σωζόμενοι ὁπόταν βούλωνται εἰς τὴν ἀληθινὴν Παιδείαν ἐλθεῖν, ὧδε πρῶτον παραγίνονται.

Πότερον οὖν ἄλλη ὁδὸς οὐκ ἔστιν ἐπὶ τὴν ἀλη- 15 θινὴν Παιδείαν ἄγουσα;

⟨Οὐκ⟩ ἔστιν, ἔφη.

XIII. Οὗτοι δὲ οἱ ἄνθρωποι οἱ ἔσω τοῦ περιβόλου ἀνακάμπτοντες τίνες εἰσίν;

Οἱ τῆς Ψευδοπαιδείας, ἔφη, ἐρασταὶ ἠπατημένοι 20 καὶ οἰόμενοι μετὰ τῆς ἀληθινῆς Παιδείας συνομιλεῖν.

Τίνες οὖν καλοῦνται οὗτοι;

Οἱ μὲν ποιηταί, ἔφη, οἱ δὲ ῥήτορες, οἱ δὲ διαλεκτι- 2 κοί, οἱ δὲ μουσικοί, οἱ δὲ ἀριθμητικοί, οἱ δὲ γεωμέ-

2 ante τῷ praeter AM omnes add παντὶ ‖ 3 κενοδοξίας sscr ψευ E¹ ψευδοπαιδείας P ‖ 4 ἄλλος] καὶ F ‖ 5 Ψευδοπαιδεία] ψευδοδοξία M | ἔστιν RFE ‖ 9 καθάριος A καθάρειος M καθαρὰ reliqui ‖ 11 ταῦτα VL | οἰκαῖοι ED οἱ καλοὶ MW¹ καῖοι W² mg | ἀνδρῶν] ἀνθρώπων CKP ‖ 14 πρότερον P | παραγίνονται πρῶτον M ‖ 15 ἔστι V¹ ἔστιν V² ἦν AM ‖ 17 οὐκ inser Sauppeus * p. 775 minime, inquit, non habent viam aliam 𝔄 ‖ 18 οἱ ante ἔσω om BR sed add R¹ mg | εἴσω EDW ‖ 20 οἱ om M ‖ 21 ἀλη- θοῦς F ‖ 22 καλοῦν V¹ καλοῦνται V²

cleansed[42] by her he is saved and becomes blessed and happy in his life. But if he does not, he is led astray once again by False Opinion."

XII.   "Heracles![43] How great this other danger is! But tell me, of what kind is False Education?" I said.
        "Don't you see that other enclosure there?"
2   "Certainly," I said.
        "Then, don't you see that outside the enclosure at the entrance stands a woman who appears to be altogether pure and neatly adorned?"
        "Certainly."
3   "Well," he said, "this woman most rash men call Education,[44] but she is not. Rather, she is False Education. In any case, those who are being saved arrive here first, whenever they wish to enter into true Education."
        "Is there, then, no other path that leads to true Education?"
        "<No,> there is <not>," he said.[45]

XIII.   "Now, who are these people who are walking to and fro inside the enclosure?"
        "They are the lovers of False Education," he said, "who have been deceived into thinking that they are consorting with true Education."
        "What are they called?"
2   "Poets," he said, "orators, dialecticians, musicians, mathematicians, geometricians,

τραι, οἱ δὲ ἀστρολόγοι, οἱ δὲ κριτικοί, οἱ δὲ ἡδονικοί, οἱ δὲ περιπατητικοὶ καὶ ὅσοι ἄλλοι τούτοις εἰσὶ παραπλήσιοι.

XIV. Αἱ δὲ γυναῖκες ἐκεῖναι αἱ δοκοῦσαι περιτρέ-
5 χειν ὅμοιαι ταῖς πρώταις, ἐν αἷς ἔφης εἶναι τὴν
Ἀκρασίαν [καὶ αἱ ἄλλαι αἱ μετ’ αὐτῶν] τίνες εἰσίν;
Αὐταὶ ἐκεῖναί εἰσιν, ἔφη.

2 Πότερον οὖν καὶ ὧδε εἰσπορεύονται;
Νὴ Δία καὶ ὧδε, σπανίως δὲ καὶ οὐχὶ ὥσπερ ἐν
10 τῷ πρώτῳ περιβόλῳ.

Πότερον οὖν καὶ αἱ Δόξαι; ἔφην.

3 Μένει γὰρ καὶ ἐν τούτοις τὸ πόμα, ὃ ἔπιον παρὰ
τῆς Ἀπάτης, καὶ ἡ ἄγνοια μένει [ἐν τούτοις νὴ Δία]
καὶ μετ’ αὐτῆς γε ἡ ἀφροσύνη, καὶ οὐ μὴ ἀπέλθῃ ἀπ’
15 αὐτῶν οὔθ’ ἡ δόξα οὔθ’ ἡ λοιπὴ κακία μέχρι ἂν ἀπογνόντες τῆς Ψευδοπαιδείας εἰσέλθωσιν εἰς τὴν ἀλη-

---

1 οἱ δὲ κριτικοὶ post περιπατητικοὶ exhibent libri, ita ut critici pessime disiungantur ab reliquarum sex artium sectatoribus (Sauppeus p. 777); sed malui ordinem mutare quam cum Sauppeo philosophorum nomina eicere; in 𝔄 critici praecedunt et musicos et peripateticos ac ioculatores ‖ 2 περιπατικοὶ AMED περιπατηκοὶ P¹ corr P² | τοιούτοις B ‖ 5 ὅμοια F ‖
* 6 καὶ — αὐτῶν del Drosihnus, αἱ ante ἄλλαι om praeter EDK omnes sed W sscr, αἱ et ante et post ἄλλαι om M | μετ’] κατ’ W ‖
* 7 αὐταὶ BRK αὗται A αὗται reliqui ‖ 9 οὐχ F ‖ 11. 12 ἔφη μὲν *
γὰρ AM ναὶ ἔφη μὲν γὰρ DW¹C¹ ναὶ ἔφημεν γὰρ VLBRFEP *
ναὶ ἔφη ἔτι μὲν γὰρ W²C²K. Recepi quae Muellerus proposuit p. 64 ‖ 12 καὶ om L ‖ 12. 13 τὸ πόμα — τούτοις om W¹ add W²
mg sed om ἐν τούτοις ‖ 13 καὶ ἐν τούτοις M ἐν τούτοις δὲ B
ἐν τούτοις om K | Καὶ ἡ ἄγνοια μένει hospiti tribuit Drosihnus; *
(Iamne etiam, quaerebam, versantur isti in ignorantia? 𝔄); sed hic utique desideraveris interrogandi particulam. Suspicor et νὴ Δία et ἐν τούτοις (quod etiam Drosihnus delevit) additamenta esse librarii, qui illud καὶ ἡ ἄγνοια μένει enuntiatum interrogativum ratus hospiti dabat ‖ 14 αὐτῆς] αὐτῶν BRFE DW¹ sed αὐτῆς W² mg ‖ 15 μέχρι A μέχρ V¹ μέχρις V² reliqui

astronomers, literary critics,[46] Hedonists,[47]
Peripatetics,[48] and all others like them."[49]

XIV.   "And who are those women who seem to be
running around like that first group, among whom you
said was Incontinence [and the others with them]?"

"They are the very same," he said.

2   "Then they are entering here, too?"

"Yes, by Zeus, but rarely, not as in the
first enclosure."[50]

"And do the Opinions, too?" I asked.

3   "Yes, for the potion these people drank from
Deceit remains in them; likewise, ignorance remains
[in them, by Zeus,] and foolishness along with it.
And neither opinion nor the remaining evil will
depart from them until they renounce False Education,
embark on the true

θινὴν ὁδὸν καὶ πίωσι τὰς τούτων καθαρτικὰς δυνάμεις. εἶτα ὅταν καθαρθῶσι καὶ ἐκβάλωσι τὰ κακὰ 4
πάνθ᾽ ὅσα ἔχουσι καὶ τὰς δόξας καὶ τὴν ἄγνοιαν καὶ
τὴν λοιπὴν κακίαν πᾶσαν, τότε ἂν οὕτω σωθήσονται.
ὧδε δὲ μένοντες παρὰ τῇ Ψευδοπαιδείᾳ οὐδέποτε
ἀπολυθήσονται οὐδὲ ἐλλείψει αὐτοὺς κακὸν οὐδὲν
ἕνεκα τούτων τῶν μαθημάτων.

XV. Ποία οὖν αὕτη ἡ ὁδός ἐστιν ἡ φέρουσα ἐπὶ
τὴν ἀληθινὴν Παιδείαν; [ἔφην].

Ὁρᾷς ἄνω, ἔφη, τόπον τινὰ ἐκεῖνον, ὅπου οὐδεὶς 10
ἐπικατοικεῖ, ἀλλ᾽ ἔρημος δοκεῖ εἶναι;

Ὁρῶ.

Οὐκοῦν καὶ θύραν τινὰ μικρὰν καὶ ὁδόν τινα πρὸ 2
τῆς θύρας, ἥτις οὐ πολὺ ὀχλεῖται, ἀλλ᾽ ὀλίγοι πάνυ
πορεύονται ὥσπερ δι᾽ ἀνοδίας τινὸς καὶ τραχείας καὶ 1
πετρώδους εἶναι δοκούσης;

Καὶ μάλα, ἔφην.

Οὐκοῦν καὶ βουνός τις ὑψηλὸς δοκεῖ εἶναι καὶ 3

1 τὰς τούτων καθαρτικὰς δυνάμεις ΑΜ τὴν τούτων καθαρτικὴν δύναμιν reliqui ‖ 2 εἶτα ὅταν καθαρθῶσι om praeter ΑΒ
ΜΆ omnes | καθαρθῶσιν Β | ἐκβάλωσι ΑΒΚ idem sed corr ex
ἐκβάλλωσι L ἐκβάλλωσι VRFWC ἐκβάλλωσιν Ρ ἐκβάλλουσι ΕD ‖
3 ὁ∗∗∗χουσι tribus litteris evanidis Α ὅσ᾽ ἂν ἔχωσι Μ ‖ 4 κακίαν
πᾶσαν Α πᾶσαν κακίαν reliqui | post τότε add γὰρ ΒRFEDW |
∗ ἂν] δὴ coni Sauppeus p. 775; sed vide quae collegit Kuehnerus
gramm. graec. II p. 170 (cf. etiam Marquardtius Galeni script.
min. I praef. XLV sq.) | οὕτω VLCKP οὕτως reliqui οὗτοι
Sauppeus | σωθήσωνται LRC σωθήσονται sscr ω F¹ ‖ 5. 6 ὧδε
. . . ἀπολυθήσονται om FEDW ‖ 5 δὲ] καὶ CP om Μ | ψευδο-
ποιΐα Μ ‖ 5. 6 οὐδέποτε ἀπολυθήσονται om Μ ‖ 6 αὐτοῖς L ‖
8 ἐστιν αὕτη ἡ ὁδός Μ ‖ 9 ἔφην Α om reliqui ‖ 10 ἄνω ἔφη Α
ἔφη ἄνω reliqui | οὐδεὶς CKP οὐδεὶς reliqui ‖ 14 ὀλίγοι πάνυ
ΑΜVL πάνυ ὀλίγοι reliqui ‖ 15 δι᾽ ἀνοδίας Α ἀνοδίας Μ δυσ-
ανόδου ceteri ‖ 17 ἔφη FC¹ corr C²

4   path, and drink their purifying powers. Then, when
     they have been purified and have cast out all the
     evils they possess--such as opinion, ignorance, and
     the rest--will they be saved. But those remaining
     here with False Education will never be freed, nor
     will any evil leave them as a result of these academic
     disciplines."

     XV.   "Now what kind of path is this that leads to
     true Education?" [I said].
             "Do you see this place up here," he said,
     "where no one dwells, but seems instead to be
     deserted?"
             "I see."
2   "Then do you also see a small gate and in
     front of the gate a path which is not much frequented;
     very few pass this way, as it were through a trackless
     waste[51] which seems both rough and rocky?"
             "Certainly," I said.
3   "And there seems to be a high hill,[52] and

ἀνάβασις στενὴ πάνυ καὶ κρημνοὺς ἔχουσα ἔνθεν καὶ
ἔνθεν βαθεῖς.

Ὁρῶ.

Αὕτη τοίνυν ἐστὶν ἡ ὁδός, ἔφη, ἡ ἄγουσα πρὸς
5 τὴν ἀληθινὴν Παιδείαν.

4   Καὶ μάλα γε χαλεπὴ προσιδεῖν.

Οὐκοῦν καὶ ἄνω ἐπὶ τοῦ βουνοῦ ὁρᾷς πέτραν τινὰ
μεγάλην καὶ ὑψηλὴν καὶ κύκλῳ ἀπόκρημνον;

Ὁρῶ, ἔφην.

10 XVI. Ὁρᾷς οὖν καὶ γυναῖκας δύο ἑστηκυίας ἐπὶ
τῆς πέτρας λιπαρὰς καὶ εὐεκτούσας τῷ σώματι, ὡς
ἐκτετάκασι τὰς χεῖρας προθύμως;

Ὁρῶ, ἀλλὰ τίνες καλοῦνται, ἔφην, αὗται;

2   Ἡ μὲν Ἐγκράτεια καλεῖται, ἔφη, ἡ δὲ Καρτερία·
15 εἰσὶ δὲ ἀδελφαί.

Τί οὖν τὰς χεῖρας ἐκτετάκασι προθύμως οὕτως;

3   Παρακαλοῦσιν, ἔφη, τοὺς παραγινομένους ἐπὶ τὸν
τόπον θαρρεῖν καὶ μὴ ἀποδειλιᾶν λέγουσαι ὅτι βραχὺ
ἔτι δεῖ καρτερῆσαι αὐτούς, εἶτα ἥξουσιν εἰς ὁδὸν καλήν.

20
4   Ὅταν οὖν παραγένωνται ἐπὶ τὴν πέτραν, πῶς ἀνα-
βαίνουσιν; ὁρῶ γὰρ ὁδὸν φέρουσαν οὐδεμίαν ἐπ᾽ αὐτάς.

Αὗται ἀπὸ τοῦ κρημνοῦ προσκαταβαίνουσι καὶ
ἕλκουσιν αὐτοὺς ἄνω πρὸς αὐτάς, εἶτα κελεύουσιν

---

1. 2 ἔνθεν καὶ ἔνθεν ΑΜΒ ἔνθεν κἀκεῖθεν reliqui ‖ 2 βα-*
θεῖς δὲ C ‖ 7 post ἄνω add γε omnes praeter A | ἐπὶ] περὶ
CKP | τὸν βουνὸν ΚΡ | τινὰ Α om reliqui ‖ 8 καὶ ante κύκλῳ
ignorant praeter ΑΜ omnes ‖ 11 τῆς πέτρας Κ τῇ πέτρᾳ ΑΜ
τὴν πέτραν reliqui | εὐτάκτους Μ | ante ὡς add καὶ praeter ΑΜ
omnes ‖ 13 καλοῦνται ἔφην] φημὶ καλοῦνται Μ ‖ 15 δὲ om V¹
add V² ‖ 16 οὕτω προθύμως praeter A omnes ‖ 18 ὅτι om ΑΜ
λέγουσαι βραχὺ ἔτι δεῖν coni Muellerus p. 64 ‖ 20 παραγίνωνται V¹
παραγένωνται V² ‖ 21 αὐτάς ΑΜC αὐτήν reliqui ‖ 22 προσκατα-
βαίνουσαι sscr σι Κ¹ καταβαίνουσι Μ ‖ 23 αὐτάς? Α αὐτάς Μ
ἑαυτάς reliqui αὑτάς Sauppeus p. 774

a very narrow ascent with a deep precipice on either side."

"I see."

"Now this," he said, "is the path that leads to true Education."

4   "It most certainly looks difficult."

"And up here do you see on top of the hill a massive towering boulder which has sheer drops all around?"

"I see," I said.

XVI.   "So, do you also see how two women, radiant and healthy in body, are standing upon the boulder and are eagerly stretching forth their hands?"

"I see them," I said, "but what are they called?"

2   "One is called Self-Control and the other Perseverance.[53]   They are sisters."

"Why are they stretching forth their hands so eagerly?"

3   "They are encouraging[54] the ones arriving at this place to be confident[55] and not to shrink back, saying that they must persevere yet a little longer, and then they will come to a good path."

4   "But when the people get to the boulder, how do they ascend? For I see no path leading up to the women."

"The women descend from the precipice and pull them up to them. Then they bid

αὐτοὺς διαναπαύσασθαι. καὶ μετὰ μικρὸν διδόασιν 5
ἰσχὺν καὶ θάρσος καὶ ἐπαγγέλλονται αὐτοὺς καταστήσειν πρὸς τὴν ἀληθινὴν Παιδείαν καὶ δεικνύουσιν
αὐτοῖς τὴν ὁδόν, ὡς ἔστι καλή τε καὶ ὁμαλὴ καὶ
εὐπόρευτος καὶ καθαρὰ παντὸς κακοῦ, ὥσπερ ὁρᾷς. 5

Ἐμφαίνει νὴ Δία.

XVII. Ὁρᾷς οὖν, ἔφη, καὶ ἔμπροσθεν τοῦ ἄλσους
ἐκείνου τόπον τινά, ὃς δοκεῖ καλός τε εἶναι καὶ λει-
μωνοειδὴς καὶ φωτὶ πολλῷ καταλαμπόμενος;

Καὶ μάλα. 10

Κατανοεῖς οὖν ἐν μέσῳ τῷ λειμῶνι περίβολον ἕτε- 2
ρον καὶ πύλην ἑτέραν;

Ἔστιν οὕτως. ἀλλὰ τίς καλεῖται ὁ τόπος οὗτος;

Εὐδαιμόνων οἰκητήριον, ἔφη· ὧδε γὰρ διατρίβουσιν 3
αἱ Ἀρεταὶ πᾶσαι καὶ ἡ Εὐδαιμονία. 15

Εἶεν, ἔφην ἐγώ, ὡς καλὸν λέγεις τὸν τόπον εἶναι.

XVIII. Οὐκοῦν παρὰ τὴν πύλην ὁρᾷς, ἔφη, ὅτι
γυνή τις ἐστὶ καλὴ καὶ καθεστηκυῖα τὸ πρόσωπον,
μέσῃ δὲ καὶ κεκριμένη ἤδη τῇ ἡλικίᾳ, στολὴν δ’ ἔχουσα
ἁπλῆν τε καὶ ἀκαλλώπιστον; ἕστηκε δὲ οὐκ ἐπὶ στρογ- 20
γύλου λίθου, ἀλλ’ ἐπὶ τετραγώνου ἀσφαλῶς κειμένου.
καὶ μετὰ ταύτης ἄλλαι δύο εἰσὶ θυγατέρες τινὲς δο- 2
κοῦσαι εἶναι.

2 καταστήσειν AMP καταστῆσαι reliqui sed sscr ειν L ‖
3 πρὸς τὴν ἀληθινήν] καὶ ἀληθεινήν M ‖ 6 ἐμφαίνει] ἐμφαίνεται
Drosihnus. Sed nescio an activi forma e Polyb. 3, 23, 5 ex-
plicari possit ‖ 7. 8 καὶ om ante ἔμπροσθεν add ante τόπον M ‖
9—11 καὶ . . . λειμῶνι om L add mg (sed in fine τοῦ λειμῶνος) ‖
11 οὖν om B | καὶ add ante ἐν K | τοῦ λειμῶνος praeter AM
omnes ‖ 16 λέγεις om CKP sed add C rec man | τὸν om C add
rec man ‖ 19 καὶ om WM ‖ κεκριμμένη VBRCP κεκρυμμένη L |
ἤδη om EDW | δ’ om P ‖ 20 ἁπλῆν τε καὶ καλλοπισμόν A, *
idem sed καλλωπισμόν M ἁπλῆν καὶ καλλωπισμόν (καλωπισμόν K)
reliqui ἀκαλλώπιστον corr B² ‖ 22 μετὰ ταύτην P μετ’ αὐτῆς M |

5   them to rest a while. Then, after a short time, they
give them strength and courage, and they promise to
conduct them down to true Education. They show them
that the path is beautiful, even, easy to travel,[56]
and free of all evil, just as you see it here."
          "By Zeus, it is plain."

XVII.   "Now do you also see in front of this grove,"
he said, "a place that appears to be beautiful,
grassy, and brilliantly lit?"
          "Certainly."
2   "And can you make out in the middle of the
meadow another enclosure and another gate?"[57]
          "So there is. But what is this place called?"
3   "The dwelling-place of the happy,"[58] he said.
"For all the Virtues and Happiness spend their time
here."
          "Very well, go on," I said. "The place is
just as beautiful as you say!"

XVIII.   "Now," he continued, "do you see that there
is beside the gate a woman, who is fair and has a
calm face? She is also at an age of maturity and
judgment and has a simple, unadorned[59] robe. She
does not stand on a round rock but on a square one
2   which is firmly set. With her there are two other
women who appear to be her daughters."

Ἐμφαίνει οὕτως ἔχειν.

Τούτων τοίνυν ἡ μὲν ἐν τῷ μέσῳ Παιδεία ἐστίν, ἡ δὲ Ἀλήθεια, ἡ δὲ Πειθώ.

3 Τί δὲ ἕστηκεν ἐπὶ λίθου τετραγώνου αὕτη;

5 Σημεῖον, ἔφη, ὅτι ἀσφαλής τε καὶ βεβαία ἡ πρὸς αὐτὴν ὁδός ἐστι τοῖς ἀφικνουμένοις καὶ τῶν διδομένων ἀσφαλὴς ἡ δόσις τοῖς λαμβάνουσι.

4 Καὶ τίνα ἐστίν, ἃ δίδωσιν αὕτη;

Θάρσος καὶ ἀφοβία, ἔφη ἐκεῖνος.

10 Ταῦτα δὲ τίνα ἐστίν;

Ἐπιστήμη, ἔφη, τοῦ μηδὲν ἄν ποτε δεινὸν παθεῖν ἐν τῷ βίῳ.

XIX. Ὦ Ἡράκλεις ὡς καλά, ἔφην, τὰ δῶρα. ἀλλὰ τίνος ἕνεκεν οὕτως ἔξω τοῦ περιβόλου ἕστηκεν;

15 Ὅπως τοὺς παραγινομένους, ἔφη, θεραπεύῃ καὶ ποτίζῃ τὴν καθαρτικὴν δύναμιν. εἶθ᾽ ὅταν καθαρθῶσιν, οὕτως εἰσάγει τούτους πρὸς τὰς Ἀρετάς.

2 Πῶς τοῦτο; ἔφην ἐγώ, οὐ γὰρ συνίημι.

Ἀλλὰ συνήσεις, ἔφη. ὡς ἄν, εἴ τις φιλοτίμως 20 κάμνων ἐτύγχανε, πρὸς ἰατρὸν ἄν δήπου γενόμενος πρότερον καθαρτικοῖς ἐξέβαλλε τὰ νοσοποιοῦντα, εἶτα

---

p. 15, 22 θυγατέραις L θυγατέρα P | δοκοῦσιν CKP ‖ 23 post εἶναι add αὐτῆς F

1 ἐμφαίνει libri ἐμφαίνεται Drosihnus, vid. supra p. 15, 6 ‖ 6 ἀφικομένοις EDW ‖ 8 εἰσὶν M ‖ 11 μὴθ᾽ ἕν A | δεινὸν om M | παθεῖν ἐν τῷ βίῳ δεινόν FEDW ‖ 13 ὦ F ὣ M om reliqui | ἔφης M ‖ 14 οὕτως (οὗτος M) ἔξω τοῦ περιβόλου ἕστηκεν AMF ἔξω τοῦ περιβόλου ἕστηκεν οὕτως reliqui ‖ 15 παραγινομένους AM παραγενομένους reliqui ‖ 17 εἰσάγει τούτους A αὐτοὺς εἰσάγῃ RFC αὐτοὺς εἰσάγει reliqui sed sscr η K corr εἰσάγῃ D ‖ 19 εἴ τις] οὗτος A | φιλότιμος M ‖ 20 ἄν om EDWM | παραγενόμενος C ‖ * 21 ἐξέβαλλε A ἐξέβαλε reliqui | τὰ νοσοποιοῦντα AML πάντα νοσοποιοῦντα V¹ πάντα τὰ νοσοποιοῦντα V² reliqui

"That appears to be the case."

"Well, the one in the middle is Education, and
the others are Truth and Persuasion."[60]

3   "But why is she standing on a square rock?"[61]

"It is a sign," he said, "that for those arriving
the path which leads to her is safe and secure,[62] and
that of all the gifts bestowed, her gift is safe for
those who receive it."

4   "And just what are the gifts that she gives?"

"Courage and fearlessness," he said.

"And what are they?"

"Knowledge," he said, "that they can never
suffer anything terrible in life."[63]

XIX.   "Heracles," I said, "how beautiful are these
gifts! But for what purpose is she standing outside
the enclosure in this way?"

"So that she can heal the ones arriving," he
said, "and give them her purifying power to drink.
Then, when they have been purified she leads them in
this way to the Virtues."[64]

2   "How can this be?" I said. "I do not understand."

"Well, you shall understand," he said. "Thus,
as it were if someone were to fall critically[65] ill,
doubtless he would first go see a doctor,[66] and, by
means of purgatives, expel the causes of the disease.

οὕτως ἂν ὁ ἰατρὸς αὐτὸν εἰς ἀνάληψιν καὶ ὑγείαν
κατέστησεν, εἰ δὲ μὴ ἐπείθετο οἷς ἐπέταττεν, εὐλόγως 3
ἂν δήπου ἀπωσθεὶς ἐξώλετο ὑπὸ τῆς νόσου —

Ταῦτα μὲν συνίημι, ἔφην ἐγώ.

Τὸν αὐτὸν τοίνυν τρόπον, ἔφη, καὶ πρὸς τὴν Παι- $\frac{5}{4}$
δείαν ὅταν τις παραγένηται, θεραπεύει αὐτὸν καὶ ποτίζει τῇ ἑαυτῆς δυνάμει, ὅπως ἐκκαθάρῃ πρῶτον καὶ
ἐκβάλῃ τὰ κακὰ πάντα ὅσα ἔχων ἦλθε.

Ποῖα ταῦτα;

Τὴν ἄγνοιαν καὶ τὸν πλάνον, ὃν ἐπεπώκει παρὰ $\frac{10}{5}$
τῆς Ἀπάτης, καὶ τὴν ἀλαζονείαν καὶ τὴν ἐπιθυμίαν
καὶ τὴν ἀκρασίαν καὶ τὸν θυμὸν καὶ τὴν φιλαργυρίαν
καὶ τὰ λοιπὰ πάντα, ὧν ἀνεπλήσθη ἐν τῷ πρώτῳ
περιβόλῳ.

XX. Ὅταν οὖν καθαρθῇ, ποῦ αὐτὸν ἀποστέλλει; 15

Ἔνδον, ἔφη, πρὸς τὴν Ἐπιστήμην καὶ πρὸς τὰς
ἄλλας Ἀρετάς.

Ποίας ταύτας;

Οὐχ ὁρᾷς, ἔφη, ἔσω τῆς πύλης χορὸν γυναικῶν, 2
ὡς εὐειδεῖς δοκοῦσιν εἶναι καὶ εὔτακτοι καὶ στολὴν 20
ἀτρύφερον καὶ ἁπλῆν ἔχουσιν· ἔτι τε ὡς ἄπλαστοί εἰσι
καὶ οὐδαμῶς κεκαλλωπισμέναι καθάπερ αἱ ἄλλαι;

Ὁρῶ, ἔφην. ἀλλὰ τίνες αὗται καλοῦνται; 3

---

1 ὁ ἰατρὸς αὐτὸν Α αὐτὸν ὁ ἰατρὸς CKP αὐτὸς ὁ ἰατρὸς
reliqui | ὑγίαν Μ ὑγίειαν Κ ὑγείαν reliqui sed supra α sscr η W² ‖
2 κατέστησαν W | ἐπύθετο C¹P ἐπείθετο corr C² ‖ 4 μὲν AMC²
om C¹ reliqui ‖ 5 τοίνυν] δὴ Μ ‖ 6 παραγένηται ΑΜ παρα-
γίνηται reliqui | αὐτὴν F ‖ 7 ἑαυτῇ V¹ ἑαυτῆς V²; vid. supra
p. 5, 2 ‖ 8 πάντα om Μ | ἦλθεν CP | ἦλθεν ἔχων FEDW ‖ 10 ὃν]
ἃ Μ ‖ 10. 11 παρὰ τῆς Ἀπάτης ἐπεπόκει Μ ‖ 13 πρώτῳ om Μ ‖
15 ὅτ᾽ Α ‖ 20 δοκοῦσιν εἶναι] δοκοῦσαι Μ ‖ 21 ἔχουσιν] ἔχουσαι
Dros. | ἄπληστοί FEDP ‖ 22 καθάπερ ΑΜ ὥσπερ reliqui ‖
23 ἔφη P

Then, in this way the doctor would put him on the
3   road to recovery and health. But if he did not
submit to those things which the doctor prescribed,
he would deservedly suffer a setback and would
undoubtedly be ravaged by the disease."[67]

"I understand so far," I said.
4   "Well then," he said, "it is just the same
whenever anyone arrives here at Education. She cures
him and gives him her own power to drink, so that she
may first purify and rid him of all the evils which
he had when he came."

"What kind are they?"
5   "The ignorance and error which he drank from
Deceit; likewise, pretentiousness, desire, incontinence, passion, avarice, and all the rest with which
he was infected[68] in the first enclosure."

XX.   "So, when he has been purified, where does she
send him?"

"Inside, to Knowledge and the other Virtues,"
he said.

"What kind are they?"
2   "Don't you see," he said, "that inside the
gate is a group of women who appear to be attractive
and seemly with simple, inexpensive dress, and that
they are not at all artificial and in no way adorned,
in contrast to the others?"[69]
3   "Oh, yes, I see," I said. "What are they
called?"

Ἡ μὲν πρώτη Ἐπιστήμη, ἔφη, καλεῖται, αἱ δὲ ἄλλαι ταύτης ἀδελφαὶ Ἀνδρεία, Δικαιοσύνη, Καλοκἀγαθία, Σωφροσύνη, Εὐταξία, Ἐλευθερία, Ἐγκράτεια, Πραότης.

4 Ὦ κάλλιστε, ἔφην ἔγωγε, ὡς ἐν μεγάλη ἐλπίδι ἐσμέν.

5 Ἐὰν συνῆτε, ἔφη, καὶ ἕξιν περιποιήσησθε ὧν ἀκούετε.

Ἀλλὰ ποσέξομεν, ἔφην ἔγωγε, ὡς μάλιστα.

Τοιγαροῦν, ἔφη, σωθήσεσθε.

XXI. Ὅταν οὖν παραλάβωσιν αὐτὸν αὗται, ποῦ
10 ἄγουσι;

Πρὸς τὴν μητέρα, ἔφη.

Αὕτη δὲ τίς ἐστιν;

Εὐδαιμονία, ἔφη.

Ποία δ᾽ ἐστὶν αὕτη;

15
2 Ὁρᾷς τὴν ὁδὸν ἐκείνην τὴν φέρουσαν ἐπὶ τὸ ὑψηλὸν ἐκεῖνο, ὅ ἐστιν ἀκρόπολις τῶν περιβόλων πάντων;
Ὁρῶ.

3 Οὐκοῦν ἐπὶ τοῦ προπυλαίου γυνὴ καθεστηκυῖα εὐειδής τις κάθηται ἐπὶ θρόνου ὑψηλοῦ κεκοσμημένη
20 ἐλευθέρως καὶ ἀπεριέργως καὶ ἐστεφανωμένη στεφάνῳ εὐανθεῖ πάνυ καλῷ;

1 ἐπιστήμη ἔφη AK ἔφη ἐπιστήμη reliqui | δ᾽ B ‖ 2 ταύτας P | ἀδελφαὶ om P | καὶ δικαιοσύνη CKP ‖ 3 πραότης] πρώτως A πρώτης VLREDW¹C¹P πρῶτον γ῾ρ ῥώτης F¹ πραότης BW²C²K ‖ 4 κάλλισται K ‖ 5 περιποιήσησθε AVLRE περιποιήσεσθε FCKM περιποιήσεσθαι P πεποιήσοσθε D πεποιήσοισθε W ‖ 7 προσέξω-
* μεν B | ἔφην ἔγωγε ὡς μάλιστα] ἔφην ὡς ἐγὼ μὴ μάλιστα A ἔφην ἔγωγε μάλιστα B ἔφην ὡς ἐγ᾽ ὦμαι (sic) μάλιστα M ἔφην καὶ ἔγωγε καὶ (add sec man) κάλλιστα L ὡς μάλιστα ἔφην ἔγωγε K ἔφην ὡς ἔγωγε μάλιστα reliqui (sed litt. ὡς ἔγω in rasura D) ‖ 10 ἄγουσι A ὑπάγουσι L ἀπάγουσιν BCPM ἀπάγουσι reliqui (in D ν erasum) ‖ 11 πρὸς] εἰς M ‖ 13 εὐδαιμονία γε F ‖ 14 δ᾽ AM δέ reliqui ‖ 15.16 τὸ ὑψηλὸν ἐκεῖνο] τὸν ὑψηλὸν τόπον M ‖ 19 τις] τε F | καὶ κεκοσμημένη F ‖ 20 περιέργως M ‖*
* 21 καλῷ A καὶ ποικίλῳ M καλῶς reliqui

"The first is called Knowledge," he said, "and the others are her sisters, Courage, Justice, Goodness, Moderation, Propriety, Freedom, Self-Control,[70] and Gentleness."

4   "Excellent sir," I said, "how great is our hope!"

"If you understand," he said, "you will also make a habit of doing what you are hearing about."[71]

"Well, we shall pay attention!" I said, "as closely as possible."

"Then you will surely be saved," he said.

XXI.   "Now, when these women have received him, where do they lead him?"

"To their mother," he said.

"But who is she?"

"Happiness," he said.

"And what kind is she?"

2   "Do you see that path there leading to this high place, which is the high citadel of all the enclosures?"

"I do."

3   "Then is there not stationed at the vestibule sitting on a high throne, an attractive woman who is adorned nobly and simply[72] and crowned with a very beautiful and flowery wreath?"

Ἐμφαίνει οὕτως.

Αὕτη τοίνυν ἐστὶν ἡ Εὐδαιμονία, ἔφη.

XXII. Ὅταν οὖν ὧδέ τις παραγένηται, τί ποιεῖ;

Στεφανοῖ αὐτόν, ἔφη, τῇ ἑαυτῆς δυνάμει ἥ τε
Εὐδαιμονία καὶ αἱ ἄλλαι Ἀρεταὶ πᾶσαι ὥσπερ τοὺς 5
νενικηκότας τοὺς μεγίστους ἀγῶνας.

Καὶ ποίους ἀγῶνας νενίκηκεν αὐτός; ἔφην ἐγώ.

Τοὺς μεγίστους, ἔφη, καὶ τὰ μέγιστα θηρία, ἃ 2
πρότερον αὐτὸν κατήσθιε καὶ ἐκόλαζε καὶ ἐποίει δοῦ-
λον, ταῦτα πάντα νενίκηκε καὶ ἀπέρριψεν ἀφ᾽ ἑαυτοῦ 10
καὶ κεκράτηκεν ἑαυτοῦ, ὥστε ἐκεῖνα νῦν τούτῳ δου-
λεύουσι, καθάπερ οὗτος ἐκείνοις πρότερον.

XXIII. Ποῖα ταῦτα λέγεις θηρία; πάνυ γὰρ ἐπι-
ποθῶ ἀκοῦσαι.

Πρῶτον μέν, ἔφη, τὴν Ἄγνοιαν καὶ τὸν Πλάνον. 15
ἢ οὐ δοκεῖ σοι ταῦτα θηρία;

Καὶ πονηρά γε, ἔφην ἐγώ.

Εἶτα τὴν Λύπην καὶ τὸν Ὀδυρμὸν καὶ τὴν Φιλαρ- 2
γυρίαν καὶ τὴν Ἀκρασίαν καὶ τὴν λοιπὴν ἅπασαν Κακίαν.
πάντων τούτων κρατεῖ καὶ οὐ κρατεῖται ὥσπερ πρότερον. 20
Ὦ καλῶν ἔργων, ἔφην ἐγώ, καὶ καλλίστης νίκης. 3

1 ἐμφαίνει οὕτως AMR¹ ἐμφαίνει οὖν οὕτως V ἐμφαίνει
οὕτως ἔχειν CKP ἐμφαίνει εἶναι οὕτως BR²FEDWC² mg
ἐμφαίνεται οὕτως Drosihnus; vid. supra p. 15, 6 ‖ 2—5 ἔφη —
Εὐδαιμονία om W ‖ 3. 4 ὅταν — ἔφη om ED ‖ 3 παραγίνεται Μ ‖
4 τε A om reliqui ‖ 5 ἀρεταὶ πᾶσαι A πᾶσαι ἀρεταί reliqui sed
add (στεφανοῦσι) W ‖ 6 νενικότας AC¹ νενικηκότας C² reliqui
sed obliteravit articulum erasit ς B² ‖ 9 αὐτὸς ED ‖ 10 νενίκη-
*κεν BEDCP ‖ 11. 12 δουλεύουσιν EWP ‖ 12 ἐκεῖνος P ‖ 13 ποῖα
ταῦτα λέγεις θηρία AM ποῖα λέγεις ταῦτα τὰ θηρία reliqui ‖
13. 14 ἐπιθυμῶ BK ‖ 16 ταῦτα θηρία A θηρία ταῦτα εἶναι reliqui ‖ 18 post ὀδυρμὸν add καὶ τὴν ὑπερηφάνειαν Μ ‖ 20 πρό-*
τερον ABM τὸ πρότερον reliqui ‖ 21 καλίστης B καλῆς τῆς Μ
καλλίστης reliqui καλλίστης τῆς corr C²

2*

"So it seems."

"It is she, indeed, who is Happiness," he said.

XXII.   "When someone arrives here what does she do?"

"Happiness crowns him with her power,"[73] he said, "as do all the other Virtues, in the same way that one crowns those who have been victorious in the mightiest contests."[74]

"Well, what kinds of contests has he won?" I said.

2   "The mightiest," he answered, "overcoming even the mightiest beasts, which previously used to devour, abuse, and enslave him. All these he has overcome and cast from himself; he has mastered himself so that these beasts are his slaves just as he was once theirs."

XXIII.   "What kinds of beasts do you mean? For I really want to know."

"In the first place," he said, "Ignorance and Deceit,[75] or don't you think that they are beasts?"

"Yes, and base ones at that," I said.

2   "Next come Grief, Lamentation, Avarice, Incontinence, and every other Vice. All these he masters and is not mastered as before."

3   "What noble feats," I said, "and what a glorious victory!

ἀλλ' ἐκεῖνο ἔτι μοι εἰπέ· τίς ἡ δύναμις τοῦ στεφάνου,
ᾧ ἔφης . . . στεφανοῦν αὐτόν;

4 Εὐδαιμονική, ὦ νεανίσκε. ὁ γὰρ στεφανωθεὶς ταύτῃ
τῇ δυνάμει εὐδαίμων γίνεται καὶ μακάριος καὶ οὐκ ἔχει
5 ἐν ἑτέροις τὰς ἐλπίδας τῆς εὐδαιμονίας, ἀλλ' ἐν αὐτῷ.

XXIV. Ὡς καλὸν τὸ νίκημα λέγεις. ὅταν δὲ
στεφανωθῇ, τί ποιεῖ ἢ ποῖ βαδίζει;

2 Ἄγουσιν αὐτὸν ὑπολαβοῦσαι αἱ Ἀρεταὶ πρὸς τὸν
τόπον ἐκεῖνον, ὅθεν ἦλθε πρῶτον, καὶ δεικνύουσιν
10 αὐτῷ τοὺς ἐκεῖ διατρίβοντας ὡς κακῶς διατρίβουσι
καὶ ἀθλίως ζῶσι καὶ ὡς ναυαγοῦσιν ἐν τῷ βίῳ καὶ
πλανῶνται καὶ ἄγονται κατακεκρατημένοι ὥσπερ ὑπὸ
πολεμίων, οἱ μὲν ὑπ' Ἀκρασίας, οἱ δὲ ὑπ' Ἀλαζονείας,
οἱ δὲ ὑπὸ Φιλαργυρίας, ἕτεροι δὲ ὑπὸ Κενοδοξίας, οἱ
15
3 δὲ ὑφ' ἑτέρων Κακῶν. ἐξ ὧν οὐ δύνανται ἐκλῦσαι
ἑαυτοὺς τῶν δεινῶν, οἷς δέδενται, ὥστε σωθῆναι καὶ
ἀφικέσθαι ὧδε, ἀλλὰ ταράττονται διὰ παντὸς τοῦ βίου.
τοῦτο δὲ πάσχουσι διὰ τὸ μὴ δύνασθαι τὴν ἐνθάδε
ὁδὸν εὑρεῖν· ἐπελάθοντο γὰρ τὸ παρὰ τοῦ Δαιμονίου
20 πρόσταγμα.

XXV. Ὀρθῶς μοι δοκεῖς λέγειν. ἀλλὰ καὶ τοῦτο
πάλιν ἀπορῶ, διὰ τί δεικνύουσιν αὐτῷ τὸν τόπον
ἐκεῖνον αἱ Ἀρεταί, ὅθεν ἥκει τὸ πρότερον.

1 ἔτι om M | post μοι add ἔφην M ‖ 2 ᾧ] ὃν M | στεφα- *
νοῦν libri στεφανοῦσθαι vulg., sed excidit, nisi fallor, τὴν
Εὐδαιμονίαν vel τὰς Ἀρετὰς | ἑαυτὸν M ‖ 4 ἔχει οὐκ M ‖ 5 αὐτῷ
WM ‖ 6 ὡς] πῶς M | νίκημα] κίνημα K ‖ 7 ἢ ποῖ om P ‖ 8 ἄγου-
σαι B ‖ 9 ἦλθεν WP | πρῶτον] πρότερον K ‖ 10 ἐκεῖ VK κακῶς *
reliqui | κακῶς] εἰκῇ M | διατρίβουσι om K ‖ 11 ἐν om K ‖
13 ὑπ' ante Ἀκρασίας B ὑπὸ reliqui ‖ 13. 14 οἱ δὲ — κενοδοξίας
om W¹ add W² mg ‖ 13 ὑπὸ ἀλαζ. M ‖ 14 οἱ (alt.)] ἕτεροι K ‖
16 αὐτοὺς M ‖ 17 τοῦ βίου om P ‖ 18 ἐνθάδε] ἐνταῦθα M ‖
21 δοκεῖ C¹P δοκεῖς corr C² δοκεῖ C³ mg | καὶ om M

But tell me still this: What is the power of the crown with which you said...[76] crowns him?"

4   "It is the power that makes happiness possible, young man.[77] For the person who has been crowned with this power becomes happy and blessed, and he places his hopes for happiness not in others but in himself."

XXIV.   "How noble is the victory you recount! But when he is crowned, what does he do or where does he go?"

2   "The Virtues take him in hand and lead him to that place from which he first came. They show him how those who spend their time there spend time wickedly and live wretchedly; how they are shipwrecked in life, wander aimlessly, and are led about in submission as if by enemies, some by Incontinence, others by Pretentiousness, Avarice, Vanity, and the other

3   Vices. From these terrors, to which they are bound, they cannot free themselves and so be saved and arrive here. Rather, they are troubled throughout their lives. They suffer this lot because they are unable to find the path here. For they have forgotten the command of the Daimon."[78]

XXV.   "You seem correct in what you say. But I am still puzzled regarding this point: Why do the Virtues show him that place from which he had come previously?"

Οὐκ ἀκριβῶς ἤδει οὐδὲ ἠπίστατο, ἔφη, οὐδὲν τῶν **2**
ἐκεῖ, ἀλλ᾽ ἐνεδοίαζε καὶ διὰ τὴν ἄγνοιαν καὶ τὸν πλάνον, ὃν δὴ ἐπεπώκει, τὰ μὴ ὄντα ἀγαθὰ ἐνόμιζεν
ἀγαθὰ εἶναι καὶ τὰ μὴ ὄντα κακὰ κακά. διὸ καὶ ἔζη **3**
κακῶς, ὥσπερ οἱ ἄλλοι οἱ ἐκεῖ διατρίβοντες. νῦν δὲ **5**
ἀπειληφὼς τὴν ἐπιστήμην τῶν συμφερόντων αὐτός τε
καλῶς ζῇ καὶ τούτους θεωρεῖ ὡς κακῶς πράσσουσιν.

XXVI. Ἐπειδὰν οὖν θεωρήσῃ πάντα, τί ποιεῖ ἢ
ποῦ ἔτι βαδίζει;

Ὅπου ἂν βούληται, ἔφη. πανταχοῦ γὰρ ἔστιν αὐτῷ **10**
ἀσφάλεια ὥσπερ τῷ τὸ Κωρύκιον ἄντρον ἔχοντι, καὶ
πανταχοῦ, οὗ ἂν ἀφίκηται, πάντα καλῶς βιώσεται
μετὰ πάσης ἀσφαλείας. ὑποδέξονται γὰρ αὐτὸν ἀσμένως
πάντες καθάπερ τὸν ἰατρὸν οἱ πάσχοντες.

Πότερον οὖν κἀκείνας τὰς γυναῖκας, ἃς ἔφης θηρία $\frac{15}{2}$
εἶναι, οὐκέτι φοβεῖται, μή τι πάθῃ ὑπ᾽ αὐτῶν;

Οὐ μὴ διοχληθήσεται οὐδὲν οὔτε ὑπὸ Ὀδύνης
οὔτε ὑπὸ Λύπης οὔτε ὑπ᾽ Ἀκρασίας οὔτε ὑπὸ Φιλαργυρίας οὔτε ὑπὸ Πενίας οὔτε ὑπὸ ἄλλου Κακοῦ οὐδενός. **3**
ἁπάντων γὰρ κυριεύει καὶ ἐπάνω πάντων ἐστὶ τῶν **20**

---

1 οὐκ] οὐδὲν M | ἔφη om ˙EDWM ‖ 4 εἶναι ἀγαθὰ F |
alterum κακά om C¹ add C² ‖ 5 οἱ post ἄλλοι om V¹B corr V² ‖
6 ἀνειληφὼς M ‖ 7 πράσσοντας P πράττουσιν D sed sscr σσ
prima ut vid. manu, πράσσουσιν reliqui ‖ 9 ποῦ M ποῖ reliqui,
sed statim optimi codd. ὅπου v. 10 et οὗ v. 12 | ἔτι om CKP ‖
10 ὅποι WKM | βούλονται P ‖ 11 τῷ om BK τὸ om FEDW
*CP | κηρύκιον V κωρύκειον BEDWR¹CP κωρύκιον R²FK κύ-
ριον M. Herodoti locum VIII 36 attulit Sauppeus p. 770 ‖
12 οὗ VBRFCKP ὅπου ED ὅποι W | πάντως BRFEDW ‖
13 μετὰ] κατὰ W | αὐτὸν om M ‖ 14 τῶν ἰατρῶν M | πάσχοντες]
κάμνοντες M ‖ 16 πάθῃ sscr οι E¹ πάθοι DW ‖ 17 οὐδὲν οὐ μὴ
διοχληθήσεται libri, ante οὐδὲν add διὸ M unde νὴ Δία coni
Schweighaeuserus ‖ 18 ὑπ᾽ Ἀκρασίας] ὑπὸ ἀκρ. K ὑπὸ κακοῦ M ‖
19 ὑπ᾽ ἄλλου B | οὐθενός VBRDECKPM ‖ 20 γὰρ om M

2   "He did not have precise knowledge of it," he
said, "nor did he understand any of the things there.
Rather, he was confused, and, owing to his ignorance
and error, which, of course, he had already imbibed,
he considered things that are not good to be good and

3   things that are not evil to be evil. Therefore, he
also lived wickedly, just like the others who spend
their time there. But now that he has received the
knowledge of what is advantageous, he lives nobly and
perceives how poorly they are doing."

XXVI.   "After he has perceived all these things,
then what does he do or where does he go next?"

          "Wherever he wishes," he said. "For every
place is as secure for him as the Corycian cavern[79]
is for the one taking refuge there. No matter where
he arrives, in every place and in every way he will
live nobly with all security. For all will welcome
him gladly just as the sick welcome the doctor."[80]

2   "Does he no longer fear that he will suffer
anything at the hands of these women whom you called
beasts?"

          "He will not be troubled in the least either

3   by Pain or by Grief, Incontinence, Avarice, Poverty,[81]
or by any other Vice. For he is master of all things
and is superior to everything

πρότερον αὐτὸν λυπούντων καθάπερ οἱ ἐχιοδεῖκται.
τὰ γὰρ θηρία δήπου τὰ πάντας τοὺς ἄλλους κακο-
ποιοῦντα μέχρι θανάτου ἐκείνους οὐ λυπεῖ διὰ τὸ
ἔχειν ἀντιφάρμακον αὐτούς. οὕτω καὶ τοῦτον οὐκέτι
5 οὐδὲν λυπεῖ διὰ τὸ ἔχειν ἀντιφάρμακον.

XXVII. Καλῶς ἐμοὶ δοκεῖς λέγειν. ἀλλ᾽ ἔτι τοῦτό
μοι εἰπέ. τίνες εἰσὶν οὗτοι οἱ δοκοῦντες ἐκεῖθεν ἀπὸ
τοῦ βουνοῦ παραγίνεσθαι; καὶ οἱ μὲν αὐτῶν ἐστεφανωμένοι ἔμφασιν ποιοῦσιν εὐφροσύνης τινός, οἱ δὲ
10 ἀστεφάνωτοι λύπης καὶ ταραχῆς καὶ τὰς κνήμας καὶ
2 τὰς κεφαλὰς δοκοῦσι τετρῖφθαι, κατέχονται δὲ ὑπὸ
γυναικῶν τινων.

Οἱ μὲν ἐστεφανωμένοι οἱ σεσωσμένοι εἰσὶ πρὸς
3 τὴν Παιδείαν καὶ εὐφραίνονται τετυχηκότες αὐτῆς. οἱ
15 δὲ ἀστεφάνωτοι οἱ μὲν ἀπεγνωσμένοι ὑπὸ τῆς Παιδείας ἀνακάμπτουσι κακῶς καὶ ἀθλίως διακείμενοι· οἱ
δὲ ἀποδεδειλιακότες καὶ οὐκ ἀναβεβηκότες πρὸς τὴν
Καρτερίαν πάλιν ἀνακάμπτουσι καὶ πλανῶνται ἀνοδίᾳ.

* 1 ἐχιόδηκτοι libri *viperarii (prehendunt manibus suis ser-
pentes)* 𝔄; de virorum doctorum coniecturis refert Drosihnus
praef. p. XII; ἐχιοδεῖκται Is. Casaubonus approbante Sauppeo,
qui praeterea proponit ἐχιοδαῖται (p. 776). An fuit apud ve-
teres opinio eos qui serpentis morsui supervixissent, ab eius
bestiae impetu immunes esse? Quod si testimoniis confirmetur,
ut ἐχιόδηκτοι sic statim (v. 4) τοῦτο (ex ἐχιόδηκτοι intell. τὸ
δεδῆχθαι) servari possit ‖ 2 δήπου om F ‖ τὰ (alterum) M om
reliqui ‖ 4 αὐτοὺς ἀντιφάρμακον F ‖ 4. 5 αὐτούς — ἀντιφάρμακον
om W¹ add W² mg ‖ 4 οὕτω] coni Schweighaeuserus τούτους *
W² supra versum, τοῦτο reliqui ‖ οὐκέτι om CKP ‖ 5 οὐθὲν
libri omnes ‖ ante ἀντιφάρμακον add τὸ M ‖ 6 καλῶς ἐμοὶ]
οὔμοι M ‖ 8 αὐτῶν om B αὐτὸν P ‖ 10 λύπης καὶ ταραχῆς VM
ἀπεγνωσμένοι τε BRFEDW οἱ μὲν ἀπεγνωσμένοι CKP ‖ 11 δὲ
καὶ BRFEDW ‖ 13—15 εἰσὶ — ἀπεγνωσμένοι om P ‖ 16 ἀνακάμπτουσιν P ‖ 17 δὲ] γὰρ W ‖ οὐκ] μὴ W om reliqui *neque
ascenderunt* 𝔄 οὐκ inseruit Sauppeus p. 775 ‖ 18 ἀνακάμπτουσιν P ἀνακάπτουσιν B

that formerly caused him distress, just like those
who have survived snakebite.[82] For indeed, those
snakes[83] which cause fatal injury to everyone else,
do not harm these people at all, since they have an
antidote. In the same way, no longer does anything
cause distress to this man because he has an antidote."

XXVII. "I think you are correct in what you say,
but answer this further question for me: Who are these
people who appear to be arriving from the hill over
there? Some of them are wearing crowns and present
an appearance of exultation, while others are without
crowns and give the appearance of grief and confusion.
They appear to have been battered in head and limb,
and are being restrained by some women."

"These wearing crowns are people who have
arrived safely[84] at Education, and they are rejoicing
at having found her. Of those without crowns, some,
having been rejected by Education, are turning back
in a sad and wretched state. Others of them, cower-
ing and failing to ascend to Perseverance, are also
turning back and wandering in a trackless waste."[85]

Αἱ δὲ γυναῖκες αἱ μετ᾽ αὐτῶν ἀκολουθοῦσαι τίνες 4
εἰσὶν αὗται;

Λῦπαι, ἔφη, καὶ Ὀδύναι καὶ Ἀθυμίαι καὶ Ἀδοξίαι
καὶ Ἄγνοιαι.

XXVIII. Πάντα κακὰ λέγεις αὐτοῖς ἀκολουθεῖν. 5

Νὴ Δία πάντα, ἔφη, ἐπακολουθοῦσιν. ὅταν δὲ
οὗτοι παραγένωνται εἰς τὸν πρῶτον περίβολον πρὸς
τὴν Ἡδυπάθειαν καὶ τὴν Ἀκρασίαν, οὐχ ἑαυτοὺς 2
αἰτιῶνται, ἀλλ᾽ εὐθὺς κακῶς λέγουσι καὶ τὴν Παιδείαν
καὶ τοὺς ἐκεῖσε βαδίζοντας, ὡς ταλαίπωροι καὶ ἄθλιοί 10
εἰσι καὶ κακοδαίμονες, οἳ τὸν βίον τὸν παρ᾽ αὐταῖς
ἀπολιπόντες κακῶς ζῶσι καὶ οὐκ ἀπολαύουσι τῶν παρ᾽
αὐταῖς ἀγαθῶν.

Ποῖα δὲ λέγουσιν ἀγαθὰ εἶναι; 3

Τὴν ἀσωτίαν καὶ τὴν ἀκρασίαν, ὡς εἴποι ἄν τις 15
ἐπὶ κεφαλαίου. τὸ γὰρ εὐωχεῖσθαι βοσκημάτων τρόπον ἀπόλαυσιν μεγίστων ἀγαθῶν ἡγοῦνται εἶναι.

XXIX. Αἱ δὲ ἕτεραι γυναῖκες αἱ ἐκεῖθεν παρα-
γινόμεναι ἱλαραί τε καὶ γελῶσαι τίνες καλοῦνται;

Δόξαι, ἔφη, καὶ ἀγαγοῦσαι πρὸς τὴν Παιδείαν τοὺς $\frac{20}{2}$
εἰσελθόντας πρὸς τὰς Ἀρετὰς ἀνακάμπτουσιν, ὅπως

---

1 μετ᾽] κατ᾽ W ‖ 5 πάντα τὰ BRFEDW | καλὰ ED καλὰ
sscr κ FW ‖ 6 καὶ ἐπακολουθοῦσιν M ‖ 6. 7 οὗτοι δὲ ὅταν M ‖
7 παραγίνωνται FM, in D utrum ε scriptum fuerit an ι cognosci
nequit ‖ 8 τὴν ante Ἀκρασίαν om M | οὐχὶ αὐτοὺς C οὐχὶ αὐτοὺς
VKP ‖ 11 εἰσι om M | αὐτοῖς K et (ex αἷς corr) RC² αὐτοῖς
repetit C mg rec ‖ 12 καταλιπόντες M ‖ 13 αὐταῖς F αὐτοῖς reliqui *recedere ab huiusmodi vita deliciarum plena in qua nos
sumus* 𝔄 ‖ 14 δὲ] γὰρ M ‖ 15 εἴπῃ V | τις ἂν B ‖ 16 τρόπον]
sscr υ supra ν W² τρόπῳ M ‖ 17 ἀπόλαυσιν .. ἀγαθῶν] καὶ
ἀπολαύειν μέγιστα ἀγαθὰ M idem sed om καὶ F ‖ 18. 19 παρα-
γιγνόμεναι K παραγενόμεναι BM | αἱ δὲ ἐκεῖθεν παραγενόμεναι
ἕτεραι γυναῖκες M | post τίνες add αὗται B ‖ 20 ἀγοῦσαι C sed
mg rec man ἀγαγοῦσαι ‖ 21 ἀνακύπτουσιν M

4   "But the women following them, who are they?"

           "Griefs," he said, "Pains, Despondencies,
Dishonors, and Ignorances."

XXVIII.   "You are saying that all evils[86] follow
them!"

           "Yes, by Zeus," he said; "they all follow.
And when these people arrive at the first enclosure
2   to Luxury and Incontinence, instead of blaming themselves,[87] they all at once slander both Education and
the ones approaching her. The latter, they say, are
miserable, wretched, and unhappy. Since these have
abandoned the life with them[88] they live wickedly,
they say, and do not enjoy the good things with them."
3   "And what kinds of things do they call good?"

           "Profligacy and incontinence, as one might
say by way of summary. For they suppose that feasting in the manner of cattle[89] is the enjoyment of the
greatest goods."

XXIX.   "Now those other women coming from over there,
cheerful and laughing, what are they called?"
2   "Opinions," he said. "Once they have led to
Education those who then proceed to the Virtues, they
come back here

ἑτέρους ἀγάγωσι, καὶ ἀναγγέλλουσιν, ὅτι εὐδαίμονες
ἤδη γεγόνασιν οὓς τότε ἀπήγαγον.

3   Πότερον οὖν, ἔφην ἐγώ, αὗται εἴσω πρὸς τὰς
Ἀρετὰς ⟨οὐκ⟩ εἰσπορεύονται;

5   [Ἔφη οὔ.] Οὐ γὰρ θέμις Δόξαν εἰσπορεύεσθαι
πρὸς τὴν Ἐπιστήμην, ἀλλὰ τῇ Παιδείᾳ παραδιδόασιν
4 αὐτούς. εἶτα ὅταν ἡ Παιδεία παραλάβῃ, ἀνακάμπτουσιν
αὗται πάλιν ἄλλους ἄξουσαι, ὥσπερ αἱ νῆες τὰ φορτία
ἐξελόμεναι πάλιν ἀνακάμπτουσι καὶ ἄλλων τινῶν γε-
10 μίζονται.

XXX. Ταῦτα μὲν δὴ καλῶς μοι δοκεῖς, ἔφην, ἐξη-
γεῖσθαι. ἀλλ᾽ ἐκεῖνο οὐδέπω ἡμῖν δεδήλωκας, τί προστάττει τὸ Δαιμόνιον τοῖς εἰσπορευομένοις εἰς τὸν Βίον
ποιεῖν.

15
2   Θαρρεῖν, ἔφη. διὸ καὶ ὑμεῖς θαρρεῖτε· πάντα γὰρ
ἐξηγήσομαι καὶ οὐδὲν παραλείψω.

Καλῶς λέγεις, ἔφην ἐγώ.

3   Ἐκτείνας οὖν τὴν χεῖρα πάλιν, Ὁρᾶτε, ἔφη, τὴν
γυναῖκα ἐκείνην, ἣ δοκεῖ τυφλή τις εἶναι καὶ ἐπὶ λίθου
20 στρογγύλου ἑστάναι, ἣν καὶ ἄρτι ὑμῖν εἶπον ὅτι Τύχη
καλεῖται;

Ὁρῶμεν.

XXXI. Ταύτῃ κελεύει, ἔφη, μὴ πιστεύειν καὶ βέ-
βαιον μηδὲν νομίζειν μηδὲ ἀσφαλὲς εἶναι, ὅ τι ἂν

1 ἀγάγωσιν EDW | ἀναγγέλουσιν V¹W ἀναγγέλλουσιν V²B
RFEDM ἀναγγέλωσιν CP ἀναγγείλωσιν K ‖ 4 οὐκ inserui | *
ἐκπορεύονται M ‖ 5 ἔφη οὔ libri, delevit Drosihnus, veniam roga
dominum tuum 𝕬 ‖ 6 παραδίδωσιν F ‖ 7 αὐτοὺς M ‖ 8 αὐταὶ F ‖
9 ἐξελούμεναι M | ἀνακάμπτουσιν CP ἀνακάπτουσιν B ‖ 11 ἔφην
om M ‖ 11.12 ἐξηγῆσθαι P ‖ 15 ἔφην P | ἡμεῖς CK idem sed
sscr v B ὑμεῖς sed v in ras P ‖ 16 ante ἐξηγήσομαι add ὑμῖν M |
παραλείψω] ἀποκρύψω M ‖ 20 ἐφεστάναι P | εἶπον ὑμῖν B ‖
23 αὕτη M ‖ 24 νομίζειν] πιστεύειν CK del. Sauppeus p. 776 | *
εἶναι] ἔχειν CK

to lead others. Moreover, they announce that those
whom they led away before have already become happy."

3   "Do they, then, <not> go in to the Virtues?"
I said.

         ["No," he said.] "For it is not right for
Opinion to enter to Knowledge,[90] but they deliver
4   their charges to Education. Then, when Education has
received them, the Opinions go back again to lead
others, just as cargo ships after unloading return
again to take on other cargo."

XXX.   "I think you have explained these matters
very thoroughly," I said, "but you have not yet made
clear to us this point, namely what the Daimon commands those entering Life to do."

2   "To be confident," he said. "Therefore, you
also be confident,[91] for I will explain everything
and omit nothing."

         "Very well," I said.

3   So he stretched forth his hand once again and
said, "Do you see that woman there who seems to be
blind and is standing on a round rock, who is called
Fortune, as I told you just a moment ago?"

         "Yes, we see her."

XXXI.   "He gives them the following injunctions," he
said: "not to place any trust in this woman, neither
to regard whatsoever one might receive from her as
safe or secure,

παρ αὐτῆς τις λάβῃ μηδὲ ὡς ἴδια ἡγεῖσθαι. οὐδὲν γὰρ 2
κωλύει πάλιν ταῦτα ἀφελέσθαι καὶ ἑτέρῳ δοῦναι.
πολλάκις γὰρ εἴωθε τοῦτο ποιεῖν. καὶ διὰ ταύτην οὖν
τὴν αἰτίαν κελεύει πρὸς τὰς παρ' αὐτῆς δόσεις ἴσους
γίνεσθαι καὶ μήτε χαίρειν ὅταν διδῷ μήτε ἀθυμεῖν 5
ὅταν ἀφέληται καὶ μήτε ψέγειν αὐτὴν μήτε ἐπαινεῖν.
οὐδὲν γὰρ ποιεῖ μετὰ λογισμοῦ, ἀλλ' εἰκῇ καὶ ὡς 3
ἔτυχε πάντα, ὥσπερ πρότερον ὑμῖν ἔλεξα. διὰ τοῦτο
οὖν τὸ Δαιμόνιον κελεύει μὴ θαυμάζειν, ὅ τι ἂν πράττῃ
αὕτη, μηδὲ γίνεσθαι ὁμοίους τοῖς κακοῖς τραπεζίταις. 10
καὶ γὰρ ἐκεῖνοι ὅταν μὲν λάβωσι τὸ ἀργύριον παρὰ 4
τῶν ἀνθρώπων, χαίρουσι καὶ ἴδιον νομίζουσιν εἶναι,
ὅταν δὲ ἀπαιτῶνται, ἀγανακτοῦσι καὶ δεινὰ οἴονται
πεπονθέναι, οὐ μνημονεύοντες, ὅτι ἐπὶ τούτῳ ἔλαβον
τὰ θέματα, ἐφ' ᾧ οὐδὲν κωλύει τὸν θέμενον πάλιν 15
κομίσασθαι. ὡσαύτως τοίνυν κελεύει ἔχειν τὸ Δαι- 5
μόνιον καὶ πρὸς τὴν παρ' αὐτῆς δόσιν καὶ μνημονεύειν,
ὅτι τοιαύτην φύσιν ἔχει ἡ Τύχη, ὥστε ἃ δέδωκεν ἀφελέσθαι καὶ ταχέως πάλιν δοῦναι πολλαπλάσια, αὖθις
δὲ ἀφελέσθαι ἃ δέδωκεν, οὐ μόνον δέ, ἀλλὰ καὶ τὰ 20

* 1 τις ignorant libri omnes, editores vulgo inserunt post
λάβῃ | λάβοι FEDW ‖ 2 πάλιν ταῦτα ἀφελέσθαι VP π. ἀφ. *
ταῦτα BREDW π. ἀφ. αὐτὰ F ταῦτα π. ἀφ. CK | διδόναι CK ‖
3 γὰρ om K | τοῦτο εἴωθε CK | οὖν CK om reliqui ‖ 4 παρ'
om CK | ἑαυτῆς CK | ἴσους VBRFEDP ὅσουν W ἥττους CK *
ἥττω M cf. quae attuli in dissertatione 'Cebetis Tab. quanam
aetate conscr. esse vid.' Marb. 1885 p. 49 ‖ 5 post γίνεσθαι add
οἷον πῶς ἴσους γίνεσθαι VBR| καὶ CK om reliqui ‖ 7 ἀλλὰ RF *
EDWPM ‖ 9 πράττοι EDWCM πρα sscr ττ' F ‖ 12 χαίρουσιν B ‖
13 δεινὰ οἴονται] δεινὸν βίον τε P ‖ 14 τοῦτο M | ἐλάμβανον M
sed ἔλαβον mg ‖ 15 κωλύει VBRFEDWCM κωλύειν KP. Estne
scribendum κωλύσει? ‖ 16 ἔχει] ἔφη BRFEDW ‖ 17 καὶ (alterum) om VBRFEDWP ‖ 18 ἔχει φύσιν CK ‖ 20 ante ἀφελέσθαι add μόνον CKM, οὐ μόνον deleto δὲ ante ἃ δέδωκεν
transponit Anonym. Litter. Centralbl. 1871 p. 1111

2   nor to consider it private property. For there is
    nothing to prevent her from taking her gifts back
    again and giving them to another; she is in the habit
    of doing this often. Consequently, he urges them to
    become indifferent toward her gifts, neither rejoicing
    when she gives nor being despondent when she takes,
3   neither blaming nor praising her. For she does noth-
    ing rationally, but everything randomly and in hap-
    hazard fashion, as I told you before. As a result,
    therefore, the Daimon urges them not to be surprised
    at whatever she does, and not to be like the evil
4   bankers.[92] For the latter, when they receive money
    from people, rejoice and consider it their own. But
    when they are called upon to give it back, they are
    annoyed and think they have suffered a terrible loss,
    not recalling that they had received the deposit on
    the condition that nothing prevents the depositor from
5   recovering it again. So then, the Daimon is urging
    them to respond in like manner also to the gift of
    Fortune and to remember that she has such a nature
    that she takes back what she has given, only to give
    it again quickly many times over. Moreover, she
    takes away not only what she has given but even

6 προϋπάρχοντα. ἃ γοῦν δίδωσι, λαβεῖν κελεύει παρ'
αὐτῆς καὶ συντόμως ἀπελθεῖν βλέποντας πρὸς τὴν
βεβαίαν καὶ ἀσφαλῆ δόσιν.

XXXII. Ποίαν ταύτην; ἔφην ἐγώ.

5 Ἣν λήψονται παρὰ τῆς Παιδείας, ἣν διασωθῶσιν
ἐκεῖ.

Αὕτη οὖν τίς ἐστιν;

2 Ἡ ἀληθὴς ἐπιστήμη τῶν συμφερόντων, ἔφη, καὶ
3 ἀσφαλὴς δόσις καὶ βεβαία καὶ ἀμεταμέλητος. φεύγειν
10 οὖν κελεύει συντόμως πρὸς ταύτην, καὶ ὅταν ἔλθωσι
πρὸς τὰς γυναῖκας ἐκείνας, ἃς καὶ πρότερον εἶπον ὅτι
Ἀκρασία καὶ Ἡδυπάθεια καλοῦνται, καὶ ἐντεῦθεν κελεύει συντόμως ἀπαλλάττεσθαι καὶ μὴ πιστεύειν μηδὲ
ταύταις μηδέν, ἕως ἂν πρὸς τὴν Ψευδοπαιδείαν ἀφί-
15/4 κωνται. κελεύει οὖν αὐτοῦ χρόνον τινὰ ἐνδιατρῖψαι
καὶ λαβεῖν ὅ τι ἂν βούλωνται παρ' αὐτῆς ὥσπερ ἐφό-
διον, εἶτα ἐντεῦθεν ἀπιέναι πρὸς τὴν ἀληθινὴν Παι-
5 δείαν συντόμως. ταῦτά ἐστιν ἃ προστάττει τὸ Δαιμόνιον. ὅστις τοίνυν παρ' αὐτά τι ποιεῖ ἢ παρακούει,
20 ἀπόλλυται κακὸς κακῶς.

XXXIII. Ὁ μὲν δὴ μῦθος, ὦ ξένοι, ὁ ἐν τῷ πίνακι
τοιοῦτος ἡμῖν ἐστιν. εἰ δὲ δεῖ τι προσπυθέσθαι περὶ
ἑκάστου τούτων, οὐδεὶς φθόνος· ἐγὼ γὰρ ὑμῖν φράσω.

---

1 διδῶ CK | κελεύει λαμβάνειν CK κελεύειν λαμβάνει M ‖
2 αὐτῆς] αὐτοῖς M | βλέποντας] ***ποντας P ἔχοντα CK ‖ *
5 παρὰ τῆς] παρ' αὐτῆς W | supra ἣν sscr ἐὰν W² ‖ 7 τίς]
τί F ‖ 8 ἔφη τῶν συμφερόντων CK ‖ 9 ἀμετάβλητος CK ‖ 11 ἐκείνας om P ‖ 12 εὐκρασία V ‖ 13. 14 καὶ . . . μηδέν eiec. Dros. ‖
14 ταύτας FEDW¹ αι sscr W² | ἕως κτλ. Ubi etiam per-
veniant . . . ., ut incumbant in eam aliquo spatio temporis A ‖
* 15 αὐτοῦ coni Sauppeus p. 776 αὐτῆς P αὐτοῖς reliqui ‖ 15. 16
κελεύει—βούλωνται om M ‖ 17 ἐπιέναι K ‖ 18 ταῦτ' CK ταυτά P |
προστάσσει C ‖ 20 κακός om M ‖ 22 καὶ τοιοῦτος W | ὑμῖν C
εἰμῖν W | δὲ] δὴ P | τι om P

6   what they possessed before. Accordingly, he is
        urging them to accept what she gives and to go away
        at once turning toward the safe and secure gift."[93]

        XXXII.   "What kind of gift is that?" I asked.
                 "The one they will receive from Education,
        if they make it there safely."
                 "And what is it?"
2   "True knowledge of what is advantageous,"[94]
        he said, "is the gift that is safe and secure and
3   which will not be regretted.[95] So the Daimon urges
        them to flee at once to this gift. When they come
        to those women, who are called, as I said before,
        Incontinence and Luxury, he urges them to place no
        trust at all in them and to depart quickly from
        here as well, going on until they reach False
4   Education. He urges them to spend some time there
        with her and to take from her whatever they wish
        as provisions for the journey; then to leave there
5   and go quickly[96] to true Education. These are the
        commands that the Daimon gives. Whoever, therefore,
        does anything contrary to these directions or
        ignores them is a wretch who perishes in wretched
        misery."[97]

        XXXIII.   "There you have it, strangers. Such is the
        fable on our tablet. But if you need to inquire
        further concerning each point in detail, I have no
        objection. I will explain to you."

Καλῶς λέγεις, ἔφην ἐγώ. *ἀλλὰ τί κελεύει αὐτοὺς* **2**
τὸ Δαιμόνιον λαβεῖν παρὰ τῆς Ψευδοπαιδείας;
Ταῦτα ἃ δοκεῖ εὔχρηστα εἶναι.

Ταῦτ᾽ οὖν τίνα ἐστί;

Γράμματα, ἔφη, *καὶ τῶν ἄλλων μαθημάτων ἃ καὶ* ⁵⁄₃
Πλάτων φησὶν ὡσανεὶ χαλινοῦ τινος δύναμιν ἔχειν
τοῖς νέοις, ἵνα μὴ εἰς ἕτερα περισπῶνται.

Πότερον δὲ ἀνάγκη ταῦτα λαβεῖν, εἰ μέλλει τις **4**
ἥξειν πρὸς τὴν ἀληθινὴν Παιδείαν; ἢ οὔ;

Ἀνάγκη μὲν οὐδεμία, ἔφη, *χρήσιμα μέντοι ἐστὶ* 10
πρὸς τὸ συντομωτέρως ἐλθεῖν. πρὸς δὲ τὸ βελτίους
γενέσθαι οὐδὲν συμβάλλεται ταῦτα.

Οὐδὲν ἄρα, ἔφην, *λέγεις ταῦτα χρήσιμα εἶναι πρὸς* **5**
τὸ βελτίους γενέσθαι ἄνδρας;

Ἔστι γὰρ καὶ ἄνευ τούτων βελτίους γενέσθαι, 15
ὅμως δὲ οὐκ ἄχρηστα κἀκεῖνά ἐστιν. ὡς γὰρ δι᾽ ἑρμη- **6**
νέως συμβάλλομεν τὰ λεγόμενά ποτε, ὅμως μέντοι γε
οὐκ ἄχρηστον ἦν ἡμᾶς καὶ αὐτοὺς τὴν φωνὴν εἰδέναι,
ἀκριβέστερον γὰρ ἄν τι συνήκαμεν, οὕτω καὶ ἄνευ
τούτων τῶν μαθημάτων οὐδὲν κωλύει ⟨βελτίους⟩ 20
γενέσθαι ....

2 παρὰ τῆς] παρ᾽ αὐτῆς P ‖ 3 ταῦθ᾽ CK ‖ 4 ταῦτ᾽ VCK
ταῦτα reliqui | ἐστιν B ‖ 6 πλάττων E. Laudatur Plat. leg.
p. 808 de | χαληνοῦ FEW | ἔχει W ‖ 8 δὲ om P | εἰ] ἢ P |
μέλλοι K ‖ 10 μὲν οὐδεμία om P | χρῆμα VRFEDW¹P χρήματα
*B¹ χρήσιμα B²W²CK ‖ 11 συντομώτερον BRFEDW¹P | πρὸς
... ἐλθεῖν om CK oblit W² | τὸ (alterum) om P ‖ 12 συμβάλλει VB
REDW¹P συμβα sscr λλ᾽ F συμβάλλεται CKW² ‖ 13 οὐδὲν KW²
*οὐθὲν W¹ reliqui | ἄρα ἔφην VP εἶναι ἔφην RFEDW ἄνδρας
ἔφην (v. 14) B ἔφην om CK ‖ 18 ante ἦν inser. ἄν Sauppeus | *
*αὐτοὺς CK αὐτὴν P αὐτῶν reliqui ‖ 19 ἀκριβεστέραν ἔχειν ἄν *
τι συνήκαμεν omisso εἰδέναι CK | οὕτως VCKP ‖ 20 οὐθὲν V *
*BREDW | κωλύει BDW κωλύσει reliqui | βελτίους inserui ‖ *
*21 post γενέσθαι nonnulla exciderunt, quorum sententia haec
erat: neque tamen inutilia haec sunt, cum viam ad morum

2   "Very well then," I said, "what does the Daimon urge them take from False Education?"

"Whatever seems to be useful."

"Such as?"

3   "Literature," he said, "and those of the other studies which even Plato[98] said have for youth the force of a bridle, so that they are not diverted to different pursuits."

4   "Then is it necessary, or not, to take these things if one intends to go to true Education?"

"None of these things is necessary," he said; "however, they are useful for the purpose of going more quickly. Yet they contribute nothing toward becoming better."[99]

5   "Then are you saying that these things are not useful in any way for the purpose of becoming better men?" I said.

"Well, it is possible to become better even without them; nevertheless, they are not useless. 6 For just as we sometimes surmise what is being said through an interpreter, nevertheless, it would not be useless for us to know the language ourselves, since we would then understand somewhat more accurately. In the same way then, nothing prevents one from becoming <better>[100] even without these academic disciplines...."

XXXIV. *Πότερον οὖν οὐδὲ προέχουσιν οὗτοι οἱ μαθηματικοὶ πρὸς τὸ βελτίους γενέσθαι τῶν ἄλλων ἀνθρώπων;*

2 *Πῶς ⟨γὰρ⟩ μέλλουσι προέχειν, ἐπειδὰν φαίνωνται* 5 *ἠπατημένοι περὶ ἀγαθῶν καὶ κακῶν ὥσπερ καὶ οἱ* 3 *ἄλλοι καὶ ἔτι κατεχόμενοι ὑπὸ πάσης κακίας; οὐδὲν γὰρ κωλύει εἰδέναι μὲν γράμματα καὶ κατέχειν τὰ μαθήματα πάντα, ὁμοίως δὲ μέθυσον καὶ ἀκρατῆ εἶναι καὶ φιλάργυρον καὶ ἄδικον καὶ προδότην καὶ τὸ πέρας* 10 *ἄφρονα.*

4 *Ἀμέλει πολλοὺς τοιούτους ἔστιν ἰδεῖν.*

Πῶς οὖν οὗτοι προέχουσιν, ἔφη, εἰς τὸ βελτίους ἄνδρας γενέσθαι ἕνεκα τούτων τῶν μαθημάτων;

XXXV. *Οὐδαμῶς φαίνεται ἐκ τούτου τοῦ λόγου.* 15 *ἀλλὰ τί ἐστιν, ἔφην ἐγώ, τὸ αἴτιον, ὅτι ἐν τῷ δευτέρῳ περιβόλῳ διατρίβουσιν ὥσπερ ἐγγίζοντες πρὸς τὴν ἀληθινὴν Παιδείαν;*

2 *Καὶ τί τοῦτο ὠφελεῖ αὐτούς, ἔφη, ὅτε πολλάκις ἔστιν ἰδεῖν παραγινομένους ἐκ τοῦ πρώτου περιβόλου* 20 *ἀπὸ τῆς Ἀκρασίας καὶ τῆς ἄλλης Κακίας εἰς τὸν τρίτον περίβολον πρὸς τὴν Παιδείαν τὴν ἀληθινήν, οἳ τούτους τοὺς μαθηματικοὺς παραλλάττουσιν; ὥστε πῶς ἔτι προέχουσιν ἄρα, εἰ ἀκινητότεροι ἢ δυσμαθέστεροί εἰσι;*

correctionem muniant; ultimum vocabulum litteris σθαι videtur terminatum fuisse; fort. ἀφικέσθαι cf. v. 11. Sauppeus p. 776 post οὕτω καί (v. 19) add ἐκεῖνα οὐκ ἄχρηστά ἐστι πρὸς τὸ βελτίους γενέσθαι, ἀλλὰ καί

1 οὖν om CKV | οὐδὲ VBRFEDP οὐδὲν reliqui ‖ 4 φαίνονται M ‖ 5 περὶ τῶν W ‖ 12 προσέχουσιν M ‖ 13 ἄνδρες BR FEP ‖ 14 τὰ ἐκ P ‖ 15 τὸν αἴτιον P ‖ 18 ἔφην VBRFEDP ἔφην οὐδὲν ἔφη W | ὅτε R sed ε in rasura ὅτι W ὅταν reliqui ὅτε Sauppeus ex coni p. 775 ‖ 19 παραγιγνομένους C ‖ 23 εἰ] * ἢ CK | εὐκινητότεροι VBFEDW ἀκινητώτεροι P ἀκινητότεροι * reliqui | ἀμαθέστεροι P

XXXIV.   "Do these scholars, then, have no advantage over the rest of mankind in the matter of becoming better?"[101]

2   "How could they conceivably have any advantage since it is quite evident that they, just like all the rest, are deceived about good and evil and

3   are still dominated by every vice?[102] For nothing prevents one from knowing literature and mastering all the academic disciplines and yet at the same time being drunken, incontinent, avaricious, unjust, treacherous, and, in short, foolish."

4   "Of course, one can see many such people."

"How then," he said, "in the matter of becoming better men are these people superior by virtue of these scholarly pursuits?"[103]

XXXV.   "Not at all, as is apparent from this argument. But why is it, then," I said, "that these people stay here in the second enclosure as though they were drawing near true Education?"

2   "And what advantage does staying there have for them," he said, "when one can often see, coming out of the first enclosure, from Incontinence and that other Vice, and arriving in the third, at true Education, those who pass by these scholars? So then, how are they really still superior, seeing that they are more intractable than slow witted?"

Πῶς τοῦτο; ἔφην ἐγώ. 3

Ὅτι οἱ ⟨μὲν⟩ ἐν τῷ πρώτῳ περιβόλῳ . . . . . ., ⟨οἱ
δ᾽ ἐν τῷ δευτέρῳ περιβόλῳ,⟩ εἰ μηδὲν ἄλλο, ὃ προσ-
ποιοῦνταί γε ἐπίστασθαι οὐκ οἴδασιν. ἕως δ᾽ ἂν ἔχωσι
ταύτην τὴν δόξαν, ἀκινήτους αὐτοὺς ἀνάγκη εἶναι πρὸς 5
τὸ ὁρμᾶν πρὸς τὴν ἀληθινὴν Παιδείαν. εἶτα τὸ ἕτερον 4
οὐχ ὁρᾷς, ὅτι καὶ αἱ Δόξαι ἐκ τοῦ πρώτου περιβόλου
εἰσπορεύονται πρὸς αὐτοὺς ὁμοίως; ὥστε οὐδὲν οὗτοι
ἐκείνων βελτίους εἰσίν, ἐὰν μὴ καὶ τούτοις συνῇ ἡ
Μεταμέλεια καὶ πεισθῶσιν, ὅτι οὐ παιδείαν ἔχουσιν, 10
ἀλλὰ ψευδοπαιδείαν, δι᾽ ἣν ἀπατῶνται. οὕτω δὲ δια- 5
κείμενοι οὐκ ἄν ποτε σωθεῖεν. καὶ ὑμεῖς τοίνυν, ὦ
ξένοι, ἔφη, οὕτω ποιεῖτε καὶ ἐνδιατρίβετε τοῖς λεγομένοις, μέχρι ἂν ἕξιν λάβητε. ἀλλὰ περὶ τῶν αὐτῶν
πολλάκις δεῖ ἐπισκοπεῖν καὶ μὴ διαλείπειν, τὰ δ᾽ ἄλλα 15
πάρεργα ἡγήσασθαι. εἰ δὲ μή, οὐδὲν ὄφελος ὑμῖν
ἔσται ὧν νῦν ἀκούετε.

XXXVI. *Ποιήσομεν.* τοῦτο δὲ ἐξήγησαι, πῶς οὐκ
ἔστιν ἀγαθά, ὅσα λαμβάνουσιν οἱ ἄνθρωποι παρὰ τῆς
Τύχης, οἷον τὸ ζῆν, τὸ ὑγιαίνειν, τὸ πλουτεῖν, τὸ 20

---

1 τοῦτ᾽ F | ἔφην τοῦτο ἐγώ CK ‖ 2 οἱ om CKM | μὲν igno-
rant libri | πρώτῳ] δευτέρῳ K | lacunam non indicant libri; *
οὐ προσποιοῦνται ἐπίστασθαι, ἃ οὐκ οἴδασιν, οἱ δ᾽ ἐν τῷ δευτέρῳ περιβόλῳ suppl Drosihnus ‖ 3 εἰ μηδὲν ἄλλο] μηδὲν ἄλλο
εἰ μὴ W ‖ 4 γε om EDW ‖ 8 οὐθὲν libri ‖ 9 ἡ om libri ‖ 11 δι᾽
ἧς R | δὲ om K ‖ 12. 13 ἔφη ὦ ξένοι K | οὕτω . . . ἐνδιατρίβετε *
Wolfius ex coni, ἐὰν μὴ οὕτως ποιῆτε καὶ ἐνδιατρίβητε K ἐὰν
μὴ οὕτω ποιῆτε καὶ μὴ ἐνδιατρίβητε W (prius μὴ supra versum
1. an 2. m.?) ἐὰν οὕτω (οὕτως VCM) ποιῆτε καὶ ἐνδιατρίβητε
reliqui. *Vos igitur . . . insistite hanc viam ac vosmet ipsos . . .
multopere exercitote 𝔄 vos . . . ita facite et . . . attendite* O ‖
14 μέχρι V¹ μέχρις V² reliqui | λαβεῖν libri ‖ 15 δὲ CK ‖ 16 ἡγεῖ-
σθαι F | ὑμῖν om CK add C mg ‖ 16. 17 ἔσται ὑμῖν M ‖ 18 ποιή-
σωμεν VP ὅτῳ ποιήσομεν K

3   "How can this be?" I asked.
           "Because those in the first enclosure.....
<while those in the second enclosure> if for no
other reason than the latter do not know what they
falsely claim to understand.[104] But as long as they
hold this opinion they are of necessity inert in
4   their start toward true Education. Then do you not
see the other reason, namely, that the Opinions from
the first enclosure are entering to them here as
well? So, they are no better than those in the
first enclosure, unless Repentance[105] is also with
them, and they are persuaded by her that they do
not have Education but False Education,[106] through
5   whom they are deceived. But since they are in such
a state of mind they can never be saved. Now, you
too, strangers," he said, "act like this and dwell
on these words until you make them your habit.[107]
And concerning these words you must attend to them
often, not neglecting them, and consider all the
rest as secondary. If you do not, there will be
no advantage for you in what you now hear."

XXXVI. "We will do it. But explain this: How are
all those things that men receive from Fortune not
good[108]--things such as living, being in good
health, having wealth,

εὐδοκιμεῖν, τὸ τέκνα ἔχειν, τὸ νικᾶν καὶ ὅσα τούτοις
2 παραπλήσια; ἢ πάλιν τὰ ἐναντία πῶς οὐκ ἔστι κακά;
πάνυ γὰρ παράδοξον ἡμῖν καὶ ἄπιστον δοκεῖ τὸ λεγό-
μενον.

5 Ἄγε τοίνυν, ἔφη, πειρῶ ἀποκρίνασθαι τὸ φαινό-
μενον περὶ ὧν ἄν σε ἐρωτῶ.

3 Ἀλλὰ ποιήσω τοῦτο, ἔφην ἐγώ.

Πότερον οὖν, ἐὰν κακῶς τις ζῇ, ἀγαθὸν ἐκείνῳ τὸ ζῆν;
Οὔ μοι δοκεῖ, ἀλλὰ κακόν, ἔφην ἐγώ.

10 Πῶς οὖν ἀγαθόν ἐστι τὸ ζῆν, ἔφη, εἴπερ τούτῳ
ἐστὶ κακόν;

4 Ὅτι τοῖς μὲν κακῶς ζῶσι κακόν μοι δοκεῖ εἶναι,
τοῖς δὲ καλῶς ἀγαθόν.

Καὶ κακὸν ἄρα λέγεις τὸ ζῆν καὶ ἀγαθὸν εἶναι;

15 Ἔγωγε.

XXXVII. Μὴ οὖν ἀπιθάνως λέγε. ἀδύνατον τὸ
αὐτὸ πρᾶγμα κακὸν καὶ ἀγαθὸν εἶναι. τοῦτο μὲν γὰρ
καὶ ὠφέλιμον καὶ βλαβερὸν ἂν εἴη καὶ αἱρετὸν καὶ
φευκτὸν τὸ αὐτὸ πρᾶγμα ἀεί.

20
2 Ἀπίθανον μέν. ἀλλὰ πῶς οὐχὶ τὸ κακῶς ζῆν, ᾧ
ἂν ὑπάρχῃ, κακόν τι αὐτῷ ὑπάρχει; οὐκοῦν εἰ κακόν
τι ὑπάρχει αὐτῷ, κακὸν αὐτὸ τὸ ζῆν ἐστιν.

1 εὐδοκεῖν V¹RFEP εὐδοξεῖν CK εὐδοκιμεῖν V² reliqui |
* τὸ ante τέκνα in ras V² δὲ add P | ante ὅσα add τὰ λοιπὰ CK |
2 ἔστιν P ‖ 3 ἡμῖν παράδοξον CK | τὸ om K ‖ 5 πειρῶ ἔφη CK
ἔφη om W ‖ 6 σε om B ‖ 8. 9 πότερον ... ἐγώ om B ‖ 8 ἐὰν]
κἂν CK | τις om K ‖ 10 τοῦτο VR¹C γ̓ρ τούτω R² mg |
12 ζῶσιν B ‖ 16 οὖν om P | post ἀδύνατον add γὰρ CK ‖
17 ante κακὸν add καὶ CK | τοῦτο] οὕτω CK ‖ 19 τὸ αὐτὸ
πρᾶγμα] ἅμὰ CK ‖ 20 οὐχὶ] οὐκ εἰ CKM sed in C κ rec man et
εἰ in rasura | κακῶς] κακὸν P ‖ 21 ὑπάρχῃ] ὑπάρχοι (οι in rasura)
K ὑπάρχει P | αὐτοῦ P | ὑπάρχει] ὑπάρχῃ P ‖ 21. 22 αὐτῷ ... τι
om CK ‖ 22 αὐτὸ ante τὸ ζῆν VBRCP αὐτὸ sscr ῶ K¹ αὐτῶ
sscr ὸ F

2   having good reputation, having children, winning
     victories, and all things like these? Or again, in
     what way are the opposite things not evil? For
     what you are saying strikes us as being quite con-
     tradictory and incredible."

             "Come, then," he said, "try to express
     your opinion about whatever questions I put to
     you."[109]

3   "I shall indeed do so," I said.

             "Now, if someone lives wickedly, is living
     a good thing for that person?"

             "I wouldn't think so; rather it seems bad,"
     I said.

             "Then, how is living a good thing at all,"
     he asked, "if indeed it is bad for this person?"

4   "I suppose that for those living wickedly
     it is a bad thing, while for those living nobly it
     is good."

             "Then do you mean to suggest that living
     is both bad and good?"[110]

             "I certainly do."

XXXVII.   "Don't speak implausibly, now. It is im-
     possible for one and the same thing to be both bad
     and good. For otherwise the same thing might be
     simultaneously useful and harmful, to be desired
     and to be avoided."

2   "Indeed, that is implausible. But surely
     living wickedly constitutes something bad in the
     person in whom it exists, doesn't it? So if it
     constitutes something bad in him, then living in
     and of itself is a bad thing."

Ἀλλ᾿ οὐ ταὐτό, ἔφη, ὑπάρχει τὸ ζῆν καὶ τὸ κακῶς ζῆν. ἢ οὔ σοι φαίνεται;

Ἀμέλει οὐδ᾿ ἐμοὶ δοκεῖ ταὐτὸ εἶναι.

Τὸ κακῶς τοίνυν ζῆν κακόν ἐστι, τὸ δὲ ζῆν οὐ 3 κακόν. ἐπεὶ εἰ ἦν κακόν, τοῖς ζῶσι καλῶς κακὸν ἂν 5 ὑπῆρχεν, ἐπεὶ τὸ ζῆν αὐτοῖς ὑπῆρχεν, ὅπερ ἐστὶ κακόν.

Ἀληθῆ μοι δοκεῖς λέγειν.

XXXVIII. Ἐπεὶ τοίνυν ἀμφοτέροις συμβαίνει τὸ ζῆν, καὶ τοῖς καλῶς ζῶσι καὶ τοῖς κακῶς, οὐκ ἂν εἴη οὔτε ἀγαθὸν εἶναι τὸ ζῆν οὔτε κακόν· ὥσπερ οὐδὲ τὸ 10 τέμνειν καὶ καίειν ἐν τοῖς ἀρρωστοῦσίν ἐστι νοσερὸν καὶ ὑγιεινόν, ἀλλὰ τὸ πῶς τέμνειν, οὐκοῦν οὕτω καὶ ἐπὶ τοῦ ζῆν οὐκ ἔστι κακὸν αὐτὸ τὸ ζῆν ἀλλὰ τὸ κακῶς ζῆν.

Ἔστι ταῦτα. 15

2

Εἰ τοίνυν οὕτως ⟨ἔχει⟩, θεώρησον, πότερον ἂν βούλοιο ζῆν κακῶς ἢ ἀποθανεῖν καλῶς καὶ ἀνδρείως.

Ἀποθανεῖν ἔγωγε καλῶς.

Οὐκοῦν οὐδὲ τὸ ἀποθανεῖν κακόν ἐστιν, εἴπερ 3 αἱρετώτερόν ἐστι πολλάκις τὸ ἀποθανεῖν τοῦ ζῆν. 20

Ἔστι ταῦτα.

Οὐκοῦν ὁ αὐτὸς λόγος καὶ περὶ τοῦ ὑγιαίνειν καὶ 4

1 ταυτὸν F τὸ αὐτὸ CK | ante ὑπάρχει add κακὸν CKM | καὶ τὸ] τῷ CK καὶ om M ‖ 2 ὑπάρχει post ζῆν transp EDW ‖ 3 οὐδὲ Κ | τὸ αὐτὸ CK ‖ 4 κακῶς om K | κακὸν om F | κακὸν ... ζῆν om CK ‖ 5 post κακόν add ἐστιν CK | εἰ om C | ante *τοῖς inser καὶ Sauppeus p. 776 | τοῖς ... κακὸν om M | καλῶς* solus K om reliqui | ἂν] δεῖ M δὴ reliqui libri, corr Sauppeus * *p. 776 ‖ 7 μοι δοκεῖς VCK δοκεῖς μοι reliqui ‖ 9 κακῶς ζῶσι καὶ τοῖς καλῶς CK ‖ 12 ἀλλὰ τὸ πῶς τέμνειν om CK ‖ 13.14 * οὐκ ... κακῶς ζῆν om CK ‖ 16 εἰ] σὺ CK considera nunc 𝔄 | οὕτω RP | ἔχει inserui ‖ 17 βούλη P ‖ 20 πολλάκις om B

"But living and living wickedly are not the same thing," he said. "Or is that not apparent to you?"[111]

"Of course I don't think they are the same."

3   "So, living wickedly is a bad thing, while living is not. For if it were bad, it would be a bad thing <even>[112] for those who live nobly, for living, which then would be a bad thing, exists for them as well."

"I think what you say is true."

XXVIII. "Thus, since living applies in both cases-- both for those who live nobly and those who live wickedly--surely it follows then that living would be neither good nor bad.[113] Just as for those who are sick, surgery and cautery[114] neither impair nor impart health, but how the surgery is performed; so also then in the matter of living, it is not living itself that is wicked, but a wicked manner of living."

2   "That is so."

"If then <this is> so, consider whether you would rather live wickedly or die nobly and courageously."

"For my part, I would rather die nobly."

3   "Then not even dying is a bad thing, if indeed dying is often preferable to living."

"That is so."

4   "Then the same argument also holds true concerning being healthy and

νοσεῖν. πολλάκις γὰρ οὐ συμφέρει ὑγιαίνειν, ἀλλὰ
τοὐναντίον, ὅταν ᾖ περίστασις τοιαύτη.

Ἀληθῆ λέγεις.

XXXIX. Ἄγε δὴ σκεψώμεϑα καὶ περὶ τοῦ πλουτεῖν
5 οὕτως, εἴγε ϑεωρεῖν ἔστιν — ὡς πολλάκις ἔστιν ἰδεῖν
— ὑπάρχοντά τινι πλοῦτον, κακῶς δὲ ζῶντα τοῦτον
καὶ ἀϑλίως.

Νὴ Δία, πολλούς γε.

2 Οὐκοῦν οὐδὲν τούτοις ὁ πλοῦτος βοηϑεῖ εἰς τὸ
10 ζῆν καλῶς;

Οὐ φαίνεται· αὐτοὶ γὰρ φαῦλοί εἰσιν.

3 Οὐκοῦν τὸ σπουδαίους εἶναι οὐχ ὁ πλοῦτος ποιεῖ,
ἀλλὰ ἡ Παιδεία.

Εἰκός γε.

15 Ἐκ τούτου ἄρα τοῦ λόγου οὐδὲ ὁ πλοῦτος ἀγαθόν
ἐστιν, εἴπερ οὐ βοηϑεῖ τοῖς ἔχουσιν αὐτὸν εἰς. τὸ βελτίους εἶναι.

Φαίνεται οὕτως.

4 Οὐδὲ συμφέρει ἄρα ἐνίοις πλουτεῖν, ὅταν μὴ ἐπί-
20 στωνται τῷ πλούτῳ χρῆσϑαι.

Δοκεῖ μοι.

Πῶς οὖν τοῦτο ἄν τις κρίνοι ἀγαθὸν εἶναι, ὃ
πολλάκις οὐ συμφέρει ὑπάρχειν;

5 Οὐδαμῶς.

2 τὸ ἐναντίον B | ᾖ] ἡ CM ‖ 5 post ὡς add οὐ praeter BK
omnes, ὡς ... ἰδεῖν eicit Anonym. Litter. Centralbl. 1871 p. 1111,
nescio an recte ‖ 6 ὑπάρχοντι M | τοῦτον om EDW ‖ 9 οὐδὲν]
* οὐδὲ C mg rec ‖ 11 οὐ om M | αὐτοὶ] οὗτοι K ‖ 13 ἀλλὰ VRKP
ἀλλ' reliqui ‖ 15 ἐκ ... λόγου cum Sauppeo (p. 776) seni tribui |*
οὐδὲ] ποῦ δὲ CM ποῦ K ‖ 19 ἄρα om W ‖ 19. 20 ἐπίστωνται V²*
ἐπίσταντι V¹ reliqui ‖ 22 κρίνοι V²BRFEDW (D οι in rasura)
κρινεῖ C κρι sscr ν' V¹ κρίνει P κρίνει sscr οι K¹ κρίνειε coni
Sauppeus p. 775}

sick. For often it is not advantageous to be
healthy, but the opposite, depending on the situa-
tion."[115]

"What you say is true."

XXXIX. "Come now and let us inquire also into the
matter of being wealthy, in this manner: whether it
is possible to see--as often is the case--if a man
is wealthy and yet lives wickedly and wretchedly."[116]

"By Zeus, one can see many many such cases."

2   "Then wealth is of no help to them for
living nobly, is it?"

"Apparently not, since they themselves are
base."

3   "Then it is not wealth but Education that
makes them good."

"In all probability."

"On the basis of this argument, then, wealth
is not a good thing, since it does not help those
who possess it to become better."[117]

"Apparently so."

4   "Then, it is not even advantageous for some
people to be wealthy when they do not understand
how to use their wealth."

"So it seems."

"Then how could anyone judge that to be
good which is often of no advantage to possess?"

5   "Impossible!"

Οὐκοῦν εἰ μέν τις ἐπίσταται τῷ πλούτῳ χρῆσθαι καλῶς καὶ ἐμπείρως, εὖ βιώσεται, εἰ δὲ μή, κακῶς. Ἀληθέστατά μοι δοκεῖς τοῦτο λέγειν.

XL. Καὶ τὸ σύνολον δέ, ἔστι τὸ τιμᾶν ταῦτα ὡς ἀγαθὰ ὄντα ἢ ἀτιμάζειν ὡς κακά, τοῦτο δέ, ἔστι τὸ 5 ταράττον τοὺς ἀνθρώπους καὶ βλάπτον, ὅτι ἐὰν τιμῶσιν αὐτὰ καὶ οἴωνται διὰ τούτων μόνων εἶναι τὸ εὐδαιμονεῖν, [καὶ] πάνθ᾽ ὑπομένουσι πράττειν ἕνεκα τούτων καὶ τὰ ἀσεβέστατα καὶ τὰ αἰσχρότατα δοκοῦντα εἶναι οὐ παραιτοῦνται. ταῦτα δὲ πάσχουσι διὰ τὴν 10/2 τοῦ ἀγαθοῦ ἄγνοιαν. ἀγνοοῦσι γὰρ ὅτι οὐ. γίνεται ἐκ κακῶν ἀγαθόν. πλοῦτον δὲ ἔστι πολλοὺς κτησαμένους 3 ἰδεῖν ἐκ κακῶν καὶ αἰσχρῶν ἔργων, οἷον λέγω ἐκ τοῦ προδιδόναι καὶ ληΐζεσθαι καὶ ἀνδροφονεῖν καὶ συκοφαντεῖν καὶ ἀποστερεῖν καὶ ἐξ ἄλλων πολλῶν καὶ 15 μοχθηρῶν.

Ἔστι ταῦτα.

XLI. Εἰ τοίνυν γίνεται ἐκ κακοῦ ἀγαθὸν μηδέν, ὥσπερ εἰκός, πλοῦτος δὲ γίνεται ἐκ κακῶν ἔργων, ἀνάγκη μὴ εἶναι ἀγαθὸν τὸν πλοῦτον.

20

---

1 εἰ om P | articulum ante πλούτῳ om CK ‖ 2 ἐμπείρως] εὐπόρως M ‖ 3 λέγειν τοῦτο sed transp. litteris β—α superscr. F¹‖ 4 virgulam post δὲ ponunt Saupp. Muell. Jerram. | ἔστι om K ‖ 5 ἀγαθὰ — ὡς om C add mg rec man | δὲ om K δ᾽ M ‖ 6 ταράττον] παρατάττων M | ὅταν libri ὅτι ἐὰν Muell. Jerram.; et istud quia, ubi 𝔄 | τιμῶσιν αὐτὰ K τιμῶνται reliqui τιμῶσι Muellerus ‖ 7 οἴονται V¹CKP οἴωνται V² reliqui | τοῦτον CP μόνον VCP | εἶναι μόνων, sed transpos. superscr. β—α K¹ ‖ 8 καὶ inclusi | ὑπομένουσι] ἐπομένως libri ὑπομένοντες Hemsterhusius, ὑπομένουσι Saupp. (p. 771), Muell. (p. 57), Jerram.; perseverant iuxta cum iis agere omnia 𝔄 | πράττουσιν K ‖ 9 αἰσχρότατα om CM καὶ τὰ αἰσχρότατα om K ‖ 10 οὐ] μὴ F | οὐ παραιτοῦνται om CK del Saupp.; et ita transeunt ad omnia illicita adque perpetrandum res turpes 𝔄 ‖ 12 ἔστιν B ‖ 13 ἔργων καὶ * αἰσχρῶν V ‖ 18 μηθὲν libri

"So, if someone understands how to use wealth
nobly and expertly, he will live well; otherwise
he will live wickedly."

"I think you are most correct in what you say."

XL.   "So, it all comes down to this: it is possible
to honor these things as being good or to disdain
them as bad. But it is just this notion that
harasses and harms men, namely, that if they honor
these things and suppose that happiness exists
through them alone, [then] they dare for their sake
to do anything--even things that seem to be most
profane and utterly shameful they do not avoid.
2   But they suffer these things because they are ignorant of what is good. They are ignorant of the
3   fact that no good thing comes from evils. And it
is possible to see many people who have obtained
their wealth by means of evil and shameful deeds,
I mean by things such as treachery, pillage,
murder, extortion, fraud, and many other vicious
acts as well."[118]

"Granted."

XLI. "Now then, if nothing good comes from evil,
as is likely, and if wealth comes from evil deeds,
then of necessity wealth is not a good thing."

Συμβαίνει οὕτως ἐκ τούτου τοῦ λόγου.

2   Ἀλλ οὐδὲ τὸ φρονεῖν γε οὐδὲ δικαιοπραγεῖν οὐκ
ἔστι κτήσασθαι ἐκ κακῶν ἔργων, ὡσαύτως δὲ οὐδὲ τὸ
ἀδικεῖν καὶ ἀφρονεῖν ἐκ καλῶν ἔργων, οὐδὲ ὑπάρχειν
5
3 ἅμα τῷ αὐτῷ δύναται. πλοῦτον δὲ καὶ δόξαν καὶ τὸ
νικᾶν καὶ τὰ λοιπὰ ὅσα τούτοις παραπλήσια οὐδὲν
κωλύει ὑπάρχειν τινὶ ἅμα μετὰ κακίας πολλῆς. ὥστε
οὐκ ἂν εἴη ταῦτα ἀγαθὰ οὔτε κακά, ἀλλὰ τὸ φρονεῖν
μόνον ἀγαθόν, τὸ δὲ ἀφρονεῖν κακόν.
10
4   Ἱκανῶς μοι δοκεῖς λέγειν, ἔφην.

2 οὐκ om V¹ add V² ‖ 3 δὲ om R ‖ 4 καλῶν] κακῶν P ‖ 5 τῷ
αὐτῷ] τὰ αὐτὰ libri, corr Schweigh. | δύνανται P ‖ 7 ἅμα] ἀλλὰ *
libri, corr Schweigh. | μετὰ] κατὰ W ‖ 8 εἴη W εἰ P ᾖ reliqui ‖
9 φρ*νειν V¹ ἀφραίνειν sscr ε supra αι V²

"Yes, it follows from this argument."

2   "Rather, neither prudent thought nor just action can be acquired from evil deeds, even as injustice and foolishness cannot from good deeds, nor can they exist together in the same person.

3   Yet nothing prevents wealth, reputation, victory, and the like from existing, together with much evil, in someone. So then, these things would be neither good nor bad, but being prudent is alone good while being imprudent is bad."[119]

4   "I think you have spoken adequately," I said.[120]

Et profligavimus eam opinionem, qua illa a pravis actionibus esse creduntur.

XLII. (Senex:) Utique multum hoc est et idem atque illud, quod diximus talia neque bona neque mala esse, idque eo magis, quod si ea ex solis actionibus pravis provenirent, essent mala tantummodo. Sed ab utroque genere omnia proficiscuntur, ideoque 2 diximus ea nec bona esse nec mala, sicuti somnus et vigilia nec bona sunt nec mala. Et similiter mea 3 quidem sententia ambulare et sedere et reliqua, quae accidunt unicuique eorum, qui aut intellegentes sunt aut ignorantes. Quae autem propria sunt alterutri, eorum alterum bonum alterum malum est, sicuti tyrannis et iustitia, quae duae res accidunt uni aut alteri; idque quia iustitia perpetuo adhaeret intellegentia praeditis, et tyrannis nullos nisi ignorantes comitatur. Nec enim fieri potest, id quod supra diximus, ut uni eidemque uno eodemque temporis momento res duae 4 ad istum modum se habentes accidant, ita ut homo unus idemque eodem temporis momento sit dormiens et vigilans utque sit sapiens et ignarus simul aut aliud quidlibet eorum, quae parem rationem habent.

(Hospes:) Ad haec ego: Toto hoc, inquam, sermone rem omnem te iam absolvisse autumo.

XLIII. (Senex:) Haec autem omnia, inquit, ego dico procedere ab illo principio vere divino.

"And we have given up that opinion, since those things are admittedly derived from evil deeds."

XLII.   "In any case this conclusion is very important and, indeed, it is the same as what we said before, that is, that such things are neither good nor bad. Moreover, if these things came solely from evil deeds, then they would be altogether bad.

2   Yet, all such things derive from both kinds of action. Consequently, we said that they are neither good nor bad, even as slumber and insomnia are

3   neither good nor bad. Furthermore, my judgment is similar in matters of walking, sitting, and the like, since they pertain to each and every individual no matter whether they are educated or ignorant. Some things, however, are appropriate to one or the other, some being good and others bad. Such are tyranny and justice, two things which pertain to one or the other type of individual. That is the case because justice is the constant companion of the one possessed of understanding, while tyranny accompanies none except the ignorant.

4   For, as we said before, it is in no way possible at any one moment for two things in such opposition to pertain to the same individual in such a way that one person might be, at the same moment in time, both asleep and awake, or wise and ignorant, or any other such things reckoned in pairs."

"As far as I am concerned," I said, "with this entire preceding discussion I think you have now brought to a fitting completion all these matters."

XLIII.   "However," he said, "I would add that all these things really derive from that divine first principle."

(Hospes:) At quidnam illud est, inquam, quod tu innuis?

2 (Senex:) Vita et mors, inquit, sanitas et aegritudo, divitiae et paupertas ac cetera, quae et bona et mala esse dixisti[1]), accidunt plerisque hominibus a non malo.

(Hospes:) Plane conicimus, inquam, id necessario ex hoc sermone sequi, talia nec bona nec mala esse, ita tamen, ut haud firmus sim in iudicio de istis.

3 (Senex:) Hoc fit, inquit, ideo, quod longe abs te abest habitus ille, quo eam sententiam animo con-
* cipias. Itaque rerum usum, quem paulo ante vobis indicavi, toto vitae vestrae curriculo persequimini, ut ea quae vobis diximus infigantur animis vestris eaque
4 re vobis accedat habitus. Si autem dubitaveritis de aliqua re, revertimini ad me, ut explicem vobis ea de re, quibus dubitatio a vobis discedat.

---

1) Sic vertendum esse, non, ut vulgo fit, *quae nec bona nec mala esse diximus,* humanissime me docuit vir clarissimus Steckius theologiae professor. Cogitatur de c. 36, 4.

"But to which principle are you referring?"
I asked.

2   "Life and death," he said, "health and sickness, wealth and poverty, which you claimed to be
both good and bad, happen to the vast majority of
people from no evil act."

"Obviously," I said, "we deduce from this
argument the necessary conclusion that such things
are neither good nor bad. As a result, however,
I am in no way confident of my judgment regarding
these matters."

3   "You find yourself in this predicament," he
said, "because missing from you is that habit by
which you might adopt this very disposition of
soul.[121] Therefore, throughout your course of
life strive to put into practice these things which
I have briefly set before you, so that my words may
be etched on your minds and become a habit for you.
4 However, if you are still perplexed about anything,
return to me that I may give you an explanation
that will dispell your doubts."

NOTES TO TEXT AND TRANSLATION

[1]The opening line is probably an imitation of the beginning of the Pseudo-Platonic *Eryxias*: 'Ετυγχάνομεν περιπατοῦντες ἐν τῇ στοᾷ τοῦ Διὸς τοῦ ἐλευθερίου. Some have classified the *Tabula* as a "Temple Dialogue" on the basis of this similarity, cf. Introduction, pp. 11f.

Another parallel to the opening is to be found in Longus' pastoral romance, *Daphnis et Chloe*. Longus may have some relationship to the work of Alciphron, whose courtesan literature also has similarities to the symbolism of the *Tabula* (cf. *C.T.* 9.1f and n. 33 below). Datable perhaps to the second or third centuries C.E., Longus' romance is introduced by a proem which gives the occasion for the writing--the author's chance observation of a painting in the sacred grove of the Nymphs at Lesbos. The story that follows, then, is supposedly based on the content of the picture and its interpretation. It will be sufficient here to quote only a few lines of the English translation by Thornley and Edmonds to indicate the similarities to the fiction behind the *Tabula*.

> 1. When I was hunting in Lesbos, I saw in the grove of the Nymphs a spectacle the most beautiful and pleasing of any that ever I cast my eyes upon. It was a painted picture, reporting a history of love (εἰκόνα γραπτήν, ἱστορίαν ἔρωτος). The grove indeed was very pleasant, thick set with trees and starred with flowers everywhere, and watered all from one fountain with divers meanders and rills. But that picture, as having in it not only an excellent and wonderful piece of art but also a tale of ancient love, was far more amiable. And therefore many, not only the people of the country but foreigners also, enchanted by the fame of it, came as much to see that, as in devotion to the Nymphs. There were figured in it young women....
> 2. When I had seen with admiration these and many other things...I had a mighty instigation to write something as to answer that picture. And therefore, when I had carefully sought and found an interpreter of the image (ἀναζητησάμενος ἐξηγητὴν τῆς εἰκόνος), I drew up these four books....
>
> (Cf. Longus, *Daphnis and Chloe*, trans. by G. Thornley, rev. by J.M. Edmonds [Loeb Classical Library; London, 1916] 6-7.)

The setting of the *Tabula* in the temple of Cronus has been interpreted in various ways, depending on the view adopted of the work as a whole. Joël (II, 326) for example, in arguing for the Cynic character of the *Tabula*, notes

that the Cynics viewed the ideal life as standing under
the aegis of Cronus (cf. Ps-Diogenes, *Ep.* 32; Lucian,
Fugitivi 17; compare the discussion of these passages by
F. Duemmler, *Akademika* [Giessen, 1889] 242-43). This interpretation thus appeals to the myth which equates the
rule of Cronus with the Golden Age. Joly (59), on the
other hand, invokes the myths about Cronus' rule in the
islands of the Blest and in Hades in support of his understanding of the *Tabula* as an enigmatic revelation of Neo-
Pythagorean eschatology. From this perspective the mention
of Cronus is placed at the very beginning of the work so as
to alert Neo-Pythagorean initiates to the idea of the Hereafter contained in the work. Von Albrecht, however, thinks
that these same myths suggest the other-worldly perspective
from which the tablet is to be viewed (758). Other scholars, such as Jerram (25) and Parsons (68), appeal to the
common equation of Κρόνος with Χρόνος and suggest the ap-
propriateness of the name "Time" for an allegory dealing
with human life. Whatever the merits of this non-
eschatological interpretation, the equation itself is both
ancient and widespread. It occurs at least as early as
the pre-Socratic philosopher Pherecydes (cf. the relevant
texts and discussion in G. S. Kirk and J. E. Raven, *The
Pre-Socratic Philosophers* [Cambridge, 1963] 54-57) and is
often repeated (cf. Aristotle, *De mundo* 7; Cornutus 6;
Plutarch, *Quaestiones Romanae* 266EF, *De Iside et Osiride*
363D; Cicero, *De Natura Deorum* II.25.64; Macrobius, *Saturnalia* I.8.6-7; 22.8).

It is precarious to place undue emphasis on this
reference to Cronus. Indeed, the myths about Cronus are
as diverse as the interpretations which appeal to them.
In the *Tabula* the references are confined to 1.1 and 2.2,
and these sections function to provide the setting for the
work and to attest the religiosity of the founder of the
temple and tablet. A deeper significance is possible but
by no means certain. The issue is complicated, moreover,
by the fact that this is a *temple* of Cronus. As Nilsson
points out, Cronus is primarily a mythological figure, not
a cultic one (*Geschichte der griechischen Religion* [Munich,
1967] I, 510). There is some evidence for a cult of Cronus
but this is meager (cf. the discussions by L. R. Farnell,
The Cults of the Greek States [Oxford, 1896] 23-34, and by
M. Pohlenz, "Kronos," in Pauly-Wissowa-Kroll, XI:2, col.
1982-86). According to Dionysius of Halicarnassus (I.35.5)
there were temples (ἱερά) dedicated to Cronus in many parts
of Italy, and Pausanius (I.18.7; VI.20.1; IX.39.4-5) and
Macrobius (I.4.7; 7.37; 10.22) provide some evidence for
cultic activities elsewhere that were associated with the
name of Cronus. But usually the interest in Cronus is confined to the attempt to link the Roman Saturnalia with the
Greek Κρόνια festivals. The obsolescence of the cult of
Cronus is admitted by Plutarch (*De Defectu Oraculorum*

421CD) and the paucity of evidence confirms this admission.
In view of this obsolescence it seems preferable to understand the mention of Cronus as the author's attempt at
placing the founding of the temple in a period when (it was
believed) the worship of Cronus was more prevalent and thus
give the work the appearance of greater antiquity. The
setting in antiquity would fit with the reference to Parmenides in 2.2. Thus, if the references to Cronus are intended to promote the antiquity and/or pseudonymity of the
work, it is a mistake to try to relate these references to
a particular myth or to connect them to the adherents of a
particular philosophical school. Cronus at any rate was
not the exclusive property of the Cynics or the Pythagoreans but was invoked even in Mithraic circles (cf. F. Cumont,
Textes et monuments, I.76). Cronus is common property and
the fact that he is not the special god of a particular
group is in keeping with the lack of technical school language found in the document. For the Cronus=Helios equation, cf. Pohlenz, 2000-1, and M. Mayer, *Die Giganten und
Titanen in der antiken Sage und Kunst* (1887) 71.

[2]For a somewhat similar opening with a following discussion inspired by a γραφή, see Achilles Tatius I.1.2ff.
Tablets as votive offerings were quite common, especially
in temples of Isis (Tibullus I.3.27; Juvenal 12.27) and of
Asclepius (Herodas IV.19; Pausanius II.27.3; 36.1; Strabo
VIII.6.15 [374]; cf. the collection of inscriptions on
tablets found in *IG* IV[2].1.121-122, reproduced and translated by E. J. Edelstein and L. Edelstein, *Asclepius: A
Collection and Interpretation of the Testimonies* [Baltimore,
1945] I, 221-37). See also Horace, *Car.* I.V.13-16; Cicero,
De Natura Deorum III.37.89ff; Ovid, *Fasti* III.268, and compare also Ps-Diogenes, *Ep.* 36 (Hercher/Malherbe). Since
such tablets normally were dedicated to Isis for deliver-
ance from shipwreck and to Asclepius for healing of disease,
the erection of this tablet may be intended to indicate
that the dedicator (2.2) had himself escaped from the moral
shipwreck (24.2) and sickness (19) which are depicted in
the painting. That is, the allegory that follows is perhaps intended to be understood as a generalization based on
the personal experience of the dedicator of the tablet.
Another possibility, however, is that the dedicator erected
the tablet subsequent to a vision in a place such as the
shrine of Trophonius. This possibility is not considered
by Joly, but it is one that is readily compatible with his
views. Pausanias IX.39.14 says that "those who have
descended into the shrine of Trophonius are obliged to
dedicate a tablet (πίνακι) on which is written all that
each has seen or heard" (trans. by W.H.S. Jones in the
Loeb edition). The myth of Timarchus recounted in Plutarch's *De Genio* (cf. n. 19) comes after he has taken such
a descent. Timarchus' descent was known to Cebes (590A)
and at the site there was, according to Pausanias IX.39.
4-5, a temple with an image of Cronus and a building sacred
to the good Daimon (cf. *C.T.* 4.3) and to Good Fortune (cf.
C.T. 8.2).

[3]The stress on the particular type of construction depicted seems inconsequential at first. It may be intended
to demonstrate the puzzlement of the observers and their
attempts to interpret the picture. A short but helpful
discussion of the similarities and differences between city
walls and gates and those of a military camp (*castrum*) is
found in R. MacMullen, *Soldier and Civilian in the Later
Roman Empire* (Cambridge, 1967) 39-41. The statement here
that the picture contains three enclosures has produced a
good bit of confusion in interpreting the movement of the
text as well as in illustrating the text. In fact there
are four enclosures, the fourth of which is apparently not
visible to the viewers here at the beginning. Cf. n. 51
to the "Introduction" and n. 57 below.

[4]In Plutarch's *De Facie* a myth is related to Sulla by
a stranger (942B). Note especially the similarity of *C.T.*
2.3.5-6 to the statement made by Sulla at 945D: ταῦτα...ἐγὼ
μὲν ἤκουσα τοῦ ξένου διεξιόντος. Cf. also Plato's *Sophista*
in which a stranger, who is a follower of Parmenides, leads
a philosophical discussion after stating that he has no
objection (οὐδεὶς φθόνος) to Socrates' request that he do
so (cf. *C.T.* 3.1.1-4).

[5]Plato, *Republica* X.3 (600B) is an early reference to
those who have adopted the Pythagorean way of life (τρόπον
τοῦ βίου). For the *Tabula* it may serve more as a literary
device to give an air of antiquity, cf. Plato, *Phaedo* 61D
and Joly, *Le Tableau*, 51 n. 5.

[6]The text derives ultimately from Plato's *Theaetetus*
183E. Here Socrates recalls that as a youth he met the
quite elderly Parmenides, who deserved to have Homer's word
δεινός applied to him (*Il.* III.172; *Od.* VIII.22, XIV.234;
cf. also *C.T.* 2.2.3). For the old man as the mediator of
ancient wisdom as a conventional literary device, cf. Niels
Hyldahl, *Philosophie und Christentum* (Kopenhagen, 1966)
160-61, and J.C.M. van Winden, *An Early Christian Philosopher* (Leiden, 1971) 53ff, both with reference to the old
man of Justin, *Dial.* 3.

[7]The riddle of the Sphinx was a widely used metaphor
in the dramatic and moralist literature. We may cite for
the sake of contrast its use in Anaxilas (Kock II, 270)
and Athenaeus, *Deipnosophistae* XIII.558d. In the latter
passage, courtesans are equated with the Sphinx. It is of
interest for our purposes because the courtesans appear in
C.T. 9 as agents of destruction.
    C.T. 3.2-4 is Joly's chief exegetical argument for
the explanation of the *Tabula* as an enigmatic, allusive
work containing a hidden Neo-Pythagorean teaching. Since
the explanation is a riddle, Joly argues that this explanation must itself be interpreted. This he proceeds to do

from a Neo-Pythagorean perspective. But as von Albrecht
(758-59) notes, Joly has overinterpreted this comparison.
The comparison functions to confront the hearers (and the
readers) in their entire being with the seriousness of
finding the solution to the riddle. The riddle to be
solved is that of human life (cf. also J. Moreau, *Revue
des etudes anciennes* 65 [1963] 432-33) and, as the parallel
text in Dio Chrysostom 10.31-32 shows, the riddle is to be
answered existentially and not with mere words (cf. n. 8).
For Dio the true answer to the Sphinx's riddle is not "man"
but the "nature of man." Thus Oedipus did *not* solve the
riddle but only deluded himself into believing that he had.
As a result he too was destroyed, and most miserably at
that. It should also be noted that in this respect the
lovers of Pseudopaideia appear as types of this deluded
Oedipus figure. Just as Dio's Oedipus erroneously considered himself to be exceedingly wise and to have escaped
from the Sphinx, these learned devotees think that they
have attained to true Paideia and as a result claim to understand what they in fact do not know (35.3-5). As a result they will not be saved, and, like Oedipus, will perish
most miserably (32.5).

[8]Compare Dio Chrysostom 10.31: ἐγὼ δὲ ἤκουσά του λέ-
γοντος ὅτι ἡ Σφίγξ ἀμαθία ἐστιν: "I have heard someone say
that the Sphinx stands for stupidity" (trans. by J. W.
Cohoon in the Loeb series). Joly (54, 83-84) considers
this passage in Dio to be a citation from the *Tabula*. This
possibility gains some credence from the similarities of
Dio 4.114-15 with *C.T.* 5-6. Yet in view of the differences
between Dio and "Cebes" the confidence of Joly is unwarranted. The more cautious assessment is that of Praechter
(*Cebetis Tabula quanam*, 102) who assumes both "Cebes" and
Dio are following a common source. This view is approved
by von Albrecht (759). Cf. p. 7 for other views. The conception of the Sphinx as a symbol of human folly recurs in
Zenobius, the *Suda*, and Photius, where the ancient proverb
of the "Cadmean victory" is applied to the Oedipus-Sphinx
confrontation (cf. Lesky, "Sphinx," in Pauly-Wissowa-Kroll,
Second Series, 6, col. 1725).

[9]The most logical candidate for the subject of
αἰνίττεται would seem to be ἀφροσύνη, the same word being
the antecedent of ὑπ' αὐτῆς in the following sentence.
Several editors have even capitalized ἀφροσύνη here and in
C.T. 3.4 as the beginning of the personification of vices
and virtues in the text. Joly (*Le Tableau*, 53 n. 5) suggests ἡ ἐξήγησις as the subject and cites the translation
of M. Meunier which gives ὁ πίναξ as the subject. The
latter seems highly unlikely. But the former is perhaps
possible as part of the ambiguity of the analogy being employed. Yet, in our view, the grammatical subject of

αἰνίττεται must remain ἀφροσύνη, and ἡ ἐξήγησις can be more properly equated with the object, τάδε, etc. This reading of the passage serves to point to the real subject of the riddle and of the *Tabula* itself, i.e., τί ἀγαθόν, τί κακόν, τί οὔτε ἀγαθὸν οὔτε κακόν ἐστιν ἐν τῷ βίῳ. This phrase was a philosophic axiom widely used in the Hellenistic period by Stoics, Cynics, and others. Its axiomatic character can be seen in Seneca, *Ep.* 89.14 (cf. 88.28); Cicero, *De fin.* IV.5f, 15., Sextus Empiricus, *Adv. Math.* XI.2-4. It is especially prominent among the Stoic and Cynic moralists as the logical premise for their respective ethics. Among the Stoics it is accompanied by the notion that some things are subject to human control and some are not (cf. Diogenes Laertius, VII.93, 104f; Epictetus III.22.13, 38). From these premises are derived the Stoic ideals of "indifference" (ἀδιάφορα) and "moral purpose" (προαίρεσις) (cf. Musonius Rufus, *Diss.* IX [ed. O. Hense, pp. 41ff]); Epictetus, II.16, II.19.13ff, II.21.2ff, II.22.1-3). Among the Cynics the axiom stands behind the renunciation of worldly needs as idealized in the term "freedom" (ἐλευθερία). Cf. Ps-Diogenes, *Ep.* 36.2, 6 (ed. Hercher); Ps-Crates, *Epp.* 7, 8, 11, 13, 15 (ed. Hercher); but also Epictetus, III.22.42ff. The connection of this axiom with ἀφροσύνη is made by a standard Stoic definition to be found in Diogenes Laertius VII.92 (cf. VII.111): καὶ τὴν μὲν φρόνησιν εἶναι ἐπιστήμην κακῶν καὶ ἀγαθῶν καὶ οὐδετέρων ("wisdom, they say, is the knowledge of things good and evil and what is neither good nor evil"). By extension, then, we may expect that ἀφροσύνη is ignorance (ἄγνοια) with respect to these same matters. It will be seen quite quickly that ἄγνοια (the result of personified Ἀπάτη) is the chief cause of vice in the *Tabula*, cf. 5.1ff; 14.3. Moreover, the entire discussion of the final chapter concludes with a reprise of this initial axiom in terms of φρόνησις and ἀφροσύνη, cf. 41.3. See also introduction p. 16, and n. 7 above (re. *C.T.* 3.2-4).

[10]Cf. 20.4 for the constellation of paying attention, understanding, and salvation, and 32.5 for the linking of misunderstanding and destruction. Compare the frequent admonition in the Gospels to give heed to the parables of Jesus. Although the word is not used, these also are understood as αἰνίγματα (Matt 13:10-18, 34-35; Mark 4:10-12; cf. also Sir 39:2-3).

[11]The translation "up here" for ἄνω is intended to reflect the fiction of the Senex pointing to and describing the picture. For discussion of the use of directional adverbs, demonstrative adjectives, etc., see the Introduction, p. 8 above.

We have chosen to transliterate the Greek term Daimon/ Daimonion as part of the personification of the *Tabula* (cf. 6.2; 24.3; 30.1; 31.3, 5; 32.5; 33.2). The term was part

of the common parlance of the Graeco-Roman world and had a
highly complex variety of meanings and uses, no one of which
seems quite right for this text. Among the meanings are:
demon, genius, fate, or deity, equivalent to Latin *numen*.

[12]For the content of the Daimon's commands, see *C.T.*
30-32. In 33-35 these commands are elaborated and de-
fended by the Senex.

[13]It is not quite correct to say, as Joly does (31 n.
2), that this is a question without an immediate response.
The question is never answered in terms of a simple direct
statement. Like the γέρων, the πρεσβύτης *shows* (δείκνύει,
4.3.5) the temple visitor the way. This description begins
immediately and continues through chap. 23. Once the goal
of the journey has been attained, the question shifts to
one concerning the where and why of future journeyings
(24.1; 26.1).

[14]The dialogue shifts here from a group of interlocutors to a single spokesman, the author of the text. The
singular will predominate in the text, but the plural is
interspersed from time to time to reinforce the fictional
setting given in chaps. 1-4. The plural is also used to
direct the reader's attention to the moral point of the
allegory, as in 20.4-5 and 30.3. Cf. n. 91.

[15]Cf. Aristaenetus I, *Ep.* 2: αἱ μείρακες..ἦθος οὐ
πεπλασμένον ἐμφαίνουσαι. For the general description of
the woman compare the Prodicus myth in Dio Chrysostom,
Or. 1.78.

[16]Cf. Dio Chrysostom 4.114-15: "Let his steps also be
guided by Delusion ('Απάτη), a very beautiful and enticing
(πιθανή) maid, decked out in harlot's finery, smiling and
promising a wealth of good things and making him believe
that she is leading him to the very embrace of happiness,
till unexpectedly she drops him into the pit, into a morass
of foul mud, and then leaves him to flounder about in his
garlands and saffron robe. In servitude to such a tyrant
and suffering such tribulation those souls wander through
life which, craven and impotent in the face of hardships,
enslaved to pleasure, pleasure-loving, and carnally-minded,
go on living a disgraceful and reprehensible life, not from
choice, but because they have drifted into it" (trans. by
Cohoon in the Loeb edition). Dio's description coincides
with the *Tabula*'s depiction of life in the "first" enclosure. Dio's 'Απάτη combines the functions of 'Απάτη and the
Δόξαι, 'Επιθυμίαι, and 'Ηδοναί. Joly (36) would see her
role as analogous to that played by Λήθη in eschatological
texts. On the relationship of "Cebes" and Dio, see n. 8.
Here it should be added that the similarity between Dio 4

and *C.T.* 5ff was noted prior to that of Dio 10 and *C.T.* 3. Gronovius (105-8) argued that Dio had imitated "Cebes." Drosihn, "Die Zeit," 14-15, on the other hand, in arguing for a second century date for the *Tabula*, reverses the relationship and has "Cebes" imitate Dio. Regarding the complex of ideas surrounding Ἀπάτη (e.g., πλανᾶν) and its role in human life see also *C.T.* 6.3, 19.5, 25.2, 40.1. For the same ideas seen together, cf. Plato *Phaed.* 81a; *Rep.* VI.505c.

[17] Praechter is virtually alone in retaining the dative δυνάμει of the manuscripts. Not only Drosihn and Sauppe but also Müller ("Relieffragment," 117), Jerram (3), and Parsons (24) change the construction to the accusative δύναμιν (cf. 19.1.4, all manuscripts). Yet δυνάμει is also the reading of all the manuscripts at 19.4.2-3, and Praechter is probably correct in resisting this modern attempt at standardization. The possibility of interpreting the dative as "by her own power she makes them drink" is excluded by a comparison of 19.1 and 19.4, where it is clear that δύναμις is what is imbibed. Finally, it should be added that the contrast to this δύναμις of Deceit is found both in the δύναμις of Paideia's drink and in the δύναμις of the wreath bestowed by Happiness (22.3-4).

[18] Compare the statement of Cicero, *Tusc. Disp.* III.I.2, "As soon as we come into the light of day...we at once find ourselves in a world of iniquity amid a medley of wrong beliefs, so that it seems as if we drank in deception with our mother's milk" (trans. by J. E. King in the Loeb edition). Cf. also Dio Chrys. *Or.* 30.36sq.

[19] Joly (33, 36, 38) correlates the varying quantities imbibed with the various degrees to which souls mix with the flesh in Plutarch's *De Genio* XXII (591Dff). The amount imbibed by those reincarnated would thus depend on the number of faults to be expiated. The varying degrees of ignorance and error cannot, in his opinion, be reconciled with the Stoic paradox of equal faults. Cf. n. 2.

[20] Dio states (4.114) that Deceit is dressed in the finery of a harlot (πορνικοῖς). Whether Dio is quoting "Cebes" or both are depending on the same source, the idea of courtesans is present in the tradition. The fact that a different Greek word is used is not significant, since different words are employed by them for the same idea. To cite only one example, "Cebes" uses ἐπαγγέλλονται (6.3.1) for "promise" whereas Dio uses ὑπισχνουμένη. Again, the fact that Dio uses this imagery of Deceit and "Cebes" of the Opinions is not a valid objection, since Dio's Deceit performs the same role as Opinions in the *Tabula*. In view of these considerations it might be possible to follow the

majority of manuscripts, taking ἐταιρῶν as the original reading and regarding ἑτέρων as the result of an early scribal error.

[21] On these actions (ἀναπηδῶσιν, πλέκονται) as characteristic of personified vices see Dio Chrys., *Or.* I,80; Ps-Diogenes, *Ep.* 28.6 (Hercher/Malherbe). Compare also the courtesan literature, e.g., Lucian, *Dial. Court.* 308 (11.1), cf. n. 33 below (on *C.T.* 9.1ff).

[22] The language of promise (ἐπαγγέλλεσθαι, ὑπνισκνεῖσθαι) is a common feature of the Prodicus myth (cf. Dio Chrys., *Or.* 4,114; Xenophon, *Mem.* II.1.23) as well as the courtesan literature. Cf. n. 33 below.

[23] Tychē's blindness was proverbial. Cf. Pliny, *Historia Naturalis* II.22; Cicero, *De Amicitia* 15.54; Ovid, *Ex Ponto* IV.8.16 (but contrast III.1.125-26); Ammianus Marcellinus 25.5.8, 31.8.8. Cf. also the references given in n. 27 below. Tychē's blindness, insanity, and placement on a globe are all mentioned in *Rhetor. ad Herenn.* II.22.36. The latter two features are found in Dio 65.12.

[24] For the word ἔργον used to describe Tychē's task, see Plutarch, *De Fortuna Romanorum* 319D; also Dio 64.5. The word ἔργον/ἔργα is sometimes used in aretalogies as the equivalent of the ἀρεταί of the deity, i.e., the miraculous manifestations characteristic of divine power. Cf. Aelius Aristides II, 357 (Keil), and the so-called "Delian Aretalogy of Serapis," line 31 and p. 26 (ed. H. Englemann).

[25] Cf. especially Dio 64.27; Ovid, *Tristia* III.7.42; Horace, *Car.* III.29.49-52; Juvenal, *Sat.* III.38-40.

[26] Dio, on the other hand, attributes the change in Tychē's action to human nature, not her own (*Or.* 65.6, 8-9), but note Dio's characterization in his version of the Prodicus myth in *Or.* 1.80-81.

[27] Tychē's portrayal as situated on a spherical object is older than the imperial period but was especially popular at this time. In addition to the references given in n. 23, see Dio 63.7; Plutarch, *De Fortuna Romanorum* (317E-318A); Galen, *Protrepticus* 2; Artemidorus Daldianus, *Oneirocrit.* II.37; Ovid, *Ex Ponto* IV.3.31-33; *Tristia* V.8.7; Ammianus Marcellinus 26.8.13, 31.1.1. The fact that "Cebes" uses the description "round rock" (λίθος στρογγύλος) instead of the more customary word "globe" (σφαῖρα) is connected with his portrayal later of true Paideia as standing on a "square rock" (λίθος τετράγωνος, 18.1-3). Since both rocks are interpreted as signs of their respective natures, the use of antonyms serves to emphasize the contrast. Hermas, *Sim.* IX, also uses these same terms antithetically.

[28]Cf. especially Dio Chrys., 65.4, 7, 10, and *C.T.*
18.3.

[29]Cf. 31.1ff. Dio, on the other hand, attributes disappointments and calamities to the failure to trust Tychē
(64.25-26; 65.1).

[30]Cf. especially Dio Chrys., *Or.* 63, for the difference in emotions depending on the presence or absence of
Tychē. See also Dio Chrys., *Or.* 1.81, of the personified
vice herself.

[31]Wealth is given a detailed discussion in chap. 39.
Its placement at the beginning of the list is in keeping
with the statement of Juvenal X.23ff that petitions for
riches are the most frequent heard in temples. Wealth was
doubtless a special concern of the social class in which
the author of the *Tabula* moved. Cf. "Introduction," n. 68
For these components in similar lists, cf. Philo, *De Abram.*

[32]Cf. 36ff.

[33]The use of the courtesans as the personification of
the vices of Incontinence, Profligacy, Covetousness, and
Flattery constitutes a *topos* based on the courtesan literature. The common literature descriptive of the dress and
appearance of courtesans (Lucian, *Piscator* 11ff; *Dial.
Court.* 6.2f(294), 7.1(296); Alciphron, *Ep. Court.* 9.1-2,
4.4, 10.1, 13.3, 12.1; Dio 4.114f) seems to be behind the
description of all the female personifications in the *Tabula* (cf. *C.T.* 4.1; 9.1; 10.1, 3; 12.2; 16.1; 18.1; 20.2;
21.3; 29.1). On the Christian side compare Clement of
Alexandria, *Paed.* III.2. Compare Philo, *Leg. Spec*, III.51,
64f, 80. The faithlessness, trickery and deceit of courtesans was also a commonplace (cf. Athenaeus, *Deipnosophistae*
XIII, 558d, 568a, 569c, 571c; Lucian, *Dial. Court.* 2.4(283)
4.1(286), 7.4(298); Alciphron, *Ep. Court.* 11.3-8, 16.6).

[34]A common depiction of the "ideal life" as conceived
by the masses. Compare the formulation by Cicero, *De Senectute* XXIII.82: *nonne melius multo fuisset otiosam et quieta
aetatem sine ullo labore et contentione traducere?*

[35]Luxury is here both a place and a person (cf. 28.1,
32.3). In the latter capacity she seems to be portrayed
here as the madame of a bordello to whom business is brough
by Incontinence and the other street courtesans. Reference
should also be made to Dio 4.84, where the first of Dio's
three types of lives is characterized as luxurious
(ἡδυπαθής) in regard to bodily pleasures. Compare also
Philo, *De sacr. Cain et Able* 32ff.

[36]The term γαργαλισμός was employed by Epicurus (cf.
H. Usener, *Epicurea* [1887] frag. 411-13) and became re-
nowned in antiquity as an Epicurean word (Cicero, *De Natura
Deorum* I.XL.113; Athenaeus XII.546E; cf. also Plutarch,
Amatorius 765C, 766E; *An Seni* 876D; *An Recte Dictum* 1129B;
Cicero, *De Sen.* XIV.47). Hence the word is closely connected with the idea of pleasure (ἡδονή, cf. Philo, *Legum
Allegoria* III.160; *Quod deterius potiori insidiari soleat*
110; *De Specialibus Legibus* IX.XVII.100). For γαργαλίζειν
as the transient lure of pleasure, compare Ps-Diogenes,
Ep. 28.5 (Hercher/Malherbe): χαρισάμενοι γὰρ τούτοις ὀλίγον
ἐγαργαλίσθητε χρόνον ὑφ' ἡδονῆς μεγάλας καὶ ἰσχυρὰς ἐναπο-
δεικνυμένης ἀλγηδόνας. See also Seneca, *Ep.* 75.6f. For a
discussion of γαργαλίζειν in connection with the moralist
sickness-health *topos*, see A. J. Malherbe, "Medical Imagery
in the Pastoral Epistles," *Texts and Testaments: Critical
Essays on the Bible and Early Church Fathers*, ed. by W.
Eugene March (San Antonio: Trinity University [1979] 19-35.
Two forms of medical *topoi* occur later in *C.T.* 19.2 and 26.1.

[37]The term ἀνανήφω is often used metaphorically to
indicate conversion. As such it is closely related to the
word μετάνοια (2 Tim 2:26; Ignatius, *Sm.* 9.1; Ps-Lucian,
De Saltatione 84). The statement of Philo (*Legum Allegoria*
II.60) is particularly revealing: the wise man, if he
should sin, ἀνανήφει, τοῦτο δ' ἐστὶ μετανοεῖ καὶ ὥσπερ ἐκ
νόσου ἀναλαμβάνει ("he comes to his senses and recovers as
from an illness"). In the *Tabula* μετάνοια and ἀνάληψις
occur at different stages. Repentance encounters people
in either the "first" (10.4-11.1) or "second" (35.4) enclosure, whereas healing and recovery result from the action
of true Paideia (19.1-5). Moreover, a person's full perception of the true nature of life with Madame Luxury comes
only after the return to the "first" enclosure (24-25).
An instructive example of this return to sobriety is
found in Lucian's account of the conversion of Polemo in
Bis Accusatus. The young and impressionable Polemo is cor-
rupted by Incontinence and Pleasure, so that he lives a
life of dissipation with courtesans. The unhappy Polemo
(16; cf. *C.T.* 10.4) is brought to his senses (17) and con-
verted by the discourses of the Academy. Finally, the term
(ἀνανήφω) probably comes from anti-Epicurean polemic. Cf.
1 Cor 15:32-34 (ἐκνήφω) and the discussion by A. J. Malherbe, "The Beasts at Ephesus," *Journal of Biblical Literature* 87 (1968) 71-80, esp. 77-78.

[38]We are reading ἐσθίειν, ὑβρίζειν, and κατεσθίειν in
a sexual sense. For the latter in this sense, compare
Athenaeus, *Deipnosophistae* VIII.582f.

[39]The subject of "retribution" has already appeared in
connection with the riddle of the Sphinx (*C.T.* 3.4), but it

is not personified. There seems to be an intentional connection between the warning as to the gravity of the picture and its interpretation and what happens to the deceive
"traveller" in the picture. For the personification of
τιμωρία here and below in *C.T.* 10.2, compare the descriptic
in Ps-Crates *Ep.* 29.1 (Hercher/Malherbe) and Philo, *De Abrar*
104.

[40] As part of his minimization of the Stoic background
of the *Tabula*, Joly (32-33) argues that the important and
positive role played by Repentance in the *Tabula* is ir-
reconcilable with the negative Stoic view of repentance as
a form of λύπη (cf. *S.V. Fr.* III.414). While repentance
may not play a positive role in most Stoic texts, it does
occur in Seneca (*paeniteat*, *De Benefic.* VII.2.2) and in
Epictetus (*Ench.* 34) as the result of indulgence in pleasure. In both cases the discussion is heavily influenced
by Cynic ideas. *Metanoia* functions positively as a turning
point following hardship in some strictly Cynic texts, cf.
Ps-Diogenes, *Ep.* 47 (Hercher/Malherbe). Compare also
Philo, *De Abram.* 26 (which incorporates the sickness-health
topos).

In regard to the translation of the word μετάνοια we
have retained the traditional rendering "Repentance." But
as von Albrecht (758) emphasizes, the meaning of the term
is objective rather than subjective. He prefers the terms
"umdenken" and *"Umstellung des Denkens"* to the more subjective words *Busse*, *Reue*, and *Repentir*. Note that in Ps-
Diogenes, *Ep.* 42 (Hercher/Malherbe), προαίρεσις designates
a deliberate choice for the Cynic life, and thus is appropriate here in the context of Repentance. Finally, it is
interesting to note that Philo, *De spec. leg.* III.51 uses
ἐπιτυγχάνειν of the courtesan's approach to those passing
by.

[41] A person is thus once again placed before the Heraclean decision. The "other Opinion" that leads to true
Paideia (cf. also *C.T.* 29.2-3) is one of those mentioned
in 6.2.6 which lead to salvation. The Opinion that leads
to Pseudopaideia is identified at 11.2.6 as False Opinion
and is among those that lead to destruction (6.2.6-7).
This False Opinion consists in thinking that one is asso-
ciating with true Paideia when one is not (13.1.4).

[42] For the development of this theme, cf. chap. 19.

[43] This exclamation might be seen in contrast to νὴ Δία
(s.v. index, Ζεύς). Whereas the latter (both for the Senex
and the interlocutor) seems to have only an exclamatory
function, the three occurrences of ὦ Ἡράκλεις seem to have
an additional function. In all three cases (*C.T.* 4.1, 12.1

19.1) it is an exclamation of the interlocutor placed at those points where the content of the expression seems to point toward the Prodicus myth.

[44]Dio 4.29-30 distinguishes divine and human education. The latter is called by most people (οἱ πολλοί) "education" since they (erroneously) posit a direct correspondence between wisdom and the reading and knowledge of literature. Compare Lucian, *Piscator* 13 for ἡ ἀληθὴς Φιλοσοφία. For the expression οἱ πολλοὶ καὶ εἰκαῖοι, see Epictetus, II.12.13.

[45]Praechter's insertion of the οὐκ into the Senex's response reflects the consensus of that period. Conjectured by Sauppe, it was endorsed by Müller (*De arte critica*, 78), Krauss (10, 32), Jerram (48), and Parsons (89). In support of the conjecture are the following considerations: (1) the reading of Elichmann's translation of the Arabic offers versional support: *minime, inquit, non habent viam aliam*; (2) those who are saved are said to come to Pseudopaideia *first* (12.3.3-4); (3) the Daimon *commands* (κελεύει) men to spend some time with Pseudopaideia and to take what she offers (32.3-4); (4) if the answer were an affirmative, the interlocutor would presumably be expected to ask concerning the other route. Since this is not the case, the following questions assume a negative answer to this question.

Joly (31-32), however, has raised serious objections to this emendation. In his view, the failure of the interlocutor to query the Senex about the other route is owing to the author's intention of reserving this issue for later treatment (compare 8.4). Positively, he points to 33.4 and 35.2 as prohibiting this emendation. In these passages the absolute necessity of a brief sojourn with Pseudopaideia is denied and a direct passage from the "first" enclosure to the "third" is affirmed. To introduce the οὐκ is then to involve the author in a self-contradiction of which he is not guilty. His guilt is that of literary imprecision.

It seems possible to offer a third solution to an apparently hopeless confusion. Textually, the insertion of οὐκ has no basis and, as Joly points out, *C.T.* 33.4 and 35.2 seem to make a sojourn *in* the "second" enclosure unnecessary. But contextually, it is still possible to assert with Praechter that the only path that leads to Paideia goes first to Pseudopeideia (12.3). If we note that Pseudopaideia stands *outside* the "second" enclosure (12.2) and that the question of the interlocutor (in 12.3) refers primarily to the path (ὁδός), it is possible to maintain both the consistency and the integrity of the text. If the οὐκ is not inserted, the Senex's response can be read, not as an affirmation that there is another route, but as an affirmation of the interlocutor's deduction, viz., that this is indeed the only path to true Paideia, cf. 14.3. Such a reading is perhaps made more plausible if the reading

ἦν (in A and M) is accepted in 12.3.5, making the clause
a so-called "imperfect of a truth just recognized" (cf.
Smyth, sec. 1902; Goodwin-Gulick, sec. 1260) as taken by
Jerram (31) and Parsons (70f). Thus, in *C.T.* 33.4 and
35.2 the crucial point is not the selection of a different
path but the decision to *stop* along the way at Pseudopaidei
and the relative merits of this decision. Other passages
in the *Tabula* further support this conclusion that the
Heraclean choice of the *Tabula* concerns how one follows the
path to Paideia. Thus, in 11.1-2 one is forced to choose
between the ἑτέραν Δόξαν which leads to true Paideia and
the ψευδοδοξίαν by which one is again led astry. Or again,
in 32.4-35.2 the real issue is whether and how much time
to spend in acquiring the μαθήματα of the "second" enclosure. Thus "Cebes" believes there to be only one path that
leads to true Paideia, but that there are several ways it
may be traveled.

Theoretically, it should be possible in the scheme of
"Cebes" for someone to imbibe so little of Deceit's potion
that he does not completely forget the Daimon's command
and to choose an Opinion that leads to salvation (6.2.6)
and thus never enter the "first" enclosure. But either
"Cebes" is not interested in treating this possibility or
his working assumption is that this never or seldom happens.
Similarly, his interest lies in those who enter the "second"
enclosure, i.e., those who pursue the various arts and sciences. His concern is that of preventing them from an extended sojourn there. Those who go directly from vice to
virtue are never treated in their own right. They are mentioned only for the purpose of demonstrating the dispensability of such studies and the consequent folly of devot-
ing an inordinate amount of time to them. Those whom "Cebes"
would influence run the danger of prolonging their studies,
not of omitting them entirely. As for the Daimon's *command*
that people should spend some time in the "second" enclosure, this is not intended by "Cebes" as unconditionally
binding.

[46]Κριτικοί is the older term for grammarians (Dio 53.1
Clement of Alexandria, *Stromata* I.16 [79,3]; Bekker, *Anecd.*
III.1140; cf. the discussion by Gudeman in Pauly-Wissowa-
Kroll XI.2 [1922] 1912-15). The choice of this term rather
than the more current γραμματικοί is probably due to the
author's desire to give the work the appearance of having
been written at an earlier period (cf. n. 1). The κριτικοί
and the poets represent the branch of study known as grammar (so H.-I. Marrou, *Saint Augustin et la fin de la culture antique* [1937] 216 n. 3). The list given by "Cebes"
thus comprises the seven liberal arts and sciences known in
antiquity as the ἐγκύκλιος παιδεία or the ἐγκύκλια μαθήματα
For a general discussion of this curriculum of pre-
professional studies, cf. Marrou, 211-35, and also his later work, *A History of Education in Antiquity* (trans. G.
Lamb [1964] 243-55, 527-30), where certain statements in
the former work are modified.

[47]The ἡδονικοί are usually identified as either
Cyrenaics or Epicureans. The Cyrenaic identification is
given by Liddell-Scott-Jones (764) with Athenaeus XIII.588A
cited as another instance of this name being applied to
them. An additional piece of evidence for this interpretation is the statement of Galen in *Histor. Philos.* 4
(Diels, 602=Kuehn, 230) that connects the ἡδονικὴ φιλοσοφία
with Aristippos. On the other hand, Marrou (*Saint Augustin*,
216 n. 3) identifies them as Epicureans. Unfortunately he
does not cite any supporting evidence for this identification. Appeal may be made, however, to the use of the Epicurean word γαργαλίζειν at 9.3.3 (cf. n. 36) and to the
Epicurean writing mentioned in Galen, *Libr. Propr.* XVI.
The designation could, of course, be less specific than the
two identifications given above. Archestratus, for example,
a contemporary of Aristotle and author of a Ἡδυπάθεια of
gastronomical delights, is called ὁ ἡδονικὸς φιλόσοφος by
Athenaeus (VII.312F; cf. also 310A). Yet the following
reference to the Peripatetics suggests that a philosophical
school is intended. Since Epicurus and Aristippus were
often mentioned together (e.g., Lucian, *Piscator* I) and
since "Cebes" may well have in mind both the Cyrenaics and
the Epicureans, we have followed a neutral course and
translated the word with "Hedonists." For the view that
οἱ δὲ ἡδονικοί is an interpolation, see the following note.

[48]Schweighaeuser (1806, p. 67) prefers the reading
περιπατικοί (AMED) and understands this as a reference to
"Doctores Scholastici," thus denying that the Peripatetics
are intended. But this is in keeping with his defense of
the traditional authorship of the *Tabula*. The reference
is clearly to the followers of Aristotle and is thus an
obvious anachronism. In view of this, most defenders of
traditional authorship sought to explain this reference to
the Peripatetics as an interpolation (so, for example,
Bähr in the first edition of Pauly [1842], II.232). But
even many of those who deny the *Tabula* to Theban Cebes believe this reference and also that to the ἡδονικοί to be
glosses that have crept into the text (so, for example,
Sauppe, 777; Susemihl, *Geschichte der griechischen Literatur in der Alexandrinerzeit* II [1892] 658). Even Praechter
in his dissertation (21f) concurs in this judgment, although
he prints them in the text. The Hedonists and Peripatetics
(along with the κριτικοί) are omitted in Chalcidius' reference to this passage and the fact that they occur in all
the manuscripts between the ἀστρολόγοι and the κριτικοί
makes them especially suspect. But the fact that members
of the pre-professional disciplines are mentioned here together with philosophers is not as objectionable as many
seem to think. It should be recalled that Posidonius (c.
135-c. 51/50 B.C.E.) sought to claim a place for the ἐγκύκλια
μαθήματα in philosophy (cf. Seneca, *Ep.* 88.21f), and Seneca
(*Ep.* 88.42ff) refers to philosophers engaging in many of the

studies that were the domain of the arts and sciences.
This would certainly be true for the Peripatetics, who,
following Aristotle, regarded the general studies as ser-
viceable (εὔχρηστα) for the attainment of virtue (Diog.
Laert. V. 31). The same sort of engagement in the arts
and sciences may have been true in practice for certain of
the Hedonists, even if this devotion was not in keeping
with the official position of their schools (cf. n. 47).

[49]For a collection of texts attacking some of the individual arts and sciences listed here, see A. Otramare,
Les origines de la diatribe romaine (1926) 44-45.

[50]This is the first use of the numbering of the enclosures which becomes standard for the rest of the text,
cf. *C.T.* 17.2 and n. 57.

[51]Cf. n. 85 below.

[52]On the steep rocky hill to virtue, cf. Hesiod, *Opera
et Dies* 289-92; Simonides 41; Xenophon, *Mem.* II.1.20;
Cyrop. II.2.24; Lucian, *Bis Acc.* 21; Silius Italicus,
Punica XV.101ff; Ps-Diogenes 37.4ff.

[53]Cf. 27.3. The combination of terms here in conjunc-
tion with the symbolism of the steep, rough road to virtue
is quite similar to the Cynic usage, cf. Ps-Crates, *Ep.* 15
(Hercher/Malherbe); Ps-Soc., *Ep.* p. 20, 22 (Hercher/Mal-
herbe); Ps-Diogenes, *Epp.* p. 30; 31.4f; 39.5 (Hercher/
Malherbe). In these texts ἐγκράτεια and καρτερία become
the watchwords of the Cynic life-style in contrast to the
life of pleasure and luxury. But see also Epictetus II.
16.14, 19f; III.22.100. The Stoic interpretation of the
Tabula stresses the similarity of this to the slogan of
Epictetus: ἀνέχου καὶ ἀπέχου, "bear (hardship) and forbear
(pleasure)." Joly (63), on the other hand, would see
Ἐγκράτεια and Καρτερία as constituting one of the three
types of daimons, *viz.*, the δαίμονες σωτηρικοί. The δαίμονες τιμωροί are found in chap. 10 whereas Paideia and
certain of the Opinions belong to the class of the δαίμονες
καθαρτικοί. In line with this is his view (46-47) that the
admonition to take courage (θαρρεῖν, 16.3.2) is to be taken
as reassurance concerning the immortality of the soul and
the afterlife.

[54]Exhortation to strive and endure with a promise of
future reward is characteristic of a *topos* derived from the
literary convention of the general's speech before going
into battle. For discussion of the genre, see Josef Alber-
tus, *Die παρακλητικοί in der griechischen und römischen Lit
eratur* (Strassburg, 1908).

[55]For confidence as a Cynic ideal, cf. Ps-Crates, *Ep.*
19 (Hercher/Malherbe), but compare Epictetus II.8.24f; Dio
Chrys., *Or.* I.71.

⁵⁶In contrast to the standard picture of the rough road to virtue (cf. *C.T.* 15.2-3), note the reversal indicated here. Compare Seneca, *De Benefic.* VII.1.7 (*planum*). We may compare also the form of the Prodicus myth found in Dio Chrys., *Or.* 1, 66ff where the road to Royalty (=Virtue) is safe and broad (ἀσφαλῆ καὶ πλατεῖαν). See also n. 85 below.

⁵⁷The *fourth* enclosure is not visible to the observer until the Senex points to it. This fact has generally been missed because the numbering of the enclosures makes a shift from 14.1 on. Chapter 35 makes it quite clear that the second enclosure of 1.2 and 9.1 is hereafter called the "first" enclosure (35.2; cf. 14.2, 19.5, 28.1). At this point, then, the third enclosure of 1.2 and 12.1, that of Pseudopaideia, is quite clearly the "second" enclosure of 25.2 (cf. 19.2), and the hidden (fourth) enclosure of 17.2 is called the "third." Cf. also n. 51 to the "Introduction."

⁵⁸The similarity in the description of the dwelling place of the Happy to that of the islands of the Blessed and the Elysian Fields has been noted for some time. Joly (57) naturally sees in this similarity a great support for his interpretation. But he pushes his thesis much too far when he suggests (63) that the εὐδαίμονες are those humans who have been stripped of body and soul and have become δαίμονες in the hereafter. An entirely different interpretation of the "eschatological" imagery found in chap. 17 is given by Büchling-Grosse (55). In their view the author uses this imagery to suggest the excellence of the happiness that can be achieved even in this life by means of following the instructions found in the *Tabula*.

⁵⁹The word ἀκαλλώπιστον, though appearing in the fragments of Heraclitus (no. 92; cf. Plutarch, *De Pyth. Or.*, 397A) is found almost exclusively in writers of the first and second centuries of the common era. (Indeed, even the Heraclitus reference is debated; the word may well be that of Plutarch himself. Cf. Kirk and Raven, 212.) The two most important texts are Lucian, *Piscator* 12 and 16, and Galen, *Protr.* 10. In Lucian a woman with apparently disheveled hair, who represents the various contemporary philosophical schools, is depicted as talking like a courtesan. However, the seeming disorder of her hair was neither accidental nor ἀκαλλώπιστον (12). That is, her seeming lack of adornment *was* her adornment. Ἀλήθεια, on the other hand, is depicted as truly unadorned (ἀκαλλώπιστον) (16). In Galen an unadorned woman in her natural beauty is contrasted to women with rouge and other makeup. Cf. also *C.T.* 20.2.

⁶⁰In Lucian's *Piscator*, Παιδεία and Ἀλήθεια are mentioned together with three others as the friends (φίλαι) of

(true) philosophy. In the *Tabula* they are mother and
daughter (18.2.1; compare Hermas, *Vision* III.8). Ἀλήθεια
does not appear again, but Paideia is later characterized
as being true (ἀληθινήν, 32.4) and her gift is described
as true (ἀληθής) knowledge (32.3). Πειθώ, the other
daughter of Παιδεία, is also mentioned only here in the
Tabula. Joly (45) arbitrarily claims that her function is
the dispensing of faith. This is most dubious. In whom
would this faith be placed? "Cebes" is concerned that
people *not* place any faith in Τύχη (7.3, 31.1), Incontinence or Luxury (32.3). Thus, if we are to seek a function for Πειθώ, it is probably indicated in 19.2-4. Just
as a physician is able to cure a sick person only if the
latter is persuaded to obey (ἐπείθετο) the former's instruction, so Παιδεία can only heal when people are persuaded to drink her medicine. Only then can she give the
knowledge that is true. Thus Πειθώ has the function of
persuading men to attain to (cf. 16.3ff) and obey (19.2-4)
Παιδεία. Compare 9.3.

[61] Cf. 7.3 and Hermas, *Vision* III.13.3.

[62] See 7.3. Compare Philo, *De Abram.* 269; cf. 263
(cf. *C.T.* 18.3, 31.1, 32.2). See also Dio Chrys., *Or.*
1.67.

[63] The positive dimension of Paideia's gift is given
in 32.2 as the true knowledge of what is advantageous.
Here the emphasis is on the certainty of Paideia's gift as
opposed to that of Τύχη (chap. 7). The gift of θάρσος
mentioned above (18.4.2, 16.5.2) is appropriate in this
context, for in Cynic thought θάρσος is the opposing force
to Τύχη (Diogenes Laertius VI.38; Ps-Diogenes 29.102
(Hercher/Malherbe); Epictetus, *Enchir.* 14; cf. von Albrecht, 759). The idea of suffering nothing terrible in
life, not even death, is stated as one of the things taught
by Socrates to Cebes in Ps-Soc., *Ep.* 14.7.

[64] On the close connection between truth (18.2), purification, and virtue, cf. Plato, *Phaedo* 69B-C. Joly (36-
37, 44), sees in the concept of κάθαρσις the Orphic-
Pythagorean doctrine of purgation. An important text for
him in this regard is Plutarch's περὶ ψυχῆς (see Vol. 15 of
the Loeb edition, pp. 316ff), where the soul of the de-
ceased comes to a country that is pure and converses with
pure men while observing the unpurified crowd on earth.
That the idea of κάθαρσις could be used eschatologically is
then clear. What is not so clear, however, is whether
"Cebes" is using the term eschatologically here. There is,
in fact, nothing in the text that *necessitates* such an interpretation (so Jerram, xxiii-xxiv). The comparison of
Paideia with the doctor in 19.2 suggests rather the widespread conception of the philosopher-physician who treats
the morally infirm. Vices are understood as diseases which

must be eradicated if the sick soul is to recover. Health,
on the other hand, is the work of virtue (Maximus of Tyre
7.12-13 Duebner). But health can only be attained by following the philosopher's instructions. As Cicero puts it,
"souls which have been ready to be cured and *have obeyed
the instructions of wise men* are undoubtedly cured" (*Tusc.
Disput.* III.III.5; trans. by J. E. King in the Loeb edition; cf. *C.T.* 19.3). Unfortunately, however, "those who
are sick in soul avoid philosophers, for they think they
are doing well in those very matters where they are at
fault" (Plutarch, *Anime an corporis affectiones sint
peiores* 501B; trans. by Helmbold in the Loeb edition).
That is, signs of health are often confused with symptoms
of disease. Avarice (φιλοπλουτία) is the most deceptive
illness of all, cf. Plutarch, *De cupiditate divitiarum* 3f
(Mor. 524A-525A) and Teles, pp. 38-40 (ed. Hense), trans.
by E. N. O'Neil (Missoula, MT: Scholars Press, 1977) 38ff.
Θύμος (cf. *C.T.* 19.5.3), for example, is mistaken for
ἀνδρεία. These moral maladies are therefore more serious
than bodily diseases and just as deadly (Cicero, *Tusc.
Disput.* III.III.5; Plutarch, *Anime*; Maximus of Tyre 7).
In the *Tabula* Paideia functions as the physician who expels
the diseases which infect the soul by giving an antidote.
It is ignorance and error which are thereby eliminated, not
the body. On the medical background of the term κάθαρσις,
see the material discussed by W. Schadewaldt, *Hellas und
Hesperien* (Zurich/Stuttgart, 1906) esp. 365-88.

[65]The word φιλοτίμως is usually interpreted contextually here, meaning "exceedingly" (Parsons, 71), "serious-
ly" (Jerram, 35), "extremely" (Hogue, "A Greek 'Pilgrim's
Progress,'" *The Union Seminary Magazine* [1902] 218),
"gravement" (P. Commelin, *Pensees de Marc Aurèle Antonin...
suives...du Tableau de Cébès* [n.d.] 333). This translation finds some support in Odaxius' rendering *graviter* and
the use of the comparative adverb φιλοτιμώτερον in Lucian,
Timon 10, and Polybius 4.32.1 may also give some linguistic basis for this rendering (cf. Drosihn, 17). The reading of M, φιλότιμος, is preferred by Guthrie, who trans-
lates it as "an ambitious man" (*The Greek Pilgrim's Progress*
[1910] loc. cit.). Several translators follow a conjecture
made by Corais and read φιλόθοινος ("a glutton"). Advocates
of this reading include Krauss (13, 32) and Meunier (*Marc-
Aurele...suives...du Tableau de Cebes* [1960] 269).

[66]This is the first of two separate medical images used
in the *Tabula* which are usually part of one larger medical
topos in the moralist literature. In one the philosopher/
moralist is pictured as the doctor of the soul (cf. *C.T.*
26.1.7 and note). Here and in the following sections the
image is of philosophy (Paideia, 18.3, 19.1) imparting virtue which brings health and purification to those sick with
vice. This complex of images was widespread and appears in
various forms. The form which appears beginning in 19.1

(cf. n. 64 above) equates the healing (θεραπεύειν) with purification (καθαίρειν) from the diseases of vice (cf. Ps.-Crates, *Ep.* 10; Ps-Diogenes, *Ep.* 28.5; 29.5; 49 (Hercher/Malherbe); Ps-Anacharsis 9 (Malherbe); Dio Chrys. *Or.* 77/78; Epictetus II.15.5). Special notice should be taken of Philo, *De Abram.* 26 where μετάνοια is equated with the healing process. In this light, then, many of the images of the vices in earlier portions of the *Tabula* lead into this medical imagery, cf. 9.3 (γαργαλίζῃ), 10.4f (μετάνοια), 11.2 (καθαρείς), 14.3f (καθαρθῶσι καὶ ἐκβάλωσι τὰ κακά). But note how these same elements play into the other *topoi* of these sections.

[67]Compare Plutarch, *Anime an corporis affectiones sin[t] peiores* 500E-501D: "For the beginning of the riddance of disease is awareness which leads the ailing part to the use of what will relieve it; but the man who through disbelief in his ailment does not know what he needs, refuses the remedy, even if it be at hand" (trans. by Helmbold in the Loeb edition). If, in addition to the metaphor of physician, one wishes to follow Joly's eschatological interpretation, a text worthy of consideration is Plutarch's *De genio Socratis* 594A. Here, those who have become daimons give assistance to and encourage those who are "straining every nerve" (φιλοτιμουμένη) to reach the upper world. Those who hear the daimon's encouragement are saved (σᾠζεται). But if the soul pays no attention to the voice, it is forsaken by the daimon and comes to an unhappy end. Cf. also Epictetus II.21.20f.

[68]For the use of ἀναπίμπλημι to describe the condition from which one must be cleansed, cf. Plato, *Phaedo* 67a: μηδὲ ἀναπιμπλώμεθα τῆς τούτου [τοῦ σώματος] φύσεως, ἀλλὰ καθαρεύωμεν ἀπ᾿ αὐτοῦ. Cf. also Iamblichus, *De mysteriis liber* V. 15.

[69]The description of the women as εὐειδεῖς, εὔτακτοι and στολήν...ἁπλῆν places them in continuity with Paideia. The description of them as ἁπλαστοι contrasts them with Deceit (chap. 5) and οὐδαμῶς κεκαλλωπισμέναι contrasts them with the courtesans of chap. 9.

[70]While the items in this virtue list are not unexpected, the inclusion of ἐλευθερία and ἐγκράτεια at this point serves an additional literary function. It ties together the various figures along the path of virtue by repeating ἐγκράτεια (for the last time, cf. 16.2) and by anticipating the characterization of Εὐδαιμονία (cf. 21.3). For this reason the deletion of Ἐγκράτεια here (as suggested by "P.C." [*Rev. de phil.*, 96] on the grounds of consistency) should not be accepted.

[71]Praechter's punctuation indicates that he views περιποιήσησθε as future indicative active in form, and an

orthographical variant for περιποιήσεσθε (the reading of mss. FCKM). This is possible and we have so translated. It is also possible, however, to read περιποιήσησθε as aorist subjunctive middle in form. In this case 20.4.2-3 would form the protasis of a conditional sentence, and 20.4.5 would serve as its apodosis. 20.4.4 would then need to be set off by dashes as the interlocutor's interruption.

[72]The characterization here is most directly related to the description of virtue in the Prodicus myth. For ἐλευθέρως, see Xenophon, *Mem.* II.1.22. For the γυνὴ εὐειδής...ἐπὶ θρόνου ὑψηλοῦ on a mountain, see Dio Chrys., *Or.* I.70ff, 74, 78f.

[73]Joly's interpretation (44, 56, 61) of this section of the *Tabula* is as follows: the vision of the Virtues (20.2-3) corresponds to the vision of the Elect and the ascent to them involves a two-part escort (παραπομπή). Paideia leads the travellers to the Virtues (19.1) and they in turn conduct them to Happiness (21.1), who receives them and bestows on them the crown of immortality. This astral immortality is indicated by the fact that Happiness is located on the highest point of all the enclosures (21.2). Such an interpretation, however, is not necessary, and strains the text at several points. First, Joly's two-stage "παραπομπή" is in fact a three-stage one. The first stage involves Opinion leading people to true Paideia (6.3; 11.1, 20; 29.3). This is accomplished with assistance by Self-Control and Perseverance toward the end of this stage of the journey (16.2-4). Thus the παραπομπή does not commence at chapter 19; only a new stage in the journey is begun here.

Second, the presentation of "Cebes" is not as precise as Joly's reconstruction. For instance, "Cebes" does not say explicitly that Happiness *receives* the person arriving, as Joly (61) claims. It is only the Virtues who are said to receive (παραλάβωσιν); Paideia's reception is at best implied. Again, Paideia is said both to lead (εἰσάγει, 19.1) and to *send* (ἀποστέλλει, 20.1) the travellers to the Virtues. Joly notes only the former. Yet if the idea of a παραπομπή is as central to the depiction as Joly would have us believe, why does he use the word ἀποστέλλει at 21.1?

Third, a simpler background for many of the details of the *Tabula*'s presentation is the Prodicus myth. In the version of this myth by Silius Italicus (XV.68-120), for example, triumph wears a crown of laurel (XV.100; cf. *C.T.* 21.3.3) and raises Virtue to heaven (cf. *C.T.* 16.4). Virtue's *domus* is pure (cf. *C.T.* 19-20) and set on a lofty hill with a steep track and rocky ascent leading up to it (cf. Dio Chrys., *Or.* I.66ff; *C.T.* 15.4, 20.2). Those who ascend are persons who refuse to reckon as good anything which fickle fortune can take away (cf. *C.T.* 7.2-3; 31).

Those who reach the top are awarded victory and its laurel (cf. *C.T.* 22) and look down on mankind below (cf. *C.T.* 24-25). Such persons are a benefit and help to their society (cf. *C.T.* 26.1). In Silius Italicus' version the final result is victory over the Carthaginians, but in Prodicus' version it is "the most blessed happiness" (Xenophon, *Mem.* II.1.33: τὴν μακαριστοτάτην εὐδαιμονίαν). That "Cebes" has earlier (chap. 6) made use of the beginning of this myth is undeniable. It is only reasonable to believe that he is now drawing upon it once more in this section and adapting it to his own purposes.

Fourth, given this background of the Prodicus myth, it is not surprising that many of the things said about the victor in the *Tabula* were said of Diogenes as well. For example, according to Dio (IX.11-12), at the Isthmian games Diogenes crowns himself and is reprimanded for this deed because he has not won any contest. To this he replied, "Many and mighty (μεγάλους) antagonists have I vanquished, not like those slaves who are now wrestling here, hurling the discus and running, but more difficult in every way-- I mean poverty, exile, and disrepute; yes, and anger, pain desire, fear, and the most redoubtable beast (θηρίον) of all, treacherous and cowardly, I mean pleasure..." (trans. by Cohoon in the Loeb edition). Moreover, he goes about in complete safety and acts as a physician to sick souls whom he sees (cf. nn. 66 and 80).

[74] The so-called *agōn topos* (*C.T.* 22.1-23.4, 26.2-3) was, like the medical imagery and the catalogues of vices and virtues, standard fare in moralist literature (cf. esp. Ps-Diog., *Ep.* 37.4f; 39.4f; 46; Ps-Heracl., *Ep.* 4.3 (Hercher); Epictetus II.19.20ff, III.22.52ff. Its usual form relates the attainment of virtue to the conquest of vice (often characterized as a beast). Hence, the athletic imagery of training and exercise for the contest is quite prominent in Stoic notions of ἄσκησις (cf. Epictetus III.15; Plutarch, *De genio Socr.* 593D-594A; Plato, *Phaedo* 114C; Musonius Rufus, *Dis.* VI [ed. O. Hense] pp. 22ff). The other standard component of the metaphor, especially in Cynic literature, is the overcoming of hardships. The metaphor is often accompanied by *peristasis* catalogues containing the very elements seen earlier in the *Tabula* at work in other contexts but now brought to bear in this new metaphor (*C.T.* 22.2, 23.1f; cf. 9.3f, 10.2ff). It should be noted, too, that for the Cynics Heracles was the prototypical victorious athlete (cf. Dio Chrys., *Or.* 8.30, 1.62f; Ps-Diog. 36.1; 6).

[75] For the personification of ἄγνοια and its use in ancient religion and philosophy, cf. K. Lehmann, "Ignorance and Search in the Villa of the Mysteries," *Journal of Roman Studies* 52 (1962) 62-68. With regard to the fact that in the shift of metaphors the vices personified as courtesans (9.1) are now depicted as beasts, note Athenaeus,

Deipnosophistae, 558d.   Thus there is a conquest not only
of the vices which accompany luxury (*viz.*, Avarice and
Incontinence) but also of those which are connected with
Retribution (*viz.*, Grief and Lamentation).

[76]The lacuna, as indicated by Praechter's apparatus,
is best resolved by the insertion of Happiness based on the
scene in *C.T.* 22.1.   The other alternative might be just to
insert the feminine pronoun as the accusative of reference
for the active infinitive: "with which you said *she* crowns
him."   The variant suggested by some of the common manuscripts, but which Praechter rejected, would be to read the
passive infinitive with αὐτόν as the accusative of reference rather than the object: "with which you said *he is
crowned*."

[77]This is the first indication that the old-young
transmission motif (cf. 1.3, 2.3, 4.3) is to be applied to
the explanation now being given to the stranger, who is
here for the first time specifically called a "young man"
(cf. 33.3) by the πρεσβύτερος (cf. 2.1).
    The thought of the following sentence seems to derive
ultimately from Plato, *Menexenus* 247E-248A: "For that man
is best prepared for life who makes all that concerns his
welfare (εὐδαιμονίαν) depend upon himself, or nearly so,
instead of hanging his hopes on other men...; because he
puts his trust in himself, he will neither be seen rejoicing nor yet grieving overmuch" (trans. by Bury in the Loeb
edition).   For a citation of this text by an author from
the same general period as "Cebes," cf. Cicero, *Tusc. Disp.*
V.12.36 (cf. the discussion by Joly, 27-29).   On this goal
of absolute self-sufficiency, cf. also Cicero, *Tusc. Disp.*
V.14.42 and *Parad. Stoic.* 17, and Seneca, *Ep.* 92.2 Epictetus (III.22.45ff and 26.34f) places it in the context of
the Cynic ideal of freedom (ἐλευθερία); cf. *C.T.* 20.3.

[78]For the description and πρόσταγμα of the Daimon,
see 4.3 and 30-32.   Note the change from Δαίμων to Δαιμόνιον, perhaps as a result of a change in the mss.; see also
30.1, 31.3, 31.5, 32.5, 33.2.

[79]Two Corycian caves were known in antiquity.   One was
located in Cilicia and was famous for its saffron (cf.
Pliny, *Historia Naturalis* XXI.17.31; Quintus Curtius, III.
4.10; Horace, *Satirae* II.4.68).   Typhon is said to have
deposited Zeus in this cave (cf. Apollodorus, *Lib.* I.6.3;
compare Pindar, *Pyth. Od.* I.15ff), and Zeus is known to
have been worshipped there (cf. J. G. Frazer, *Adonis, Attis,
Osiris* [3rd ed., 1961] Book I, 152-61).   For a full description of the Cilician Corycian cave, see Strabo, *Geog.* 14.5.5
and Pomponius Mela, *Chronogr.* I.13.   The other Corycian cave
was located in Phocis on Mt. Parnassus.   According to one
legend, it received its name from the nymph Corycia (Pausanias, X.6.3; X.32.2).   In addition to this particular

derivation, the association of the Parnassian cave with
nymphs is widely attested (cf. for example, Aeschylus,
Eumen. 22; Sophocles, *Antigone* 1128). Owing to the association with nymphs, the cave and the whole mountain were
considered sacred (*Strabo,Geog.* IX.3.1; Pausanias X.32.7).
This may have been one of the reasons why most of the male
inhabitants of Delphi took refuge in the cave and peaks of
Mt. Parnassus when the Persians marched against their city
(cf. Herodotus VII.36). In any case, the author of the
Tabula seems to have regarded the cave as an inviolable
sanctuary, and the brevity of the reference suggests that
it was commonly regarded as such. The literary texts of
Pausanias have recently been borne out by excavation of
the cave on Mt. Parnassus. See M. E. Caskey, "News Letter
From Greece," *American Journal of Archeology* 75 (1971) 395f.

[80]There is a double metaphor here. The first part of
the Senex's response should be seen in the light of the
Cynic ideal of freedom (ἐλευθερία), cf. *Ps-Socratic Epp.*
1.2ff; Ps-Diogenes, *Ep.* 36; 37.3; 38.4; 39 (Hercher/Mal-
herbe); Epictetus III.22.23, 45, 69ff. In connection with
ἀσφάλεια see also Dio Chrys., *Or.*4.8 (Diogenes) and the
speech of Cebes and Simmias to Socrates in Plato's *Criton*
45C. The second element of the metaphor turns once again
to medical imagery (cf. 19.2), but now the philosopher himself is the physician of sick souls, cf. Epictetus II.13.12,
14.21; III.10.12ff, 16.11f, 21.20, 22.72, 23.27; Musonius
Rufus, *Dis.* I (ed. O. Hense) p. 1, 9ff; V, p. 20, 6f; VI,
p. 23, 18; Dio Chrys., *Or.* 77/78; Seneca, *Epp.* 22.1, 27.1,
40.5, 72.5; Ps-Diogenes, *Ep.* 28; 39.4 (Hercher/Malherbe);
Diogenes Laertius VI.30, 36. We may take special note of
Dio Chrys., *Or.* 9.2, in which Diogenes the Cynic is pictured as physician; he looks upon mankind and its folly as
one who has overcome that folly and now offers aid to the
rest. It should be emphasized, however, that for the
Tabula the stress seems to be on the personal victory.

[81]The word occurs only here in the *Tabula*. It was a
technical term in the Cynic literature, and it served to
oppose the Cynic life-style to the life of pleasure and
wealth. Poverty was often portrayed as one of the hardships which accompanied the Cynic life so that he might
attain endurance and indifference. The fact that πενία
occurs here in connection with vices personified earlier
in the text, tends to change somewhat the perspective on
the function of the vices. It is not atypical for the
Tabula to introduce unique readings for such a purpose; cf.
Introduction, n. 69.

[82]For ἐχιοδεῖκται (as printed by Praechter), we read
ἐχιόδηκτοι as attested in all the Greek manuscripts, implied by the reading of Odaxius: *qui a vipera morsi ali-
quando fuerint*, and recorded in the margin of Odaxius (cf.
Finch, "Value of Odaxius' Translation," 28). There has

been a reluctance on the part of many scholars to accept
this reading and most have chosen to emend the text so as
to secure a reference of some sort to "snake-handlers" or
"snake-charmers." But the proposals are quite numerous.
In addition to the two cited by Praechter they include:
(1) ὀφιογενεῖς (Caselius and Drosihn; cf. Strabo 13.1.14);
(2) ἐχιολέκται (Coray); (3) ἐχιοδῆκται or (4) ἐχιοδηγοί
(Schneider); (5) ἐχιοθῆροι (Salmasius, on the basis of the
Arabic); (6) ἐχιοδιῶκται (M. Casaubon); (7) ἐχιοδέκται
(Johnson); (8) ἐχιοθέλκαι (Hertlein; Krauss). If Praechter's emendation is accepted, it is necessary to read the
sentence as does A. D. Nock: "...and is superior to all
that formerly distressed him, as those who exhibit snakes
(are to their snakes). Nothing distresses him any more
because he has a remedy" (*Conversion*, 180). In this way
the basis of the analogy is restricted to the idea of superiority, since snake-handlers presumably would have had
an antidote, making the possibility of being bitten of
little concern. The received reading ἐχιόδηκτοι, however,
should be accepted for the following reasons. First, the
word ἐχιόδηκτοι is known and occurs in writers from the
period of "Cebes" (Joly, 15). These include Dioscorides
(*De materia medica* 1.13) and Strabo, 13.1.14 (588). Moreover, the meaning of the term is quite clearly "bitten by
a snake" (cf. also Theognostus, *Canones* 96). Second, the
proposed emendations fail to take the πρότερον with sufficient seriousness. The importance of a "then...now" context is suggested by *C.T.* 25.2f; the same notion is apparent here in the resolution of the comparison using οὐκέτι.
The ἐχιόδηκτοι serve as a valid point of comparison only if
they had formerly suffered distress (cf. 22.2), but no
longer. Such a reading has the additional advantage of
incorporating both the ideas of superiority and of former
condition. Third, the idea of the body forming an immunity
against poisons is not unknown in antiquity. It is related
of Mithridates that, following a military defeat, he tried
to commit suicide by taking a poison. Whereas his daughters
died from the poison, Mithridates did not because he had
become immune, owing to the drugs he habitually drank as a
protection against poisoners (Appian, XII, 16.111). In line
with this, "Cebes" quite clearly believes that the person
who survives snakebite develops an immunity and is safe from
the effects of a new bite. (This third point is that of
Gruebler, 98). Therefore, like such people, the victor is
immune from the stings inflicted by the metaphorical snake.

[83]On θηρία as a designation for snakes, see Hermas,
Shep., *Sim.* IX.26.7; cf. IX.1.9. For the sequence ἐχιόδηκτοι...θηρία...κακοποιοῦντα, compare Acts 28:3-5: ἔχιδνα...
θηρίον...ἔπαθεν οὐδὲν κακόν. See also Philo, *De spec. leg.*
III.104; Ps-Diogenes, *Ep.* 29.4 (Hercher/Malherbe). For
snakes as θηρία, cf. Aelian, *H.A.* 17.37.

[84]For the idiom σῴζειν πρός ("to arrive at"), see
Xenophon, *Cyrop.* V.4.16. Compare *Anab.* VI.4.8 (with εἰς)
and VI.5.20 (with ἐπί). Cf. also *Anab.* III.1.6; *Hellen.*
I.6.7; and Euripides, *Phoenissae* 725.

[85]The use of ἀνοδία here represents an interesting
element in moralist literature. The term does not seem
unusual in the context of the Prodicus myth as used in
15.2. The road to virtue is customarily pictured as rough
and rocky while the road to vice is smooth. But here in
27.3 an unusual shift in that polarity occurs. Now the
ἀνοδία is the course of those who fail to ascend to Perseverance. Cf. 16.3ff for the beginnings of this reversal
at the point when the summit is reached and Virtue is attained. This same use of the term is found also in Philo,
Vita Mosis 2.138 (II.156, ed. Cohn and Wendland) referring
to the rough road of vice and the smooth road of virtue.
See also Philo, *De agricultura* 22.101 (I.316, ed. Cohn and
Wendland). Compare this usage to Hermas, *Man.* VI.1.3. See
also Hermas, *Vis.* III.7.1 for the use of ἀνοδία in conjunc-
tion with πλανᾶν referring to those who fail to come to
repentance. J. M. Cotterill noted some of these similarities and suggested that Philo was the first to use ἀνοδία
in the context of the Prodicus myth. See J. M. Cotterill
and C. Taylor, "Plutarch, Cebes, and Hermas," *Journal of
Philology* 31 (1910) 20. This exact phrase is employed by
Hermas (*Vision* I.1.3; cf. also *Vision* VI.3.1) to describe
the district through which a spirit took him. It is said
to be a precipitous (κρημνώδης; cf. *C.T.* 15.3.2) place
through which it is impossible to walk.

[86]There is a variety of editorial decisions that must
be made at this point; at stake is whether the dialogue in
28.1-2 continues the allegorical personification or not.
We have followed Praechter in adopting the usual reading
(since Drosihn) without capitalization, "all evils" (πάντα
κακά). Taken in this way the point of reference is in
direct contrast to ἀγαθά (28.3.1; cf. 34.2, 36.1, 3.3, 8.3)
In this vein Praechter sees no need to capitalize ἀσωτίαν,
ἀκρασίαν (28.3.2), or ἀγαθά (28.3.1) even though these
terms are part of the personification in the preceding
sections. Another possibility seems to have been generally
accepted to the time of Schweighaeuser. The latter capitalized ἀγαθά, ἀσωτίαν, and ἀκρασίαν in 28.3, thereby re-
turning the dialogue to the allegory of the picture. Following Schweighaeuser's logic it might be asked whether
κακά (28.1.1) should be capitalized as well. The insertion
of the definite article in a number of the Mss. (cf.
Praechter's apparatus) gives some credence to this suggestion. Moreover, it would not be totally out of place to
take the neuter κακά as a reference to the personified
vices. On two previous occasions the author has concluded
a list of personified (feminine) vices with the neuter

κακόν (in the singular, 26.2, in the plural, 24.2). In
either case it is important to notice that the word-play
on ἀκολουθεῖν (and its cognates) provides the continuity
for the section.

[87]Compare Epictetus II.19.26, 21.2f; III.22.48; cf.
especially Ps-Heraclitus, *Ep.* 4.4 (Malherbe). For an extended dramatization of this kind of indictment see Lucian,
Bis accus. 16 (with ἄθλιος and κακοδαίμων).

[88]Praechter has taken the minority reading παρ' αὐταῖς on the basis of 9.2, understanding it with τὴν 'Ἡδυπάθειαν καὶ τὴν 'Ακρασίαν (cf. 9.1, 32.2). But the majority reading παρ' αὐτοῖς is quite possible. In this case
the logical antecedent for αὐτοῖς would be οὗτοι (28.1.3)
which is resumed with λέγουσι (28.2.1). The clause, ὡς...
ἀγαθῶν, is the indirect statement (λέγουσι) of the ones
who have returned to the first enclosure.

[89]For the idea, cf. Plato, *Republica* IX.586A, where
people πλανῶνται διὰ βίου and "with eyes ever bent upon the
earth and hands bowed down over their tables they feast
like cattle (βοσκημάτων δίκην) grazing and copulating"
(trans. by P. Shorey in the Loeb edition). Aristotle (*Eth.
Nic.* I.V.1-3) says that the majority love the enjoyable
life (τὸν βίον ἀγαπῶσι τὸν ἀπολαυστικόν) and thereby reveal themselves as utterly servile, since they prefer the
life of cattle (βοσκημάτων βίον προαιρούμενοι). Pleasure,
according to Seneca, is the good of cattle (*Ep.* 92.6). Dio
77/78.29 suggests that the person who envies the feasting
of a Sardanapalus is envious of the happiness of goats and
asses. Compare also Sallust, *Cat.* I.1-II.19; *Jug.* I.1-II.4.

[90]The distinction between knowledge and opinion is in
keeping with the thought of Parmenides, but the positive
role here accorded Opinion is neither Parmenidean nor Stoic.
The view is essentially Platonic, as both Jerram (xxvi) and
Joly (30) indicate.

[91]The shift in person here seems stark at first glance,
yet it appears to be intentional. Since the initial section
(5.1) there has been a single interlocutor with the exception of a similar shift in 20.4. While the fiction of the
setting is heightened by such a shift, there is another
function as well. For in both 20.4 and 30.2 the structural
shift occurs precisely at those points where the moral of
the allegory is being proffered to the reader. In 20.4 the
point of understanding the allegory is heightened further
by the interlocutors' interruption of the conditional paraenesis. Here in 30.2 it should be noted that θάρσος is not
only a command but also a gift. Apparently an individual
must first show sufficient courage to achieve self-control
and perseverance (16.3) and then he is fortified for the
rest of the journey (16.5, 18.4). The exhortation to the

interlocutors is not merely a stylistic device to maintain
the reader's attention. Rather, the interlocutors' own
weariness and lack of perseverance parallels that of the
pilgrims in the picture. Like them, they too must be
exhorted (cf. 16.3) so that they can reach the end of the
explanation. In chaps. 36-41 (43) they are given the
knowledge of what is advantageous in life--the gift of
Paideia. To reach the end of the explanation is tantamoun
to arriving at Paideia. Now the decision rests on the interlocutors whether to obey the instructions and move on
to virtue and happiness or to disobey and suffer the con-
sequences.

[92] The "wicked banker" had become proverbial and there
had developed a literary *topos* with its own technical vocabulary, which is fully employed here. For the vocabular
and discussion, see Maurer's "παρατίθημι" article in *TDNT*
VIII (1972) 162-64, and C. Spicq, "Saint Paul et la loi de
Depots," *Revue Biblique* 40 (1931) 481-502. The most strik
ing parallel to the analogy made by "Cebes" is found in th
pseudo-Plutarchian *Consolatio ad Apollonium* 28 (116 AB):
"We ought not, therefore, to bear it with bad grace if the
gods make demand upon us for what they have loaned us for
a short time. For even the bankers, as we are in the habi
of saying frequently, when demand is made upon them for th
return of deposits (ἀπαιτούμενοι τὰ θέματα), do not chafe
at the repayment, if they be honourable men. To those who
do not make repayment with good grace one might fairly say
'Have you forgotten that you accepted this on condition
that (ἐπὶ τῷ) you should return it?' Quite parallel is th
lot of all mortals. For we hold our life, as it were, on
deposit from the gods, who have compelled us to accept the
account, and there is no fixed time for its return, just a
with the bankers and their deposits, but it is uncertain
when the depositor will demand repayment" (trans. by F.
Babbitt in the Loeb edition). For Ps-Plutarch's thought,
cf. Cicero, *Tusc. Disp.* I.39.93.   Cf. also Philo, *Spec.
leg.* IV.30; Plato, *Leg.* VII.42C; Teles, 36f (ed. Hense).
For the technical use of the term λαμβάνειν/λαβεῖν in this
context, meaning "to receive on deposit," cf. Conon, *Diege-
sis* 38 (in Jacoby, *Fragmente der griechischen Historiker* I
203f).

[93] The same attitude is enjoined with respect to the
gifts of Tychē and Pseudopaideia. Neither poverty nor lac
of education is a necessary precondition of virtue and happiness. Wealth and education fall into the category of the
Stoic ληπτά, i.e., things which are not to be regarded as
the end of action but are not to be rejected if offered
(von Arnin, 104). This attitude on the part of "Cebes" is
what causes Praechter to regard Cebes as more Stoic than
Cynic. But both Joël (322-33) and Joly (30) think that
Praechter has exaggerated Cynic intransigence on these
issues.

[94]Seneca's *De benefeiciis* VII.1.7 contains a similar statement by Demetrius the Cynic concerning the person who has attained the Cynic goal. After dedicating himself to virtue and following the smooth road to her, he arrives at a safe retreat and attains a "perfect knowledge of what is useful and essential" (*consummavitque scientiam utilem ac necessariam*). He attained this goal with only a few maxims of philosophy.

[95]Compare Athenaeus, *Deip.* XII.6 (quoting Antisthenes). For ἀμεταμέλητος as the gift of which God does not repent (hence understood as the "irrevocability" of God's gifts), cf. Rom 11:29 and Athanasius, *Orationes adversus Arianos* III.25. The term is discussed fully by C. Spicq in *Revue Biblique* 67 (1960) 210-19; for the passage in the *Tabula*, cf. 213.

[96]The word probably reflects the Cynic slogan related to the ideal of renouncing all concern with luxury and wealth in order to move directly to virtue through training in endurance. See Ps-Crates, *Epp.* 13, 16, 21; Ps-Diogenes, *Ep.* 30 (Hercher/Malherbe).

[97]ἀπόλλυται κακὸς κακῶς: The person thus dies as he has lived--wretchedly. This combination, rendered wonderfully by Odaxius' *miser miserrime moritur*, is a favorite of Lucian. Drosihn (27) cites *Dial. mort.* 15(5).2; *Icarom.* 33; *De Parasito* 57; *Philopseudes* 20; *Piscator* 44.

[98]Cf. *Leges* 808DE: "With the return of daylight the children should go to their teachers, for just as no sheep or other witless creature ought to exist without a herdsman, so children cannot live without a tutor, nor slaves without a master. And, of all wild creatures, the child is the most intractable; for insofar as it, above all others, possesses a fount of reason that is as yet uncurbed, it is a treacherous, sly and most insolent creature. Wherefore the child must be strapped up, as it were, with many bridles (διὸ δὴ πολλοῖς αὐτὸ οἷον χαλινοῖς τισὶ δεῖ δεσμεύειν)--first, when he leaves the care of nurse and mother, with tutors, to guide his childish ignorance, and after that with teachers of all sorts of subjects and lessons (μαθήμασιν), treating him as becomes a freeborn child" (trans. by Bury in the Loeb edition); cf. also Xenophon, *Mem.* IV.I.3-4; Isoc., *Pan* 10. For the relevance of this quotation in regard to the issues of authorship and date of the *Tabula*, see the Introduction. This section of the *Leges* may have inspired other thoughts and images found in the *Tabula*. Compare, for example, *Leges* 807A (ἐν τρόπῳ βοσκήματος) with *C.T.* 28.3 (βοσκήματων τρόπον).

[99]The ἐγκύκλιος παιδεία was commonly viewed as preparatory to philosophical study. At debate was the issue whether this general education was an essential or a

dispensable prerequisite for philosophy. The Academy
tended to view such studies as a necessity (Diogenes Laertius IV.10, 36; Stobaeus, *Flor. app.* 16.26.27), as did the
Peripatetics (Diog. Laert. V. 31). The Epicureans, Sceptics and Cynics, on the other hand, adopted a critical
perspective concerning them. Epicurus argued that none
of the subjects is of any assistance in the perfection of
wisdom (Sextus Empiricus, *Adversus Mathematicos* I.1; for
Epicurus' position, cf. also Diog. Laert. X.6; Plutarch,
Non posse suav. viv. sec. Epic. 1092D-1096E). Torquatus
in Cicero's *De finibus* (I.21.71-72) adds that Epicurus
considered as education only that which schools us in happiness (*nullam eruditionem esse duxit nisi quae beatae
vitae disciplinam iuvaret*) and rejected the general education as contributing nothing toward making life pleasanter
and better (*nihil afferent quo iucundius, id est quo melius
viveremus*). This rejection naturally led to the accusation
that the Epicureans attracted the uneducated (Cicero, *De
fin.* II.4.12). This charge they, of course, shared with
the Cynics. The Cynics rejected the customary subjects of
instruction because of the danger of being distracted and
perverted (διαστρέφοιντο) by them (Diog. Laert. VI.104).
Indeed, the fact that the professors were no paragons of
virtue (Diog. Laert. VI.27-28) served to confirm the danger. The Sceptics based their opposition to general studies on the same ground as they did their criticism of philosophy, *viz.*, the impossibility of finding the truth known
or taught by them (Sextus Empir., *Adv. Math.* I.6).

The question seems to have been a topic of debate for
Stoics. According to Diogenes Laertius VII.32, Zeno ac-
cused the general education of being useless (ἄχρηστον).
Chrysippus, on the other hand, is said (VII.129) to have
adopted the diametrically opposite view that this course
of studies was useful (εὐχρηστεῖν). In keeping with this
is the statement by Quintilian (I.10.1f, 15) that even the
Stoics granted that the wise man might devote some of his
attention to such studies as music. This ancient debate
among Stoics has now become one *about* the Stoics' views on
this subject. Praechter (*Die griechisch-römische Popular-
philosophie und die Erziehung*, Programm-Nu. 553. Bruchsal,
1886, pp. 23ff) argues that the Stoics assigned the ἐγκύκλια μαθήματα to the category of preferred (προηγμένα), indifferent (ἀδιάφορα) things. Marrou, on the other hand,
believes that it was especially the post-Chrysippean Stoic
who insisted upon the essentiality of such studies (*Histor*
of Education, 244).

This debate is carried over into the question of the
philosophical background of "Cebes." With which of the
philosophical schools does the *Tabula* have the greatest
affinities? Praechter can accommodate it within his under
standing of the Stoics' position whereas Marrou assigns th
aspect of the *Tabula* to the author's Cynic tendencies (cf.
also his *Saint Augustin*, 215-16). Joël, of course, would
see not only "Cebes'" views about the general studies but

his whole thought as Cynic. The author comes closest to a
Cynic view when he affirms that people *frequently* (πολλάκις) go directly from the "first" to the "third" enclosure,
thereby bypassing the general education. But the author's
distance from Cynicism is revealed in the statement that
the various disciplines assist people in going more rapid-
ly (συντομωτέρως) to true Paideia (33.4). Cynicism was
known as the "shortcut to virtue" (σύντομον ἐπ' ἀρετὴν
ὁδόν, Diog. Laert. VI.104) precisely because it *rejected*
the arts and sciences as a requisite preliminary to the
attaining of virtue. The μαθήματα are among the things
that add polish, not strength, to the one who has attained
to a perfect knowledge of what is useful and essential
(Seneca, *De benef.* VII.I.7). "Cebes" affirms, on the con-
trary, that the quickest way to the Virtues is via general
education. He borrows the term σύντομος from Cynicism but
he uses it in a non-Cynic way (also Joly, 34). "Cebes"
may agree with the Cynics that such studies are dispens-
able--indeed, they belong to Pseudopaideia!--and acknowledge
that many arrive at virtue without the benefit of these
disciplines. But for all these utterances he is not prepared to deny them a place. He maintains their utilitarian
value and is not afraid that the wise man will be perverted
by them. He does not, however, go so far as Dio and claim
that it is *necessary* (ἀναγκαία) for those who have acquired
divine (=true) education to add to it frail, human education (*Or.* 4.29).

   Joly (75-77) attempts to demonstrate that "Cebes" is
best understood as a Neo-Pythagorean even in his views about
the arts and sciences. This is no small task, especially
when one recalls the Pythagorean devotion to the sciences
and that some of the Pythagoreans were known as the μαθημα-
τικοί. Joly makes some valuable observations but it cannot
really be said that he overcomes what he himself regards as
the most serious objection to his interpretation. The fact
remains that the author who most closely approximates the
viewpoint of "Cebes" is a Stoic, *viz.*, Seneca. And Seneca's
perspective (*Ep.* 88) has obviously been influenced by his
contact with Demetrius the Cynic (*De benef.* VII.1.7). Similarly, other Stoics who show strong "cynicizing" tendencies
are found frequently to recommend the acquisition of a few
philosophic maxims which are immediately put into practice
(cf. Epictetus II.21.15f, IV.21.8f; *C.T.* 19.3). To be
sure, "Cebes" is more negative than Seneca in his assessment of ἐγκύκλια μαθήματα--a fact recognized by Joly (32)
as well. But the concerns and issues that give rise to
their discussion are the same and the solutions they give
are remarkably similar. Such similarities should not be
minimized for the sake of establishing an alternative interpretation.

   Finally, it should be added that "Cebes" is Socratic
to the extent that he accords a limited place to the general studies. Socrates recommended the study of geometry,
astronomy, and arithmetic as an appropriate enterprise, but

he restricted involvement to the learning of the basics of
these disciplines. After a rudimentary knowledge in each
had been acquired, one was to move on to other useful
studies (Xenophon, *Mem.* IV.7.2-8). Thus what Socrates
recommended in regard to the individual μαθήματα, "Cebes"
recommends for them as a whole.

[100] <βελτίους> γενέσθαι.... Clearly an elliptical expression as Praechter suggests. The addition of βελτίους,
if only in sense, is given support by the readings of the
Latin of Odaxius (*meliores*) and An (*meliorem*). The ellipsis is probably resolved on the basis of 33.4 as follows:
οὕτω καὶ ἄνευ τούτων τῶν μαθημάτων οὐδὲν κωλύει <βελτίους>
γενέσθαι <ὅμως μέντοί γε χρήσιμα ἐστὶ πρὸς τὸ συντομώτερον
ἐλθεῖν πρὸς τὴν ἀληθινὴν Παιδείαν>. The point of the comparison is then as follows: Just as the knowledge of a
foreign language is useful for increasing the accuracy of
one's understanding of what is said, so also the knowledge
of the general studies is useful for increasing the rapi-
dity of one's journey to true Paideia. But just as one,
without knowing the language, can grasp the meaning of a
statement with the help of an interpreter, so also one can
arrive at true Paideia without knowing the μαθήματα. Apparently all that one needs is the help of a few short
maxims (cf. the speech of Demetrius in Seneca, *De ben.*
VII.1.7). For another instance showing the superiority of
personal knowledge over the use of an interpreter, see
Xenophon, *Cyrop.* I.VI.2.

[101] Cf. Seneca, *Ep.* 88.2.

[102] Cf. Dio Chrys., *Or.* 4.30.

[103] Cf. *C.T.* 14.5.

[104] The passage is highly enigmatic and, by all accounts, hopelessly corrupt. It is impossible to conceive
how the subject of οἴδασιν and ἔχωσι (35.3.4) could be anything but a reference to those in the second enclosure (cf.
the reading of K). Almost all editors have assumed a lacuna in the text and have supplied it in various ways.
Drosihn's proposal (see Praechter's apparatus), which was
quite similar to one made by Schweighaeuser, won the com-
mendation of H. Müller (268). Other editors, however, take
εἰ μηδὲν ἄλλο with οἱ ἐν τῷ πρώτῳ περιβόλῳ (cf. K. Müller, *De
arte*, 80f). It should be noted that actually there is no
lacuna in any of the Mss. It may be the case, then, that
the key to understanding is the ellipsis precipitated by
the question (πῶς τοῦτο;) of the interlocutor. Use of
ellipsis in service of the dialogue is not uncommon to the
author of the *Tabula*. Πῶς τοῦτο; may be seen in a similar
construction in 19.2. In the latter case it is instructive
to note that the question of the interlocutor serves to
continue the dialogue by focusing the attention of the Sene

on one part of his foregoing remarks. Thus, following a
general statement the main point is underscored, using the
πῶς τοῦτο; of the interlocutor as the bridge. In 19.2,
then, the point being picked up is really the penultimate
statement of the Senex in 19.1, i.e., regarding the purifying potion. The necessity of this draught is emphasized
by the medical imagery of the Senex's response. By analogy
we may expect a similar function of πῶς τοῦτο; in 35.3.
This impression is strengthened by the fact that the response is introduced by ὅτι (cf. 3.1). The focus of the
section in 35.3ff is on those in the second enclosure and
why they do not progress beyond that point while others
(from the first enclosure) pass by. It seems that the
proper referent for πῶς τοῦτο; is the phrase οἵ τούτους
τοὺς μαθηματικοὺς παραλλάττουσιν (35.2), or more specifically just παραλλάττουσιν. Thus, by ellipsis the question
of the interlocutor may be understood in the following way:
"How can this be--*they pass by?*" Understanding the ellipsis in this way would also seem to resolve the problems in
the "hopelessly corrupt" following lines. Rather than the
elaborate emendations proposed by Drosihn or Praechter, we
would propose to resolve the ellipsis by supplying the
sense of παραλλάτουσιν with its implied object αὐτούς.
Thus, both of the referents necessary for the comparison
by the Senex are present: "Because those in the first enclosure *pass them by* if for no other reason than the latter
do not know what they falsely claim to understand."
     The source of the thought is obviously Socratic. Cf.,
e.g., Plato, *Apol.* 21C-D, 22CD, 23C-D (προσποιούμενοι μὲν
εἰδέναι, εἰδότες δὲ οὐδέν), 29A (δοκεῖν γὰρ εἰδέναι ἐστιν
ἃ οὐκ οἶδεν), 29B (καὶ τοῦτο πῶς οὐκ ἀμαθία ἐστὶν αὕτη ἡ
ἐπονείδιστος, ἡ τοῦ οἴεσθαι εἰδέναι ἃ οὐκ οἶδεν) and Xenophon, *Mem.* III.9.6 (ἃ μὴ οἶδε δοξάζειν τε καὶ οἴεσθαι
γιγνώσκειν).
     In the contemporary period we may note the same sort
of charges being levelled at those who claim knowledge but
who in fact do not put their knowledge to work, cf. Ps-
Heraclitus 4.5 (Malherbe); Epictetus II.15.13f, 21.15ff.
     For the use of εἰ μηδὲν ἄλλο in a similar context,
compare Isocrates, *Pan.*10.

[105]In Chapter 11, Repentance is connected with deli-
very from Pseudodoxia, here with escape from Pseudopaideia.
In the former case Μετάνοια is used, here Μεταμέλεια, with
no apparent difference in meaning. Cf. n. 40.

[106]We read παιδεία and ψευδοπαιδεία with capitals as
the personifications common to the text. Drosihn, Schweighaeuser, and most others read thus, in contrast to Praechter.
For the notion of recognizing Pseudopaideia for what she
really is, see 13.1.

[107]On the thought, cf. Seneca, *De Ben.* VII.II.1: "These
are the things that my friend Demetrius says the tiro in

philosophy must grasp with both hands, these are the precepts that he must never let go, nay, must cling fast to, and make a part of himself, and by daily meditation reach the point where these wholesome maxims occur to him of their own accord, and are promptly at hand whenever they are desired, and the great distinction between base and honourable action presents itself without delay" (trans. by J. W. Basore in the Loeb edition). Cf. also Lucian, *Nigrinus* 6-7; and Heb 5:14. Cf. *C.T.* 20.4.

[108]"Cebes" now proceeds to treat this question, which was raised and postponed in 8.4. Life, health, and victory are not mentioned in the list in 8.4. Life is inserted here at the beginning since it is the first topic to be discussed.

[109]At this point there is a stylistic shift in the form of the dialogue; the author has the old man interrogate the youth in typical Socratic fashion (cf. Plato, *Meno* 77B-78C; *Criton* 48E-49A; Dio Chrys., *Or.* 69.4).

[110]This an exceedingly common *topos* in ancient philosophy. Cf., for example, Pseudo-Plato, *Eryxias*, for the argument of Critias and Prodicus that things are good to the good but evil to the evil. Here, in regard to riches, Socrates reports that Prodicus affirmed that "they were a good to good men and to those who knew in what way they should be employed, while to the bad and the ignorant they were an evil. The same is true, he went on to say, of all other things; men make them to be what they are themselves" (397E; trans. by B. Jowett, *The Dialogues of Plato* [New York, 1937] Vol. II, 812).

[111]Compare Plato, *Criton* 48B and Ps-Crates, *Ep.* 6 (Hercher/Malherbe).

[112]Sauppe conjectured καί before τοῖς, which now receives some support from An (*et bene viventibus*). Cf. Finch, "Codex Vaticanus Latinus 4037," 82. On this basis we assume its presence for our translation.

[113]Thanks to a suggestion by Professor E. N. O'Neil one might consider whether to emend Praechter's punctuation of this sentence to make it a question: οὐκ ἂν εἴη...οὔτε κακόν; ("is it not then true that living can be neither good nor bad?").

[114]For the use of τέμνειν and καίειν in connection with the medical imagery, see Ps-Diogenes, *Epp.* 28.7, 29.5 (Hercher/Malherbe); Dio Chrys., *Or.* 77/78, and nn. 66, 80 above.

[115]The two pairs, life and health, death and sickness, treated here first, also occur first in the list of Stoic neutral (οὐδέτερα) things in Diog. Laert. VII.101.

[116]The premise of this and the following discussion
of wealth (so central to the purpose and theme of the entire *Tabula*) is very similar to that of Plutarch's *De cupiditate divitiarum* (Mor. 523C-528B). Note especially 523D:
"Nevertheless many cases could be cited of men who would
rather be rich though miserable (κακοδαιμονοῦντες)....Hav-
ing wealth is not the same as being superior to it, nor
possessing luxuries the same as feeling no need of them"
(trans. by De Lacy and Einarson, Loeb Classical Library).
For discussion of Plutarch's treatise, see E. N. O'Neil,
"De cupiditate divitiarum (Moralia 523C-528B)," in *Plutarch's Ethical Writings and Early Christian Literature*
ed. H. D. Betz (Studia ad Corpus Hellenisticum Novi Testamenti 4; Leiden, 1975) 289-362.

[117]Cf. Xenophon, *Mem.* IV.2.9 where Socrates commends
Euthydemus because νομίζεις ἀργύριον καὶ χρυσίον οὐδὲν βελτίους ποιεῖν τοὺς ἀνθρώπους. For a discussion about wealth
as a good or evil, cf. Ps-Plato, *Eryxias*. Note especially
403. For a more general statement, see Terence, *Heaut.*
194-95.

[118]Seneca, *Ep.* 87, gives several syllogisms that seek
to establish that wealth is not a good. Of particular interest is 87.22: "Good does not result from evil. But
riches result from greed; therefore, riches are not a good"
(trans. by R. M. Gummere in the Loeb edition). Moreover,
Seneca gives the argument of Posidonius that wealth, as a
gift of Tychē (cf. *C.T.* 8.4, 36.1), cannot be a good since
it leads to evil practices (*Ep.* 87.35; cf. also Epictetus,
II.16.3, 19.13f). Even more stringent attacks on wealth
based on the same logic can be found among the Cynics; see
Ps-Diogenes, *Epp.* 28.5, 50 (Hercher/Malherbe); *Ps-Socratic
Epp.* 6.6, 12; Ps-Anacharsis, *Ep.* 9 (Malherbe); Ps-Crates,
Ep. 7 (Hercher/Malherbe). Note that 40.2 prepares for the
conclusion of 41.3. Confusion and ignorance concerning
what constitutes the good is the root of all evil.

[119]The thought is ultimately Socratic; cf. Diogenes
Laertius II.31; Plato, *Euthydemus* 281E. But here as a con-
clusion it serves as a reprise of the discussion in 3.3.
Cf. n. 9 above.

[120]The Greek text preserved in the extant Greek mss.
used by Praechter breaks off at this point. The longer
Latin ending which follows is based exclusively on Elichmann's rendering of an Arabic paraphrase, cf. Introduction,
p. 28 above. Generally, the Latin ending has not been
regarded as genuine. In more recent work on manuscripts
unknown to Praechter, however, C. E. Finch has found a
longer ending in Codex Vaticanus Latinus 4037, which has
strong similarities to *C.T.* 43.3. Finch thinks there must
have been a longer ending in the Greek original from which

both the Arabic and the Anonymous (Codex An; cf. Sigla)
borrowed. Cf. C. E. Finch, "The Translation of Cebes'
Tabula in Codex Vaticanus Latinus 4037," *TAPA* 85 (1954)
84-87. Cora Lutz concurs that some such hypothesis is
necessary to account for the similarity; cf. C. E. Lutz,
"The Salmasius-Elichmann Edition of the *Tabula* of Cebes,"
Harvard Library Bulletin 27 (1979) 165-71. For the text
of Cod. Vat. Lat. 4037 at this point, see the Supplemental
Notes *ad loc*. *C.T.* 43.3.

[121]Cf. Plato, *Philebus* 11D.

SUPPLEMENTARY NOTES TO THE TEXT
AND CRITICAL APPARATUS

2.1.1: οὖν. A's reading of οὖν is now supported by An,
which has *igitur*. Cf. Finch, "Codex Vaticanus Latinus 4037," 81.

2.1.2: πρὸς ἀλλήλους πολὺν χρόνον. To those mss. with the
variant reading πολὺν χρόνον πρὸς ἀλλήλους, add E.
Cf. Finch, "Codex Vat. Gr. 1823," 181 n. 17.

2.3.3: πολυχρονιώτατον. As Praechter's apparatus indicates, the text of A is mutilated at this point.
Scholars' assessment of what is still legible and of
A's original reading, however, is debated. Schweighäuser (1806, pp. 61-62) gives only πολὺ χρονίω, stating
that this is mutilated from πολυχρονιώτερον. The reading given by Müller in *De arte critica* (29, 59, 61) and
"Zur Kritik" (248) is πολυχρονιώτ...ος ων [*sic*]. Müller
was dependent here on H. Dulac's collation of A. Dulac
argued that the lacuna was too small to have contained
νεώτερος and suggested that the original reading of A
was πολυχρονιώτατος ὤν. Müller, however, in his 1884
article in the *Philologische Rundschau* states that he
himself has now seen codex A and is convinced that its
original reading was πολυχρονιώτερος ὤν. From a consideration of this reading and that of V (πολὺν χρόνον
νεώτερος ὤν), he decides that the reading of the archetype was what Sauppe had proposed in 1872: πολυχρόνιον
νεώτερος ὤν (cf. Praechter's apparatus). The textual
decision involves a basic choice between the speaker's
amazement at the man's advanced age and his amazement
for a great length of time (cf. also 2.1.2). In addition to Sauppe and Müller, those who prefer the latter
alternative include Drosihn, Jerram, and Parsons. In
favor of Praechter's understanding, however, is the
ultimate derivation of the text from Plato's *Theatetus*.
See n. 6 in the "Notes to Text and Translation."

3.1.9: καὶ πικροὶ καὶ ἀμαθεῖς. These words have occa-
sioned much debate among critics. As early as 1561
Wolf conjectured πονηροί for the πικροί of the mss.
Drosihn (3) printed καὶ πικροὶ καὶ ἀμαθεῖς in the
text but indicated in his apparatus that they were a
gloss to ἄφρονες. Krauss (30) followed Drosihn and
pointed to the resulting balance of φρόνιμοι-ἄφρονες
and εὐδαίμονες-κακοδαίμονες. Sauppe (774-75) agreed
with Drosihn that ἀμαθεῖς was a gloss to ἄφρονες but
argued that πικροί could not be. In its place he
conjectured μιαροί (cf. Praechter's apparatus). This
conjecture was regarded as certain by H. Grübler (*Revue
des études grecques* 7 [1894] 98). Jerram (26) retains
πικροί but understands it as equivalent to πικρόχολοι.
3.3.6-7: καθάπερ οἱ ἐπὶ τιμωρίᾳ παραδιδόμενοι. Drosihn's
deletion of these words is based on his view that this
is an anticipatory gloss introduced from 9.4. In this
he is followed by Jerram, Krauss, and Parsons.
4.1.4-6: Οὐκ...ἐστιν. E. N. O'Neil suggests that the οὐκ
here serves to introduce a question, so that a question
mark needs to be placed after the ἐστιν (4.1.6).
4.3.3-5: προστάττει...δεικνύει. Praechter in his apparatus gives either δείκνει δὲ or δεικύει δὲ as the reading of A. According to M. Schanz, however, the reading
of A is probably δεικνυσί (cf. Müller, "Zur Kritik,"
248). Müller (*De arte critica*, 61-62) and Krauss (6,
30) delete the verb entirely, making the following
words dependent on προστάττει (4.3.3).
5.1.5: ἤ. Müller (*De arte critica*, 18) supports Sauppe's
conjecture here by the suggestion that an original ἤ
was mistaken for an abbreviation of καί in the ms.
6.1.3: ἑτέρων. The reading ἑτέρων (AV[1]) is also printed
by Jerram (3, 48) and Parsons (24, 88), whereas Krauss
(30-31) changes it to ἑτέρας. The variant ἑταιρῶν
(printed by Drosihn) is considered by Sauppe (775) as
a gloss deriving from 9.1.3. Müller (*Phil. Rund.* 4

[1884] 1420-21) concurs in this judgment about ἑταιρῶν, yet he also rejects ἑτέρων as meaningless. Editors seem to have neglected the relevance of Dio Chrys., *Or.* 4.114, for deciding the textual problem here. Cf. n. 20 in the "Notes to the Text and Translation."

6.3.7: ὅποι ἂν τύχῃ. Praechter is incorrect in stating that ὅποι ἂν τύχωσι is Sauppe's conjecture. Sauppe mistakenly gives this as the reading of A and M.

7.1.1: τούτους. To Praechter's apparatus add the variant τοῦτο, after the reading *hoc* of Odaxius and An. This is probably the reading of the archetype of the CK(P) family (cf. Finch, "Odaxius," 28, and "Codex Vaticanus Latinus 4037," 83). The reading τοῦτο was preferred by Wolf and printed by Thieme (14) and others.

7.1.5: ἀλλὰ καὶ κωφή. As Praechter's apparatus indicates, there are primarily two ways in which editors have resolved the textual difficulty of 7.1.1-5. Praechter's solution is that of moving the ἀλλά from its location in the mss. after τυφλή and placing it after μαινομένη (cf. 7.1.4-5). The alternative solution is to leave 7.1.4-5 intact and delete the καὶ μαινομένη in 7.1.2. This solution, advocated by Drosihn, was followed by Jerram (48), Krauss (31), Parsons (89), and Müller ("Relieffragment," 118).

8.4.6: γινώμεθα. According to Schweighäuser (1806, p. 65), Drosihn (8), and Müller ("Zur Kritik," 248), the reading of A is γινόμεθα, not γινώμεθα.

9.2.6: αὐταῖς. The reading of An (*secum*) provides some support for Sauppe's emendation (cf. Finch, "Codex Vaticanus Latinus 4037," 82). The reading αὐταῖς is given by Praechter as unique to A. But according to Schweighäuser (1806, p. 65), Drosihn (8), and Müller ("Zur Kritik," 249), this is also the reading of M.

10.1.2: ἄνω. Both on p.vi and in the apparatus Praechter states that the word ἄνω is absent in V. This is incorrect. As Müller's collation indicates (*De arte critica*, 24) and as Finch ("Notes on Codex V," 240) confirms, ἄνω is present in V. The combined witness of AV all but eliminates the opinion of "P. C." that ἄνω should be deleted (cf. *Revue de philologie* 19 [1895] 96).

10.3.5: αὕτη. Schweighäuser (1806, p. 66) and Drosihn (10) give αὐτή as the reading of A whereas Müller (*De arte critica*, 25; *Phil. Rund.* 4 [1884] 1421) gives it as αὕτη. Sauppe (773) corrects it to αὕτη and this is probably the source of Praechter's reading. But see also Schweighäuser (1806, p. 66).

10.4.5: ἐπιτύχῃ. The conjecture of Johnson (ἐπιτύχῃ for ἀποτύχῃ) has been widely adopted. In support of it Müller (*De arte critica*, 67 n. 1) appeals to 9.4.7, where most manuscripts read ἀπολίπῃ rather than ἐπιλίπῃ.

10.4.6: ἐκ προαιρέσεως. Drosihn's (10) deletion of these words as a gloss may find some support from the fact that they do not appear in V (cf. Finch, "Notes on Codex V," 240). But προαίρεσις is not inappropriate in this context. See n. 40 in the "Notes to Text and Translation."

11.1.1: Εἶτα τί γίνεται, ἐάν. An alternative in punctuation is found in Gronovius and others. It involves ending the Senex's response with γίνεται and beginning the Senex's response with ἐάν (cf. 11.2.1-2). To the mss. which entirely omit the words of 11.1.1-2 through parablepsis involving συναντήσῃ, add S (cf. Finch, "Codex Vat. Gr. 1823," 177).

12.3.7: <Οὐκ> ἔστιν. See n. 45 to the "Notes to the Text and Translation."

14.1.3: [καὶ αἱ ἄλλαι αἱ μετ' αὐτῶν]. To Praechter's apparatus add the reading of O: *reliquas* (cf. Jerram, 49).

14.1.4: Αὗταί ἐκεῖναί εἰσιν. In support of Praechter's
text add the reading of O: *illae ipsae sunt* (cf.
Drosihn, 10). Cf., however, the criticism of "P. C."
(96).

14.2.2: Νὴ Δία. Odaxius omits the words from Νὴ Δία
(14.2.2) to νὴ Δία (14.3.2). This omission was explained by Müller (*De arte critica*, 72) as an over-
sight on the part of Odaxius or the typesetters. But
Finch shows that the omission is almost certainly
traceable to a gap in the Greek text used by Odaxius
(cf. "Odaxius," 27).

14.2.4-14.3.1: ἔφην. Μένει.... Both in the apparatus and
on p.x of his edition, Praechter incorrectly gives E
as reading ναὶ ἔφημεν. The reading of E is the same
as that of DW^1C^1: ναὶ ἔφη μέν. Cf. Finch, "Codex Vat.
Gr. 1823," 181 n. 17.

14.3.2: 'Απάτης, καὶ ἡ ἄγνοια μένει [ἐν τούτοις νὴ Δία].
As Praechter's apparatus indicates, the alternate punctuation of Drosihn is to end the Senex's response with
'Απάτης and to make καὶ ἡ ἄγνοια ἐν τούτοις the question of the interlocutor. In this way the Senex's response once again begins with Νὴ Δία (cf. 14.2.2;
28.1.2). This alternative is supported by Sauppe
(769-70), Krauss (11), and "P. C." (*Revue de phil*. 19
[1895] 96). The reservations of Boll (*Blätter für das
Gymnasial-Schulwesen* 31 [1895] 471) to Praechter's
text are based on the reading of the Arabic (cf.
apparatus).

14.4.3: ἄν. Sauppe (775) had conjectured δή for the ἄν
of the manuscripts. This conjecture is supported by
the reading of O: *tum demum ita* (cf. esp. Jerram, 49).

15.3.1-3: Οὐκοῦν...βαθεῖς. In view of "Cebes'" tendency
to use οὐκοῦν to introduce questions (cf., for example,
15.2.1 and 15.4.2), the punctuation here should probably be changed to a question mark.

18.1.4: ἀκαλλώπιστον. In preferring ἀκαλλώπιστον,
Praechter is following Drosihn (16), Krauss (12), and
Müller ("Relieffragment," 122). The appeal of this
solution is that it has the noun στολήν followed by
two adjectives, as is the case in 20.2. But the
reading of almost all the mss. is the noun καλλωπισμόν. The latter is printed by Schweighäuser (1806,
pp. 27, 69) and others, who understand a supplied
ἁπλοῦν (derived from the ἁπλῆν) as modifying the noun.
In this case there is a statement made about the sim-
plicity of both the garment and the adornment (cf.
Horace, *Carm*. I.5.5). Cf. n. 59 in the "Notes to
Text and Translation."

19.2.3: γενόμενος. The reading of C^1 is γενόμενος and
thus supports Praechter's text. Only C^2 has παραγενό-
μενος (cf. Finch, "Cod. Gr. 1823," 181 n. 18).

20.4.4: 'Αλλὰ ποσέξομεν, ἔφην ἔγωγε, ὡς μάλιστα. A print-
er's error has resulted in the omission of the ρ from
προσέξομεν in Praechter's text. At least two scholars
have expressed dissatisfaction with the final four
words of this line in Praechter's text. "P. C." (96)
proposes ἔφην, ὡς ἐγῷμαι, μάλιστα. Radermacher
("Varia," *Rheinisches Museum* 55 [1900] 149) conjectures
ἔφην, ὡς ἐγῷμ' ᾗ μάλιστα.

21.3.3: ἐλευθέρως. H. van Herwerden ("Ad Cebetis Tabulam,"
Mnemosyne II:22 [1894] 263) would emend the text to
read ἐλευθερίως. While Praechter himself considers
this emendation as "probably correct" (cf. his "Bericht
über die Literatur zu den nacharistotelischen Philosophen," in Bursian's *Jahresbericht über die Fortschritte der classischen Altertumswissenschaft* 26
[1898] 45), Boll (471 n. 1) considers this a superflu-
ous conjecture.

21.3.4: καλῷ. Praechter's apparatus incorrectly gives A
as the only manuscript containing καλῷ. According to
Finch ("Notes on Codex V," 241), ms. V also reads
καλῷ, not καλῶς.

22.2.4: καὶ κεκράτηκεν ἑαυτοῦ. H. van Herwerden (263) suggests the deletion of these words on the ground that they are supposedly inappropriate for the context. But neither Praechter ("Bericht," 45-46) nor Boll (471 n. 1) commend this proposal. Moreover, the words prepare for 23.2 and serve as a contrast to those in 24.2 who are subjugated (κατακεκρατημένοι) by vices.

23.2.3: ὥσπερ πρότερον. The best manuscript of the *Tabula*, codex A, breaks off at this point. For the remainder of the text we are dependent on less reliable manuscripts. See the "Introduction" (pp. 27-28) for a short discussion of the various manuscripts and attendant problems.

23.3.3: ἔφης...στεφανοῦν. E. N. O'Neil makes the attractive suggestion that ἐκείνην has been omitted because of the ἐκεῖνο in the preceding line. In this case the lacuna would be the result of a simple case of haplography. See n. 76 in the "Notes to Text and Translation."

24.2.3: ἐκεῖ. The manuscript support for this reading is, unfortunately, not as strong as Praechter's apparatus indicates. Codex V, cited erroneously by Praechter as evidence for ἐκεῖ, reads κακῶς. Only K reads ἐκεῖ, and since K is either a direct (Müller and Praechter) or an indirect (Finch) copy of C from a relatively late date, it is obvious that K introduced the ἐκεῖ in an attempt to relieve the redundancy (a twofold "live wretchedly") of the text it had received. It achieved this by substituting ἐκεῖ for the first κακῶς and omitting διατρίβουσι. Another attempt to relieve the redundancy is seen in codex M, where εἰκῇ is substituted for the second κακῶς. While the textual support for ἐκεῖ is thus extremely weak, its adoption does serve to bring the text of 24.2.3 into conformity with the οἱ ἐκεῖ διατρίβοντες of 25.3.2.

26.1.4: Κωρύκιον. To the list of mss. that have the correct spelling of "Corycian," delete F and add the
margin of Odaxius. Cf. Finch, "Odaxius," 27-28.

26.3.2: ἐχιοδεῖκται. See n. 82 in the "Notes to Text and
Translation."

26.3.5: οὕτω. Although most manuscripts read τοῦτο,
Praechter adopts the conjecture of οὕτω proposed by
Schweighäuser. This reading provides the appropriate
resolution of the comparison made above with καθάπερ.
It is supported by the readings of Odaxius (*ita*) and
An (*igitur*). Moreover, as Jerram (50) points out, the
manuscripts vary at 37.1.2 between οὕτω and τοῦτο. Cf.
also Finch, "Codex Vaticanus Latinus 4037," 82, and
"Odaxius," 28.

29.3.2: <οὐκ>. Praechter's insertion of οὐκ is criticized
by "P. C." (96).

31.1.2: νομίζειν. Sauppe's deletion (cf. apparatus) is
based partially on the erroneous assumption that ἔχειν
is the reading of all manuscripts. Sauppe was following Drosihn's edition at this point, and Drosihn mistakenly cites ἔχειν (31.1.2) as the reading of manuscripts B and D.

31.1.3: τις. The insertion of τις receives some support
from the *quis* contained in An. Cf. Finch, "Codex
Vaticanus Latinus 4037," 82.

31.2.2: πάλιν ταῦτα ἀφελέσθαι. Manuscript S may now be
added to VP as supporting this order. Cf. Finch,
"Codex Vat. Gr. 1823," 182.

31.2.4-5: ἴσους γίνεσθαι. In support of this reading,
Praechter in his dissertation (*C.T. quanam aetate*,
48-49) cites Diogenes Laertius VII.117, Tel. apud Stob
Flor. p. 125, 17 Meincke, and other passages. He thus
rejects the contention of Müller (*De arte critica*, 56;
Phil. Rund. 4 [1884] 1421-22) that the words are a
gloss deriving from V. Also, Praechter fails to cite
a conjecture by Wolf that has been accepted by many

editors. This is ἀηττήτους γίνεσθαι ("become invinc-
ible"), emended from ἥττους/ἥττω. Cf. Plato, *Repub.*
II.15 (375B) and Epictetus, I.18.21.

31.2.5: καί. The retention of καί in the text receives
additional support from the *additque* in An (cf. Finch,
"Codex Vaticanus Latinus 4037," 81). Nevertheless,
Finch is correct in arguing that it should be deleted
and the sentence punctuated with a dash after γίνεσθαι.
Thus the reading should be ...ἴσους γίνεσθαι--μήτε
χαίρειν.... Cf. Finch, "Codex Vat. Gr. 1823," 184.

31.6.2: βλέποντας. Finch explains the reading of P in the
following manner. The scribe of S wrote π for β when
transcribing and thus produced πλέποντας. The scribe
of P naturally failed to make any sense of this and
thus left blank spaces for three letters (= the three
stars of Praechter's apparatus) and wrote only ποντας
(cf. Finch, "Codex Vat. Gr. 1823," 178). The variant
ἔχοντα (or ἔχοντας), supported also by Odaxius' *accep-
tis*, is sometimes preferred (in the sense "with it").
Compare 31.6 and 32.4.

32.4.1: αὐτοῦ. Most of the mss. read αὐτοῖς, whereas
Praechter adopts the conjecture of Sauppe. The latter's conjecture of αὐτοῦ in place of αὐτοῖς was based
primarily on the observation that κελεύειν takes an
accusative object in 16.4.4-5 and 33.2.1. One would
thus expect the accusative rather than the dative here
in 32.4.1 as well. Sauppe's conjecture is supported
by both O (*ibi*) and An (*ubi*). Cf. Finch, "Odaxius," 28.

33.4.4: συντομωτέρως. The only ms. that has this reading
is V. Since S may now be added to the list of those
with συντομώτερον, this is the reading that should be
adopted (so Finch, "Codex Vat. Gr. 1823," 184).

33.5.1: ἄρα, ἔφην. Add S to those mss. that support
Praechter's text. Cf. Finch, "Codex Vat. Gr. 1823,"
182.

33.6.3-4: οὐκ ἄχρηστον ἦν...ἄν τι συνήκαμεν. See the discussion of the mss. by Jerram (51), who notes that

εἰδέναι looks suspiciously like a gloss to explain
ἔχειν (cf. the apparatus). In fact, the text printed
by Praechter seems to rest on and represent a confla-
tion of two very similar text traditions. Compare,
for example, the readings of mss. C and V. Praechter
apparatus, moreover, may be supplemented as follows:
(1) the reading of P (αὐτήν) is to be understood in
relation to the reading of S (αὐτόν); cf. Finch,
"Codex Vat. Gr. 1823," 179; (2) for Sauppe's conjecture of ἄν before ἦν, compare An (*esset*); (3) for the
reading of C (αὐτούς), compare An (*ipsos*); (4) for th
reading of C (ἀκριβέστερον ἔχειν ἄν τι συνήκαμεν),
compare An (*vocem diligentiorem habere si quid per-
ceperimus*). Cf. Finch, "Codex Vaticanus Latinus 403'
81-82.

33.6.4: οὕτω. The variant οὕτως must now be taken with
greater seriousness since this is also the reading of
S. Cf. Finch, "Codex Vat. Gr. 1823," 182.

33.6.5: κωλύει. To the mss. that have this reading add V
and An (*prohibet*). Cf. Finch, "Notes on Codex V,"
241, and "Codex Vaticanus Latinus 4037," 82.

33.6.5-6: <βελτίους> γενέσθαι.... See n. 100 in the "Note
to Text and Translation."

35.2.5: παραλλάττουσιν. After παραλλάττουσιν, An gives t
following addition: *Iu<venis>: Quos mathematicos stul
tos intelligis? Se<nex>: Non esset breve admodum opu
quales sint dicere. Tamen, ut rem breviter perstring
paucis accipe: qui infinita serie numerorum eademque
non necessaria in rebus haud laude dignis nimium oper
ponunt; qui terre, maris, celique dimensionibus infin
ta prope modum mendacia quotidie cudunt, astra metiri
conantes cum ipsi se ipsos quales sint in terris pror
sus ignorent; qui aurium pruritus secuti ac mollis sc
vocis delectati virilem illam atque valentem animi
beneformati harmoniam depravarunt, corruperunt, effe-
minarunt, idque non inscitia minus ex qua mala omnia*

ferme oriuntur quam huius temporis infelicis ac miseri corruptis moribus; qui denique ventoso cerebro syderum planetarumque influxibus humane vite cursum referunt effectusque subiiciunt. Cf. Finch, "Codex Vaticanus Latinus 4037," 82-83, who also refers to Xenophon, *Memorabilia* IV.7.5 in connection with the preceding addition.

35.2.6: εἰ ἀκινητότεροι. The combination εἰ ἀκινητότεροι is found only in R and S, but it is preferred also by Finch (cf. "Codex Vat. Gr. 1823," 183).

35.3.2-3: περιβόλῳ......, <οἱ δ' ἐν τῷ δευτέρῳ περιβόλῳ,>. See n. 104 in the "Notes to Text and Translation."

35.5.3-4: οὕτω ποιεῖτε...ἕξιν λάβητε. Praechter's reading of οὕτω ποιεῖτε is an alteration (following Wolf) of the received Greek text. Some support for this solution is provided by the versions (cf. apparatus). A second solution to the textual problems is offered by K. K. Müller. In his view, there is a lacuna in the text following ἕξιν, which he supplies in the following way: ἕξιν <λάβητε, σωθήσεσθε. οὐκ εἰσάπαξ δὲ ἐστιν ἕξιν> λαβεῖν. Cf. *Phil. Rund.* 4 (1884) 1419. A third possible solution involves the assumption of an ellipsis in the author's text/thought. The text may be understood as follows: καὶ ὑμεῖς τοίνυν <οὐκ ἂν ποτε σωθεῖτε>, ὦ ξένοι, ἔφη, ἐὰν (μὴ) οὕτω ποιῆτε καὶ ἐνδιατρίβητε τοῖς λεγομένοις, μέχρι ἂν ἕξιν λάβητε (cf. 35.5.2).

36.1.4: τὸ τέκνα ἔχειν. For a discussion of the reading of V at this point, cf. Finch, "Codex Vat. Gr. 1823," 183.

37.3.2: τοῖς ζῶσι καλῶς κακὸν ἂν. See n. 112 in the "Notes to Text and Translation" for the insertion of καὶ in the text before τοῖς ζῶσι. In support of καλῶς, one may now add S^2 (cf. Finch, "Codex Vat. Gr. 1823," 177). Both here with ἂν and in 35.2.1 with ὅτε, Praechter credits Sauppe with these proposals. But Porson had

already proposed these same emendations in 1815. Cf.
Jerram (49, 52) and Müller (*De arte critica*, 55 n. 1)

37.3.4: μοι δοκεῖς. On the basis of S's variant (δοκοῖς
μοι) Finch inclines toward the order δοκεῖς μοι. Cf.
Finch, "Codex Vat. Gr. 1823," 184-85.

38.1.5: οὐκοῦν. In "Codex Vat. Gr. 1823" (176), Finch
states that S breaks off after the οὐκοῦν of 38.1.5.
This is incorrect, for the text actually breaks off
after the οὐκοῦν of 38.3.1. We are grateful to Professor Finch for supplying us with this corrected information in a private letter of 21 November 1979.

39.2.3: Οὐ. Müller (*De arte critica*, 41) emends οὐ to
οὔτως. Jerram (21, 52) follows this suggestion, but
he prints οὔτω.

39.3.4: ἐκ τούτου ἄρα τοῦ λόγου. Sauppe (cf. apparatus)
is not the first to attribute these words to the Senex
Gronovius (81), for example, had already chosen this
option. Schweighäuser (1806, p. 53), however, attributed these words to the interlocutor and many prefer
this alternative. 35.1.1 and 41.1.4 would confirm
this attribution were it not for the fact that ἄρα is
absent in both these instances. But as Müller (*De
arte critica*, 50-51, and *Phil. Rund.* 4 [1884] 1422)
points out, ἄρα does not have a fixed position in all
the manuscripts. V, our best manuscript for this section of the *Tabula*, has the ἄρα before the ἐκ. Müller
makes the very plausible suggestion that ἄρα was omitted by a scribe and then reinserted at a different and
incorrect point in the manuscript. Given the uncertainty concerning the original position of ἄρα, he
would prefer to delete it and print Εἰκός γε ἐκ τούτου
τοῦ λόγου as the response of the interlocutor. To
have the Senex's response begin with οὐδέ would be
striking but not unusual (cf. 39.4.1). Perhaps the
original place of the ἄρα was at some point after the
οὐδέ and before the εἴπερ (compare 35.2.6: ἄρα εἰ).

But, given the use of ἄρα in the Hellenistic period, it could just as easily have begun the Senex's response (cf. LSJ, 233).

39.4.1: ἐπίστωνται. Schweighäuser (1806, p. 79) had already conjectured this reading before codex V was discovered.

40.2.2: ἄγνοιαν. Manuscripts C and K break off at this point. The Latin codex An, which is a translation of a Greek ms. of the CK(P) family, has a short ending appended here. Finch has suggested that there is a great deal of similarity between the ending of An and that of the Arabic in Elichmann's Latin at 43.3.3-43.4.3. The text of the ending of An is given in the note to 43.3.3.

41.3.3: ἅμα. Schweighäuser's conjecture of ἅμα receives some support from the reading of Odaxius: *multa cum pravitate*. Cf. Jerram, 52, and Finch, "Odaxius," 28.

43.3.3-43.4.3: *Itaque...discedat*. The Latin ms. An gives (at 40.2.2 sqq.) a conclusion which, according to Finch, is similar in content to the conclusion found in Elichmann's translation of the Arabic paraphrase and printed here by Praechter. The text of An reads as follows: *Quod ut tandem vos assequamini, studiosi iuvenes, cunctis viribus contendite eo animo ac mente, ut nihil unquam virtute potius, nihil excellentius, nihil homine libero dignius, nihil denique beatius esse putetis. Valete*. Finch sees in this similarity evidence for a longer ending in the Greek text tradition from which An derives. Cf. Finch, "Codex Vaticanus Latinus 4037," 84-87. Cf. also n. 120 in the "Notes to Text and Translation."

INDEX VERBORUM

*ἀβέβαιος
   -ως 7.2

ἀγαθός 3.3(bis); 8.2,3,4; 25.2(bis); 28.2,3(bis); 34.2;
     36.1,3(bis),4(bis); 37.1; 38.1; 39.3,4; 40.1,2(bis);
     41.1(bis),3(bis)
   βελτίων 33.4,5(bis),<6>; 34.1,4; 35.4; 39.3
   *βέλτιστος 6.3

ἀγανακτέω
   ἀγανακτοῦσι 31.4

ἄγε v. ἄγω

ἀγνοέω
   ἀγνοοῦσι 40.2

ἄγνοια 5.3; 14.3   -αν 6.3; 14.4; 19.5; 25.2; 40.2
   "Αγνοια -αν 23.1   -αι 27.4

ἄγω
   ἄγουσι 21.1; 24.2   ἄγονται 24.2
   ἀγάγωσι 29.2
   ἄγουσα 12.3; 15.3   -αν 11.1   ἄξουσαν 11.2
     -ουσαι 6.3; 29.4   ἀγαγοῦσαι 29.2
   ἄγε 36.2; 39.1

ἀγών   -ας 22.1(bis)

ἀδελφή 10.3   -αί 16.2; 20.3

ἀδικέω
   -εῖν 41.2

ἄδικος 34.3

*'Αδοξία   -αι 27.4

ἀδύνατος 37.1

ἀεί 37.1

*ἄθλιος 28.2
   -ως 24.2; 27.3; 39.1

ἀθυμέω
    ἀθυμοῦσιν 8.1
    ἀθυμεῖν 31.2

'Αθυμία 10.3   -αι 27.4

αἴνιγμα   -ματι 3.2

*αἰνίττομαι
    αἰνίττεται 3.3

αἱρετός 37.1; 38.3

αἰσθάνομαι
    αἰσθάνεται 9.3

αἰσχρός 10.1,3; 40.1,3

αἰτέω
    αἰτοῦσι 8.1

αἰτία   -αν 31.2

αἰτιάομαι
    αἰτιῶνται 28.2

αἴτιος 35.1

*ἀκαλλώπιστος 18.1

ἀκίνητος 35.2,3

ἀκολουθέω
    ἀκολουθεῖν 28.1   ἀκολουθοῦσαι 27.4

ἀκούω
    -ετε 20.4; 35.5   ἠκηκόειν 2.3
    ἀκοῦσαι 3.1(bis); 23.1

ἀκρασία   -αν 19.5; 28.3
    'Ακρασία 9.1; 32.3   -ας 24.2; 26.2; 35.2
        -αν 14.1; 23.2; 28.1

ἀκρατής 34.3

ἀκριβής 33.6
    -ῶς 25.2

*ἀκρόπολις 21.2

ἀλαζονεία   -αν 19.5
    'Αλαζονεία   -ας 24.2

'Αλήθεια 18.2

ἀληθής   32.2; 37.3; 38.4; 39.5

ἀληθινός   6.3; 11.1,2; 12.3(bis); 13.1; 14.3; 15.1,3;
    16.5; 32.4; 33.4; 35.1,2,3

ἀλλά   1.2; 2.2; 3.1,3; 4.1; 5.2; 6.1,3; 8.1; 9.3; 12.3;
    15.1,2; 16.1; 17.2; 18.1; 19.1,2; 20.3,4; 23.3,4;
    24.3; 25.2; 28.2; 29.3; 30.1; 31.3; 33.2; 35.1,4,5;
    36.3(bis); 37.2(bis); 38.1(bis),4; 39.3; 41.3
    ἀλλ' ἔτι   27.1
    ἀλλ' οὐδέ   41.2
    ἀλλὰ καί   7.1; 25.1; 31.5

ἀλλήλων   2.1

ἄλλος   1.1; 7.2; 8.4; 9.1; 10.3(bis); 12.1,3; 13.2; [14.1];
    18.2; 20.1,2,3; 22.1; 25.3; 26.2,3; 29.4(bis); 33.3;
    34.1,2; 35.2,3,5; 40.3

*ἄλσος   -ους 17.1

ἅμα (adv.)   41.2,3
    ἅμα δὲ καί   11.1

ἀμαθής   3.1

ἀμελέω
    ἀμέλει   34.4; 37.2

ἀμεταμέλητος   32.2

ἀμφιέννυμι
    ἠμφιεσμέναι   10.1

ἀμφότερος   38.1

ἄν   4.1,3; 6.3; 9.1,3; 14.3,4; 18.4; 19.2(ter),3; 26.1(bis);
    28.3; 31.1,3; 32.3,4; 33.6; 35.3,5(bis); 36.2; 37.1,
    2,3; 38.1,2; 39.4; 41.3

ἄν = ἐάν   10.4

ἀναβαίνω
    -ουσι 16.4
    ἀναβεβηκότες   27.3

*ἀνάβασις   15.3

ἀναγγέλλω
    -ουσιν 29.2

ἀναγκάζω
    -εται 9.4

ἀνάγκη   33.4(bis); 35.3; 41.1

ἀνάθημα   2.2   -ματα 1.1

ἀνακάμπτω
   ἀνακάμπτουσι   27.3(bis); 29.2,4(bis)
   ἀνακάμπτοντες   13.1

ἀνάκειμαι
   -ειτο 1.1

ἀναλαμβάνω
   -λαβών 4.2

ἀνάληψις   -ιν 19.2

ἀναλίσκω
   -λώσῃ 9.4

ἀνανήφω
   ἀνανήψῃ   9.3

*ἀνάπαλιν   3.4

ἀναπηδάω
   ἀναπηδῶσι   6.2; 9.2

*ἀναπίμπλημι
   ἀνεπλήσθη   19.5

ἀνατίθημι
   ἀνέθηκε   2.2

'Ανδρεία   20.3

ἀνδρεῖος
   -ως   38.2

*ἀνδροφονέω
   -εῖν 40.3

ἄνευ   33.5,6

ἀνήρ   2.2   ἄνδρα   2.3   -ῶν 12.3   -ας 33.5; 34.4

ἄνθρωπος   -ον 9.3   -οι 13.1; 36.1   -ων [8.1]; 31.4;
     34.1   -οις 3.2(bis); 8.3   -ους 5.2; 40.1

ἀνοδία   -ας 15.2   -ίᾳ 27.3

*ἀντιφάρμακον   26.3(bis)

*ἄντρον   26.1

ἄνω   4.3; 9.1; 10.1; 15.1,4; 16.4

ἀξιόω
  -οῦσι 9.2

ἀπάγω
  -ουσι 6.2(bis)   ἀπήγαγον 29.2

ἀπαιτέω
  -τῶνται 31.4

ἀπαλλάττω
  -τεσθαι 32.3

ἅπας   23.2; 26.3

ἀπατάω
  -τῶνται 35.4
  ἠπατημένοι 13.1; 34.2

ἀπάτη   -την 6.2
  'Απάτη 5.2   -της 6.3; 14.3; 19.5

ἄπειμι
  ἀπιέναι 32.4

*ἀπερίεργος
  -γως 21.3

ἀπέρχομαι
  ἀπέλθῃ 14.3
  ἀπελθεῖν 31.6

*ἀπίθανος 37.2
  -νως 37.1

ἄπιστος 36.2

*ἄπλαστος 20.2

*'Απληστία 9.1

ἁπλοῦς 18.1; 20.2

ἀπό   14.3; 16.4; 22.2; 27.1; 35.2

ἀποβάλλω
  -βάλλοντες 8.3

ἀπογινώσκω
  ἀπογνόντες 14.3   ἀπεγνωσμένοι 27.3

*ἀποδειλιάω
  -δειλιᾶν 16.3
  -δεδειλιακότες 27.3

ἀποθνήσκω
   ἀπέθνησκεν 3.3
   ἀποθανεῖν 38.2(bis); 38.3(bis)

*ἀπόκρημνος 15.4

ἀποκρίνω
   -κρίνασθαι 36.2

ἀπολαμβάνω
   ἀπειληφώς 25.3

ἀπόλαυσις   -σιν 28.3

*ἀπολαύω
   -ουσι 28.2

ἀπολείπω
   -λιπόντες 28.2

ἀπόλλυμι
   -λυται 3.3,4; 32.5   ἀπώλετο 3.2
   -λυσθαι 6.2

ἀπολύω
   -λυθήσονται 14.4

*ἄπονος 9.2

ἀπορέω
   -ρῶ 25.1
   -οῦντες 2.1   -ούντων 2.1

ἀπορρίπτω
   ἀπέρριψεν 22.2

ἀποστέλλω
   -στέλλει 20.1

ἀποστερέω
   -ρεῖν 9.4; 40.3

*ἀπροβούλευτος 8.1

ἀπωθέω
   ἀπωσθείς 19.3

ἄρα 33.5; 35.2; 36.4; 39.3,4

ἀργύριον 31.4

Ἀρετή   -ταί 17.3; 22.1; 24.2; 25.1   -τάς 19.1; 20.1;
    29.2,3

*ἀριθμητικός   13.2

ἁρπάζω
   -ζει   7.2

ἀρρωστέω
   -τοῦσιν   38.1

ἄρτι   30.3

ἀσεβής   40.1

ἄσμενος
   -ως   26.1

*ἀστεφάνωτος   27.1,3

*ἀστρολόγος   -οι   13.2

ἀσφάλεια   26.1   -ας   26.1

ἀσφαλής   7.3; 18.3(bis); 31.1,6; 32.2
   -ῶς   18.1

ἀσχημονέω
   -εῖν   9.4

*ἀσχολία   3.1

ἀσωτία   -αν   28.3
   ᾿Ασωτία   9.1

ἀτιμάζω
   -ζειν   40.1

*ἀτρύφερος   20.2

*αὖθις
      αὖθις δέ   31.5
      καὶ αὖθις   8.4

αὐτός   3.4; 22.1; 25.3; 38.4   αὐτό (nom./acc.) 3.2; 37.1
      (bis); 37.2(ter); 38.1
   αὐτοῦ   2.3; 10.3(bis)   αὐτῆς   3.3; 7.2,3; 8.2; 9.3;
      11.2; 14.3; 27.2; 31.1,2,5,6; 32.4
   αὐτῷ   10.3,4; 11.1(bis); 24.2; 25.1; 26.1; 37.2(bis);
      41.2   αὐτῇ   7.3
   αὐτόν   2.3(bis); 11.1,2; 19.2,4(bis); 20.1; 21.1;
      22.1,2; 23.3; 24.2; 26.1,3; 39.3   αὐτήν   8.1,2(bis);
      18.3; 31.2
   αὐτοί   39.2   αὐταί   14.1
   αὐτῶν   7.2; 8.1(bis),2; 9.3; 10.1; 14.[1],3; 26.2;
      27.1,4; 35.5

αὐτοῖς   8.2,3; 9.2,4; 16.5; 28.1; 37.3   αὐταῖς   10.3;
    28.2(bis)
αὐτούς   4.3(bis); 6.2; 14.4; 16.3,4(bis),5; 26.3;
    29.3; 33.2,6; 35.2,3,4   αὐτάς   16.4   αὐτά   32.5;
    40.1

αὐτοῦ (adv.)   32.4

*αὐτοῦ   1.2; 9.2; 16.4; 23.4
    v. ἑαυτοῦ

ἀφαιρέω
    -εῖται   7.2   ἀφείλετο   8.2
    ἀφέληται   31.2
    ἀφελέσθαι   31.2,5(bis)

ἀφικνέομαι
    ἀφίκετο   2.2
    ἀφίκηται   26.1   -ωνται   32.3
    ἀφικέσθαι   24.3
    ἀφικνουμένοις   18.3

ἀφοβία   18.4

*ἀφρονέω
    ἀφρονεῖν   41.2,3

ἀφροσύνη   3.2,4; 14.3

ἄφρων   3.1; 34.3

ἄχρηστος   33.5,6

βαδίζω
    -ζει   24.1; 26.1
    -ζειν   4.3; 5.1
    -ζοντας   28.2

βαθύς   15.3

βασιλεία   -αι 8.4

βέβαιος   7.3; 18.3; 31.1,6; 32.2

*βέλτιστος   v. ἀγαθός

βελτίων   v. ἀγαθός

βίος   -ου 24.3   -ῳ 3.3(bis),4; 11.2; 18.4; 24.2
    -ον 2.2; 6.3; 9.2; 10.4; 28.2
    Βίος   4.2   -ῳ 4.3; 6.3   -ον 4.2,3; 5.2,3; 30.1

βιόω
    βιώσεται   26.1; 39.5
    βιώσεσθε   3.1

βλαβερός   9.4; 37.1

βλάπτω
    βλάπτον   40.1

βλέπω
    βλέποντας   31.6

βοηθέω
    -θεῖ   39.2,3

*βόσκημα   -μάτων 28.3

βούλομαι
    -λεται 8.1
    -ληται 26.1   -λωνται 12.3; 32.4
    -λοιο 38.2

βουνός   15.3   -νοῦ 15.4; 27.1

βραχύς   16.3

γάρ   3.1,2(bis); 7.3; 9.3; 16.4; 17.3; 23.1,4; 24.3;
      26.1(bis),3(bis); 28.3; 30.2; 31.2(ter); 33.1,6(bis);
      34.<2>,3; 36.2; 39.2; 40.2
    γάρ καί   2.3; 14.3; 33.5; 37.1
    γάρ οὐ   38.4
    καί γάρ   31.4
    οὐ γάρ   19.2; 29.3
    οὐδὲ γάρ   2.1,2
    οὔτε γάρ   1.2

*γαργαλίζω
    -λίζῃ 9.3

γέ   35.3; 39.1,3; 41.2
    εἴγε   39.1
    καί...γέ   2.3; 6.3; 14.3; 15.4; 23.1
    μέντοι γέ   33.6

γελάω
    -λᾶν 8.2   -ῶσαι 29.1

γεμίζω
    -ονται 29.4

γέρων   1.3; 4.3

*γεωμέτρης   -τραι 13.2

γίνομαι
   γίνεται   3.4; 11.1,2(bis); 23.4; 40.2; 41.1(bis)
     γίνονται   7.3   γεγόνασιν   29.2
   γινώμεθα   8.4
   γίνεσθαι   31.2,3   γένεσθαι   33.4,5(bis),6; 34.1,4
   γενόμενος   19.2   -νοι 3.1

γινώσκω
   -εις 2.3
   γνῷ   3.4

γόνυ   -ασιν 10.2

γοῦν   31.6

γράμμα
   -ματα 33.3; 34.3

γραφή   1.1   -φῆς 2.1   -φήν 2.2; 4.2

γράφω
   γεγραμμένον   1.2

γυμνός   10.3

γυνή   5.1; 7.1; 12.2; 18.1; 21.3   γυναῖκα   30.3
   -κες 10.1; 14.1; 27.4; 29.1   -κῶν 1.3; 6.1; 20.2;
   27.2   -ξί 9.4   -κας 9.1; 16.1; 26.2; 32.3

δαιμόνιος   -νιε 6.2
   Δαιμόνιον   30.1; 31.3,5; 32.5; 33.2   -ου 24.3

Δαίμων   4.3

δέ   1.1,2(ter),3(bis); [2.3]; 3.1,2(bis),3,4(bis);
   4.3(ter); 5.3; 6.1(bis),2(bis),3; 7.1(bis),2;
   8.1(ter),2(ter),3,4; 9.1(ter); 10.1,2(bis),3(ter);
   11.1,2; 12.1,3; 13.1,2(novies); 14.1,2,4; 16.2(bis)
   18.1(ter),2(bis),3,4; 19.3; 20.3; 21.1(bis); 24.1,
   2(quater),3; 25.3; 27.2,3(bis),4; 28.1,3; 29.1;
   31.4,5; 33.1,4(bis),5; 34.3; 35.3,<3>,5(ter);
   36.1,4; 37.3; 39.1,5; 40.1(bis),2(bis); 41.1,2,3(bi

δεῖ   3.1; 4.2,3(bis); 16.3; 33.1; 35.5

δεικνύω
   -νύει 4.3   -νύουσιν 16.5; 24.2; 25.1
   -νύων 4.3

δεινός   2.1,2; 18.4; 24.3; 31.4

δεῦρο   2.2

δεύτερος   35.1,<3>

δέω
   δέδενται   24.3

δή   25.2; 39.1
   μὲν δή   30.1; 33.1
   τότε δὴ καί   2.3

δηλονότι   8.4

δηλόω
   δεδήλωκας   30.1

δήπου   19.2,3; 26.3

διά   prep. c. gen. 15.2; 24.3; 33.6; 40.1
   prep. c. acc. 6.2,3; 24.3; 25.1,2; 26.3(bis); 31.2,3;
      35.4; 40.2

*διάκειμαι
   διακείμενοι   27.3; 35.5

 διαλέγω
   διελέγετο   2.3
   διαλέγεσθαι   8.4

 διαλείπω
   -πειν   35.5

*διαλεκτικός   13.2

*διαναπαύω
   -σασθαι   16.4

 διασῴζω
   διασωθῶσιν   32.1

*διατριβή   9.3

 διατρίβω
   -βουσι   17.3; 24.2; 35.1
   -βοντες 25.3   -βοντας 24.2

 δίδωμι
   -σι 7.2(bis); 8.3; 18.4; 31.6   -δασι 16.5
      δέδωκε   7.2; 8.2; 31.5(bis)
   διδῷ   31.2
   δοῦναι   31.2,5
   διδομένων   18.3

*διέξειμι
   -ιόντος 2.3

διηγέομαι
  διήγησαι   3.1
  διηγούμενος   4.1

*δικαιοπραγέω
  -πραγεῖν 41.2

Δικαιοσύνη   20.3

διό
  διό καί   7.2; 9.4; 25.3; 30.2

*διοχλέω
  -ληθήσεται 26.2

δοκέω
  -εῖς 25.1; 27.1; 30.1; 37.3; 39.5; 41.4   -εῖ 8.3; 9.3;
    12.2; 15.1,3; 17.1; 23.1; 30.3; 33.2; 36.2,3,4;
    37.2; 39.4   -οῦσι 8.1; 10.1; 20.2; 27.1
    ἐδόκει   1.2,3
  δοκοῦσα 7.1   -ούσης 15.2   -οῦντα 40.1
  -οῦντες 8.2(bis); 27.1   -οῦσαι 14.1; 18.2

δόξα
  opinio 14.3   -αν 35.3   -ας 14.4
  Δόξα   -αν 11.1,2; 29.3   -αι 6.2; 14.2; 29.2; 35.4
  bona fama 8.4   -αν 41.3

δόσις 7.3; 18.3; 32.2   -ιν 31.5,6   -εις 31.2

δουλεύω
  -ουσι 22.2
  -ειν 9.4

δοῦλος   -ον 22.2

δύναμαι
  -ται 2.1; 41.2   -ανται 24.3   ἠδυνάμεθα 1.1
  -ασθαι 24.3

δύναμις 23.3   -μει 5.2; 19.4; 22.1; 23.4   -μιν 19.1;
    33.3   -μεις 14.3

δύο 1.2; 16.1; 18.2

*δυσειδής 10.3

δυσμαθής 35.2

δῶρον   δῶρα 19.1

ἐάν 3.3,4; 9.3; 11.1,2; 20.4; 35.4; 36.3; 40.1
    v. ἄν and ἤν

ἑαυτοῦ   5.2; 10.2; 19.4; 22.1,2(bis); 24.3; 28.2

ἐγγίζω
   -οντες 35.1

ʼΕγκράτεια   16.2; 20.3

ἐγώ   33.1
   ἔφην ἐγώ   2.3; 3.1(bis); 5.1; 7.3; 12.1,2; 17.3;
      19.2,3; 22.1; 23.1,3; 29.3; 30.2; 32.1; 33.2;
      35.1,3; 36.3(bis)
   ἔγωγε   20.4(bis); 36.4; 38.2
   ἐμοί   27.1; 37.2   μοί   23.3; 25.1; 27.1; 30.1;
      36.3,4; 37.3; 39.4,5; 41.4
   ἡμῶν   2.1; 4.1   ἡμῖν   1.2(bis); 3.1; 30.1; 33.1; 36.2
      ἡμᾶς   4.1; 33.6

ἔθω   v. εἴωθα

εἰ   4.1,3; 19.2; 33.4; 35.2,3; 37.2,3
   εἰ δέ   33.1
   εἰ δὲ μή   3.1,2; 11.2; 19.3; 35.5; 39.5
   εἰ μέν   3.1; 39.5
   εἰ μὲν οὖν   3.2
   εἰ μή   3.1
   εἴπερ   36.3; 38.3; 39.3
   εἰ τοίνυν   38.2; 41.1

*εἴγε   v. γέ

εἶδον
   ἰδεῖν   34.4; 35.2; 39.1; 40.3

*εἶεν   17.3

*εἰκαῖος   12.3

εἰκῆ   6.3; 7.2; 31.3

εἰκός   41.1
   εἰκὸς γέ   39.3

εἰμί
   ἐστί   2.2; 3.1,2,3; 4.1; 5.2,3; 6.3; 7.1,3; 8.3(bis);
      9.4; 10.1,3(bis); 12.1; 15.1,3; 18.1,2,3,4(bis);
      21.1(bis),2,3; 26.3; 32.1,5; 33.1,2,4,5; 35.1;
      36.3(bis); 37.2,3(bis); 38.1,3(bis); 39.3; 40.1
   ἔστι   3.2; 4.1; 7.1; 8.4; 12.3(ter); 16.5; 17.2; 26.1;
      36.1,2; 38.1,2,3; 40.3
   ἔστι   c. inf. 33.5; 34.4; 35.2; 39.1(bis); 40.1,3; 41.2
   ἐσμέν   20.4   εἰσί   4.2; 8.2(bis); 13.1,2; 14.1(bis);
      16.2; 18.2; 20.2; 27.1,2,4; 28.2; 35.2,4; 39.2
      ἦν   1.1,2(bis); 33.6; 37.3   ἦσαν   1.1   ἔσται   35.5
      ἔσεσθε   3.1

ἦ   38.4
εἴη   37.1; 38.1; 41.3
ἔστω   8.4
εἶναι   1.2; 7.1; 8.3; 9.3; 12.2; 14.1; 15.1,2,3;
    17.1,3; 18.2; 20.2; 25.2; 26.2; 28.3(bis); 30.3;
    31.1,4; 33.2,5; 34.3; 35.3; 36.4(bis); 37.1,2;
    38.1; 39.3(bis),4; 40.1(bis); 41.1
    ὤν   2.3   οὖσα   3.1   ὄντα   25.2(bis); 40.1

εἴπερ   v. εἰ

εἶπον
    εἶπον   30.3; 32.3   εἶπε   5.1
    εἴποι   28.3
    εἰπέ   23.3; 27.1

εἰς   4.1,2,3; 5.2,3; 6.2(bis),3; 9.3; 10.4(bis); 11.1(bis),
    2; 12.3; 14.3; 16.3; 19.2; 28.1; 30.1; 33.3; 34.4;
    35.2; 39.2,3

εἰσάγω
    -άγει   19.1

*εἰσάπαξ   3.3

εἴσειμι
    εἰσιόντι   1.3

εἰσέρχομαι
    εἰσέλθωσιν   4.3; 14.3
    εἰσελθεῖν   9.3
    εἰσελθόντας   29.2

εἴσοδος   [-δου 1.3]   -δον 12.2

εἰσπορεύω
    -εται 5.1   -ονται 14.2; 29.3; 35.4
    -ηται 6.2
    -εσθαι 4.2; 29.3
    -ομένοις 4.3; 30.1   -ομένους 5.2; 6.3

*εἴσω   29.3

εἶτα   5.2,3; 6.2; 7.3; 9.2,3; 10.4; 11.1,2; 14.4; 16.3,4;
    19.1,2; 23.2; 29.4; 32.4; 35.4

εἴωθα
    εἴωθε   31.2
    εἰώθασι   9.1

ἐκ (ἐξ)   10.4; 11.1; 24.3; 35.1,2,4; 39.3; 40.2,3(ter);
    41.1(ter),2(bis)

ἕκαστος (subst.)   8.1   -ου 33.1   -ον 6.2

ἐκβάλλω
    ἐξέβαλλε 19.2
    ἐκβάλῃ 19.4   ἐκβάλωσι   14.4

ἐκεῖ   24.2; 25.2,3; 32.1

ἐκεῖθεν   27.1; 29.1

ἐκεῖνος 18.4   -η 3.2; 7.1   -ου 17.1   -ῳ 36.3
        -ον 12.1; 15.1; 24.2; 25.1   -ην 21.2; 30.3
        -ο 21.2; 23.3; 30.1   -οι 31.4   -αι 14.1(bis)
        -α (nom./acc.) 22.2; 33.5   -ων 35.4   -οις 22.2
        -ους 26.3   -ας 26.2; 32.3

ἐκεῖσε   28.2

ἐκκαθαίρω
    ἐκκαθάρῃ   19.4

ἐκλύω
    ἐκλῦσαι   24.3

*ἐκποιέω
    ἐκποιήσει   8.4

*ἔκπτωσις   -σεις 7.3

ἐκτείνω
    ἐκτετάκασι   16.1,2
    ἐκτείνας 4.2; 30.3   ἐκτετακότες   8.1,[2]

ἐλάττων   v. μικρός

'Ελευθερία   20.3

ἐλεύθερος
    * -ως 21.3

ἕλκω
    -ουσιν 16.4

ἐλλείπω
    ἐλλείψει   14.4

ἐλπίς   ἐλπίδι 20.4   ἐλπίδας   23.4

ἐμβάλλω
    ἐμβέβληκας   4.1

*ἔμπειρος
    * -ρως 39.5

ἔμπροσθεν   1.1; 17.1

*ἐμφαίνω
    -νει 16.5; 18.2; 21.3

*ἔμφασις   -σιν 1.3; 27.1

*ἔμφρων 2.2

ἐν 1.1(ter),2,3; 3.3(bis),4; 4.3(bis); 5.1; 6.3; 10.2,4;
     11.2; 14.1,2,3[bis]; 17.2; 18.2,4; 19.5; 20.4;
     23.4(bis); 24.2; 33.1; 35.1,3[bis]; 38.1

ἐναντίος 36.2; 38.4

*ἐνδιατρίβω
    -τρίβετε 35.5   -τρῖψαι 32.4

*ἔνδον
    adv. 1.3; 20.1
    prep. c. gen. 6.1

*ἐνδοιάζω
    ἐνεδοίαζε 25.2

ἕνεκα 14.4; 34.4; 40.1
    ἕνεκεν 9.4; 19.1

ἐνθάδε 24.3

ἔνθεν 15.3(bis)

ἔνιοι 39.4

ἐνταῦθα 10.4

ἐντεῦθεν 32.3,4

ἐξαιρέω
    -αιρεῖ 11.1 cj.
    ἐξελόμεναι 29.4

ἐξαίρω
    -ρει 11.1 apparatus

ἐξηγέομαι
    ἐξηγήσομαι 30.2
    ἐξήγησαι 36.1
    ἐξηγεῖσθαι 30.1

ἐξήγησις 3.1,2   -σεως 3.2

ἕξις   ἕξιν 20.4; 35.5

*ἐξόλλυμι
    ἐξώλετο 19.3

ἔξω
    prep. c. gen. 9.1; 12.2; 19.1

ἔοικα
  ἐοικυῖα 3.2

ἐπαγγέλλω
  -ονται 6.3; 16.5

ἐπαινέω
  -νεῖν 31.2

ἐπακολουθέω
  -θοῦσιν 28.1

ἐπάνω
  prep. c. gen. 26.3

ἐπεί   37.3(bis); 38.1

*ἐπειδάν 26.1; 34.2

ἐπείπερ 4.1

ἐπί   prep. c. gen. 1.2,3; 3.2; 5.1; 7.1,3; 15.4; 16.1;
       18.1(bis),3; 21.3(bis); 28.3; 30.3; 38.1
      prep. c. dat. 3.3; 31.4(bis)
      prep. c. acc. 6.3; 12.3; 15.1; 16.3,4(bis); 21.2

ἐπιθυμέω
  -μοῦμεν 3.1

ἐπιθυμία   -ίαν 4.1; 19.5
  'Επιθυμία   [-ίαν 11.1]   -ίαι 6.2

*ἐπικατοικέω
  -κεῖ 15.1

*ἐπικίνδυνος 3.1

ἐπιλανθάνομαι
  ἐπελάθοντο 24.3

ἐπιλείπω
  -λίπη 9.4

ἐπιορκέω
  -κεῖν 9.4

ἐπιποθέω
  -ποθῶ 23.1

ἐπισκοπέω
  -πεῖν 35.5

ἐπίσταμαι
  -ταται 39.5   ἠπίστατο 25.2
  -ωνται 39.4
  -τασθαι 35.3

ἐπιστήμη   18.4; 32.2   -μην 25.3
 'Επιστήμη   20.3   -μην 20.1; 29.3

ἐπιτάττω
  ἐπέταττεν   19.3

*ἐπιτίμιον   4.1

ἐπιτυγχάνω
  ἐπιτύχῃ   10.4

*ἐπιχώριος   2.1

*ἔπομαι
  * ἐπομένως   40.1 apparatus

*ἐραστής
  -ταί 13.1

ἔργον   7.2   -ῳ 2.2   -ων 23.3; 40.3; 41.1,2(bis)

ἔρημος   15.1

*ἑρμηνεύς
  -ως 33.6

ἔρχομαι
  ἦλθε   19.4; 24.2
  ἔλθωσι   32.3
  ἐλθεῖν   12.3; 33.4

ἐρωτάω
  -τῶ 36.2

ἐσθίω
  ἤσθιεν   9.3

ἔσω   c. gen. 13.1; 20.2

*ἑταίρα
  ἑταῖραι   9.1

ἕτερος   1.2; 4.3; 6.1; 7.2; 10.4; 11.1; 12.1; 17.2(bis);
    23.4; 24.2(bis); 29.1,2; 31.2; 33.3; 35.4

ἔτι   6.1; 16.3; 20.2; 23.3; 26.1; 27.1; 34.2; 35.2

εὖ   39.5

εὐανθής   21.3

*εὐγένεια   8.4

εὐδαιμονέω
  -νεῖν   40.1

ἔχω
  -ει 3.1,2; 4.1; 5.1; 7.2; 23.4; 31.5; <38.2>
    -ουσι 8.1; 14.4; 20.2; 35.4; 39.3   ἔξουσιν 9.2
  ἔχωσι 35.3
  ἔχειν 18.2; 26.3(bis); 31.5; 33.3; 36.1
  ἔχων 1.2; 4.3; 19.4   -ουσα 1.1; 10.2(bis); 15.3;
    18.1   -οντι 26.1   -οντα 4.1; 9.2   -ουσῶν 6.1

ἕως 9.3; 32.3; 35.3

ζάω
  ζῇ 25.3   ζῶσι 24.2; 28.2   ἔζη 25.3
  ζῇ 36.3
  ζῆν 36.1,3(bis),4; 37.2(quater),3(ter); 38.1(quin-
    quies),2,3; 39.2
  ζῶντα 39.1   ζῶσι 36.4; 37.3; 38.1

Ζεύς
  πρὸς Διός 3.1
  νὴ Δία 14.2,[3]; 16.5; 28.1; 39.1

ζηλόω
  ἐζηλωκώς 2.2

ἤ 5.1,3; 23.1; 24.1; 26.1; 32.5; 33.4; 35.2; 36.2;
    37.2; 38.2; 40.1

ἡγέομαι
  ἡγοῦνται 28.3
  ἡγεῖσθαι 31.1   ἡγήσασθαι 35.5

ἤδη 18.1; 29.2

Ἡδονή   -αί 6.2

*ἡδονικός 13.2

Ἡδυπάθεια 32.3   -θειαν 9.3; 28.1

ἡδύς 9.2,3

ἦθος   ἤθει 5.1

ἥκω   ἥκει 25.1   ἥξουσιν 16.3
  ἥξειν 33.4

ἡλικία   -ίᾳ 18.1

*ἤν = ἐάν 32.1

*Ἡρακλῆς   -εις 4.1; 12.1; 19.1

ἥττων 6.1

θάνατος   -του 26.3

θαρρέω
   -ρεῖτε 30.2
   -ρεῖν 16.3; 30.2

θάρσος   16.5; 18.4

θαυμάζω
   ἐθαύμασα 2.3
   θαυμάζειν 31.3

θέμα   -ματα 31.4

*θέμις   29.3

θεραπεύω
   -πεύει 19.4
   -πεύῃ 19.1

θεωρέω
   -ρεῖ 25.3   ἐθεωροῦμεν   1.1
   -ρήσῃ 26.1
   -ρησον 38.2
   -ρεῖν 39.1

θηρίον   -ρία 22.2; 23.1(bis); 26.2,3

θρίξ   τρίχας   10.2

θρόνος   -νου 21.3   -νον 5.1

θυγάτηρ   -τέρες 18.2

θυμός   -μόν 19.5

θύρα   -ρας 15.2   -ραν 15.2

*θύριον   10.1

ἰατρός   19.2   -τρόν 19.2; 26.1

ἴδιος   1.1; 31.1,4

ἱερόν   2.2   ἱερῷ 1.1

ἱεροσυλέω
   -λεῖν 9.4

ἱκανός
   -νῶς 41.4

ἱλαρός   29.1

ἵνα 33.3

ἴσος   31.2

ἵστημι
 ἕστηκε   7.3; 12.2; 18.1,3; 19.1   -κασιν 9.2
 ἑστηκώς   4.3; 8.1   -κυῖα 7.1   -κυίας 9.1; 16.1
  ἑστώς   1.3
 ἑστάναι   30.3

ἰσχύς   -ύν 16.5

καθαίρω
 καθαρθῇ   20.1   -θῶσι 14.4; 19.1
 καθαρθείς   11.2

καθάπερ   3.3; 20.2; 22.2; 26.1,3

*καθάριος   12.2

καθαρός   16.5

*καθαρτικός   14.3; 19.1,2

κάθημαι
 -ηται 5.1; 21.3

καθίστημι
 κατέστησεν   19.2
 καταστήσειν   16.5
 καθεστηκυῖα   18.1; 21.3

καί   1.1(quater),2,3[bis]; 2.2(quater),3(quater); 3.1
 (quinquies),2,4(ter); 4.1,2(bis),3; 5.1,3; 6.2(ter),
 3(quinquies); 7.1(quater),2(quinquies),3; 8.1,2
 (bis),[2],4(septies); 9.1(bis),2(quinquies),3,
 4(quinquies); 10.1(quinquies),<1>,2,3(quater),
 4(bis); 11.1(bis),[1],2(bis); 12.2(ter),3; 13.1,2;
 14.[1],2(quater),3(quinquies),4(quater); 15.2(quinquies),3(quater),4(quater); 16.1(bis),3,4,5(septies)
 17.1(quater),2,3; 18.1(ter),2,3(bis),4(bis); 19.1,
 2,4(ter),5(septies); 20.1,2(quater),4; 21.3(bis);
 22.1(bis),2(quinquies); 23.1(bis),2(quinquies),3,
 4(bis); 24.2(quinquies),3; 25.2(ter),3(bis); 26.1,
 3(bis); 27.1(quater),2,3(ter),4(quater); 28.1,
 2(quinquies),3; 29.1,2(bis),4; 30.2(bis),3(bis);
 31.1,2(quater),3,4(ter),5(quater),6(bis); 32.2(ter),
 3(quinquies),4; 33.3(bis),5,6(bis); 34.2(ter),
 3(sexies); 35.2(bis),4(ter),5(ter); 36.1,2,4(bis);
 37.1(quinquies),2; 38.1(quinquies),2,4(bis);
 39.1(bis),5; 40.1(quinquies),[1],3(septies); 41.2,
 3(ter)

καίω
 καίειν   38.1

κακία   14.3   -ίας 34.2; 41.3   -ίαν 14.4
  Κακία   -ίας 35.2   -ίαν 23.2

*κακοδαιμονία   -ίᾳ 10.4
  Κακοδαιμονία   -ίαν 10.4

*κακοδαίμων   3.1; 28.2

κακοπάθεια   -ειαν 9.2

κακοποιέω
  -οῦντα 26.3

κακός   3.3(bis); 8.2; 11.1; 14.4(bis); 16.5; 19.4;
     25.2(bis); 28.1; 31.3; 32.5; 34.2; 36.2,3(bis),
     4(bis); 37.1,2(ter),3(quinquies); 38.1(bis),3;
     40.1,2,3; 41.1(bis),2,3(bis)
  Κακός   24.2; 26.2
  κακῶς   3.1; 24.2; 25.3(bis); 27.3; 28.2(bis); 32.5;
     36.3,4; 37.2(bis),3; 38.1(bis),2; 39.1,5

καλέω
  καλοῦσι   8.2(bis); 12.3   -εῖται 4.2,3; 5.2; 7.1; 9.1;
     10.2,3; 16.2; 17.2; 20.3; 30.3   -οῦνται 6.2;
     8.1(bis); 13.1; 16.1; 20.3; 29.1; 32.3
  καλουμένην   11.1

καλλωπίζω
  κεκαλλωπισμέναι   20.2

*καλλωπισμός   -μόν 18.1 apparatus

Καλοκάγαθία   20.3

καλός   16.3,5; 17.1,3; 18.1; 19.1; 20.4; 21.3; 23.3(bis);
     24.1; 41.2
  καλῶς   7.2; 25.3; 26.1; 27.1; 30.1,2; 33.2; 36.4;
     37.3; 38.1,2(bis); 39.2,5

κάμνω
  -νων 19.2

καρτερέω
  -ρῆσαι 16.3

*Καρτερία   16.2   -ίαν 27.3

κατά   prep. c. acc. 3.3; 5.1(bis)

*καταβιβρώσκω
  καταβρωθείς 3.3

*κατακρατέω
  κατακεκρατημένοι 24.2

καταλάμπω
 -πόμενος 17.1

κατανοέω
 -νοεῖς 17.2

καταστρέφω
 -φει 10.4

καταφθείρω
 -θείρεται 3.3

κατεσθίω
 κατήσθιε 22.2   κατησθίετο 9.3

κατέχω
 -ονται 27.2
 -ειν 34.3
 -μενοι 34.2

Κέβης   -βητος titulum

κεῖμαι
 -μένου 18.1   -μενον 5.1

κελεύω
 -ει 5.1; 31.1,2,3,5,6; 32.3(bis),4; 33.2   -ουσιν 16.4

Κενοδοξία   -ίας 24.2

κεφάλαιον   -ου 28.3

κεφαλή   -λήν 10.2   -λάς 27.1

κίνδυνος 12.1

κλαίω
 -ουσι 8.3
 -ειν 8.2

*κνήμη   -μας 27.1

κολάζω
 ἐκόλαζε 22.2

Κολακεία 9.1

κολακεύω
 -ουσι 9.2

κομίζω
 -σασθαι 31.4

κοσμέω
 κεκοσμημένη 21.3   κεκοσμημένας 9.1

λιπαρός   16.1

λογισμός   -μοῦ 31.2

λόγος   38.4   -γου 35.1; 39.3; 41.1   -γῳ 2.2

λοιπός   10.4; 14.3,4; 19.5; 23.2; 41.3

λυπέω
    -πεῖ 26.3(bis)
    -ποῦντων 26.3

λύπη   -πης 27.1
    Λύπη   10.2   -πης 26.2   -πην 23.2   -παι 27.4

*λυσιτελής   6.3

μάθημα   -μάτων 14.4; 33.3,6; 34.4   -ματα 34.3

μαθηματικός   34.1; 35.2

μαίνω
    -νομένη 7.1(bis)

μακάριος   3.4; 11.2; 23.4

*μάλα
    καὶ μάλα 9.1; 10.<1>,2; 12.2(bis); 15.2; 17.1
    καὶ μάλα γέ 15.4
    ὡς μάλιστα 20.4

μάστιξ   -τιγα 10.2

μέγας   3.1; 4.1; 7.3; 12.1; 15.4; 20.4
    μείζων 1.2
    μέγιστος 22.1,2(bis); 28.3

μέθυσος   34.3

μείζων   v. μέγας

μέλλω
    -λει 33.4   -λουσι 4.3; 34.2   -λοντες 4.2

μέν   9.3
    μέν...δέ 1.1; 7.1,2; 8.1,4; 33.1,4; 34.3
    μέν...ἀλλά 37.2; cf. also 30.1
    ἐὰν μέν...ἐὰν δέ 3.3
    ἐὰν μέν...εἰ δὲ μή 11.2
    εἰ μέν...εἰ δὲ μή 3.1,2; 39.5
    ὁ μέν...ἡ δέ 10.3
        τὸν μέν...τὸν δέ 1.2
        ἡ μέν...αὐτὸς δέ 3.4
        ἡ μέν...ἡ δέ 9.1; 10.2; 16.2; 18.2

ἢ μέν...αἱ δέ   20.3
οἱ μέν   12.3
οἱ μέν...οἱ δέ   6.1; 8.1,2,3; 13.2; 24.2; 27.1,2,3;
    <35.3>
τοῖς μέν...τοῖς δέ   36.4
αἱ μέν...αἱ δέ   6.2
ὅταν μέν...ὅταν δέ   31.4
πρῶτον μέν...εἶτα   23.1
τοῦτο μέν   37.1
ταῦτα μέν   19.3; 30.1

μέντοι   33.4
    μέντοι γέ   33.6

μένω
    -νει   14.3(bis)
    -νειν   9.2
    -νοντες   14.4

μέσος   17.2; 18.1,2

μετά   prep. c. gen. 10.3,4; 13.1; 14.[1],3; 18.2; 26.1;
    27.4; 31.2; 41.3
    prep. c. acc. 16.5

*Μεταμέλεια   35.4

Μετάνοια   10.4; 11.1

μέχρι   prep. c. gen. 9.3; 26.3
    conj. 14.3; 35.5

μή   3.1(bis),2,3,4; 10.4; 11.2; 14.3; 16.3; 19.3; 24.3;
    25.2(bis); 26.2(bis); 31.1,3; 32.3; 33.3; 35.4,
    5(bis); 37.1; 39.4,5; 41.1

μηδέ   31.1(bis),3; 32.3

μηδείς   18.4; 31.1; 32.3; 35.3; 41.1

μηνύω
    -ει   7.2

μήτε   31.2(quater)

μήτηρ
    -τέρα   21.1

μικρός   3.3; 10.1; 15.2; 16.5
    ἐλάττων   1.2

μνημονεύω
    -ειν   31.5
    -οντες   31.4

μόνος   7.1; 31.5; 40.1; 41.3

μορφή   -φήν 8.1   -φάς 6.1

μουσικός   13.2

*μοχθηρός   40.3

*μυθολογία   2.1   -γίας 2.1,3   -γίαν 8.4

μῦθος   3.1; 33.1   -θους 1.1

ναυαγέω
   -γοῦσιν 24.2

ναῦς   νῆες 29.4

νεανίσκος   -νίσκε 23.4

νέος   2.3; 33.3

*νεώς   νεώ 1.1

νή
   νὴ Δία   14.2,[3]; 16.5; 28.1; 39.1

νικάω
   νενίκηκε   22.1,2
   νικᾶν   36.1; 41.3
   νενικηκότας   22.1

νίκη   -ης 23.3

*νίκημα   24.1

νομίζω
   -ζουσιν 31.4   ἐνόμιζεν 25.2
   -ζειν 31.1

*νοσερός   38.1

νοσέω
   -σεῖν 38.4

*νοσοποιέω
   -οῦντα 19.2

νόσος   -σου 19.3

νῦν   22.2; 35.5
   νῦν δέ   8.4; 25.3

ξένος   1.1; 2.1,2; 3.1; 33.1; 35.5

ὁ, ἡ, τό   passim

ὅδε
    τάδε   3.3

ὁδός   6.3; 12.3; 15.1,3; 18.3   ὁδόν   4.3; 5.1; 14.3;
       15.2; 16.3,4,5; 21.2; 24.3

'Οδύνη   10.2   -νης 26.2   -ναι 27.4

'Οδυρμός   10.3   -μόν 23.2

ὅθεν   24.2; 25.1

οἶδα
    οἴδασι   2.1; 35.3   ᾔδει 25.2
    εἰδέναι   4.2; 33.6; 34.3

οἰκητήριον   17.3

οἶκος   -κον 10.4

οἴομαι
    -ονται 31.4
    -ωνται 40.1
    -όμενοι 13.1

οἶος
    οἶον   3.1; 9.4; 36.1; 40.3

ὀλίγος   15.2

ὅλος   3.3

ὁμαλός   16.5

ὅμοιος   8.1; 10.3; 14.1; 31.3
    -ως 34.3; 35.4

ὅμως   33.5,6

ὀπίσω   10.1

*ὅποι   6.3

ὁπόταν   12.3

ὅπου   15.1; 26.1

ὅπως   19.1,4; 29.2

ὁράω
    ὁρῶ   5.2; 6.1; 7.1; 15.1,3,4; 16.1,4; 20.3; 21.2
        ὁρᾷς   5.1; 6.1,3; 9.1; 10.1; 12.1; 15.1,4; 16.1,5;
        17.1; 18.1; 20.2; 21.2; 35.4   ὁρῶμεν   4.2; 30.3
        ὁρᾶτε   4.2; 30.3   ἑωρᾶτο   1.3   ἑωρακώς   2.3
    v. εἶδον

ὀρθός
   -ῶς 25.1

ὁρμάω
   -μᾶν 35.3

ὅς   2.2; 17.1   ἥ 5.1; 12.2; 30.3   ὅ (nom./acc.) 3.2;
      14.3; 21.2; 35.3; 39.4   οὗ 5.1   ᾧ 1.1(bis); 23.3;
      31.4; 37.2   ὃν 5.1; 6.3; 19.5; 25.2   ἥν 30.3;
      32.1; 35.4   οἵ 28.2; 35.2   ἃ (nom./acc.) 7.2;
      8.1,2,3(bis); 18.4; 22.2; 31.5(bis),6; 32.5; 33.2,3
      ὧν 7.2; 8.2; 19.5; 20.4; 24.3; 35.5; 36.2
      αἷς 14.1   οἷς 19.3; 24.3   οὓς 1.1; 29.2
      ἃς 26.2; 32.3

ὅσος   -σοι 13.2   -σα 8.4; 9.4(ter); 14.4; 19.4;
      36.1(bis); 41.3

ὅσπερ
   ὅπερ 37.3

ὅστις 32.5   ἥτις 15.2   ὅ τι 31.1,3; 32.4

ὅταν   6.2; 7.3; 9.3,4(bis); 14.4; 16.4; 19.1,4; 20.1;
      21.1; 22.1; 24.1; 28.1; 29.4; 31.2(bis),4(bis);
      32.3; 38.4; 39.4

ὅτε   35.2

ὅτι   3.1(bis); 4.2; 7.3; 8.3; 9.2,3; 16.3; 18.1,3; 29.2;
      30.3; 31.4,5; 32.3; 35.1,3,4(bis); 36.4; 40.1,2

οὗ   26.1

οὐ   (οὐκ, οὐχ, οὐχί) 1.1; 3.3; 4.1(bis); 5.3; 6.1,3;
      7.1,3; 8.1,4; 9.3; 12.1,3(bis),<3>; 14.2,3; 15.2;
      18.1; 19.2; 20.2; 23.1,2,4; 24.3; 25.2; 26.2,3;
      27.3; 28.2(bis); 29.3,<3>,[3]; 31.4,5; 33.4,5,6;
      35.3,4(bis),5; 36.1,2,3; 37.2(ter),3; 38.1(bis),4;
      39.2,3(bis),4; 40.1,2; 41.2,3

οὐδαμῶς   20.2; 35.1; 39.5

οὐδέ   7.3; 14.4; 25.2; 34.1; 37.2; 38.1,3; 39.3,4;
      41.2(quater)
   οὐδὲ γάρ   2.1,2

οὐδείς   3.1; 15.1; 33.1
   οὐδεμία 33.4   -αν 9.2; 16.4
   οὐδέν (nom./acc.) 2.1; 14.4; 25.2; 26.2(bis),3; 30.2;
      31.2,3,4; 33.4,5,6; 34.3; 35.4,5; 39.2; 41.3

οὐδέποτε   14.4

οὐδέπω   30.1

οὐκέτι   9.3; 26.2,3

οὐκοῦν   12.2; 18.1; 21.3; 37.2; 38.3,4; 39.2,3,5
   οὐκοῦν καί   10.1; 15.2,3,4
   οὐκοῦν οὕτω καί   38.1

οὖν   2.1,3; 3.3,4; 4.2; 5.1(bis),3; 6.2; 7.2; 8.1,3(bis),
   4; 9.1,2,3,4; 10.4; 12.3; 13.1; 14.2(bis); 15.1;
   16.1,2,4; 17.1,2; 20.1; 21.1; 22.1; 26.1,2; 29.3;
   30.3; 31.2,3; 32.1,3,4; 33.2; 34.1,4; 36.3(bis);
   37.1; 39.4
   μὲν οὖν   3.2

οὔτε   1.2(bis); 3.3(bis); 14.3(bis); 26.2(sexies);
   38.1(bis); 41.3

οὗτος   4.2,3; 8.1; 10.3; 12.1; 17.2; 22.2   αὕτη 2.1;
   5.2(bis); 7.2; 10.1,3; 15.1,3; 18.3,4; 21.1(bis),3;
   31.3; 32.1   τοῦτο (nom./acc.) 2.2; 4.2; 5.3(bis);
   7.3(bis); 19.2; 24.3; 25.1; 27.1; 31.2,3; 35.2,3;
   36.1,3; 37.1; 39.4,5; 40.1
   τούτου   35.1; 39.3; 41.1   ταύτης   2.1,3; 3.2; 18.2;
   20.3
   τούτῳ   22.2; 31.4; 36.3   ταύτῃ   23.4; 31.1
   τοῦτον   4.2; 26.3; 39.1   ταύτην   9.1; 11.2; 12.3;
   31.2; 32.1,3; 35.3   τουτί   3.1
   οὗτοι   4.2; 8.1,2(bis); 13.1(bis); 27.1; 28.1; 34.1,4;
   35.4   αὗται 6.2(bis); 9.1,2; 10.2; 16.1,4; 20.3;
   21.1; 27.4; 29.3,4   ταῦτα (nom./acc.) 3.3; 4.1;
   8.3(bis),4; 18.4; 19.3,4; 22.2; 23.1(bis); 30.1;
   31.2; 32.5; 33.2(bis),4(bis),5; 38.2,3; 40.1,2,3;
   41.3
   τούτων   8.4; 9.4; 10.4; 14.3,4; 18.2; 23.2; 33.1,5,6;
   34.4; 40.1(bis)
   τούτοις   8.4; 9.4; 10.4; 13.2; 14.3[bis]; 35.4; 36.1;
   39.2; 41.3   ταύταις 9.4; 32.3
   τούτους   7.1; 19.1; 25.3; 35.2   ταύτας 20.1

οὕτω(ς)   4.1(bis); 8.3,4; 14.4; 16.2; 17.2; 18.2; 19.1
   (bis),2; 21.3; 26.3; 33.6; 35.5(bis); 38.1,2;
   39.1,3; 41.1

ὄφελος   35.5

ὀχλέω
   -λεῖται 15.2

ὄχλος   1.2; 4.2; 5.1; 6.2; 8.1   -λῳ 1.3

παιδεία
   -αν 35.4
   Παιδεία   18.2; 29.4; 39.3   -ας 13.1; 27.3; 32.1
      -ᾳ 29.3   -αν 11.1,2; 12.3(ter); 15.1,3; 16.5;
   19.4; 27.2; 28.2; 29.2; 32.4; 33.4; 35.1,2,3

πάλαι   2.2

πάλιν   7.2; 8.2; 10.4; 11.2; 25.1; 27.3; 29.4(bis);
        30.3; 31.2,4,5; 36.2

πανταχοῦ   7.2; 26.1(bis)

*παντοδαπός   6.1

πάνυ   3.1; 12.2; 15.2,3; 21.3; 23.1; 36.2

παρά   prep. c. gen. 6.3; 7.2(bis),3; 8.2(bis); 9.2,4;
        14.3; 19.5; 24.3; 31.1,2,4,5,6; 32.1,4; 33.2; 36.1
     prep. c. dat. 8.3; 9.2; 14.4; 28.2(bis)
     prep. c. acc. 4.2; 5.1; 12.2; 18.1; 32.5

παραγίνομαι
     -νονται 12.3
     -γένηται 19.4; 22.1   -γένωνται 16.4; 28.1
     -γίνεσθαι 27.1
     -γινόμεναι 29.1   -μένους 16.3; 19.1; 35.2

παραδίδωμι
     -διδάσιν 29.3   -δίδοται 10.4   -δίδονται 9.4
     -διδόμενοι 3.3

παράδοξος   36.2

παραιτέομαι
     -τοῦνται   40.1

παρακαλέω
     -οῦσιν 16.3

παρακούω
     -ει 32.5   -ετε 3.4

παραλαμβάνω
     -λάβῃ 29.4   -λάβωσιν 21.1

παραλείπω
     -λείψω 30.2

παραλλάττω
     -τουσιν 35.2

παραπλήσιος   8.4; 9.4; 13.2; 36.1; 41.3

παρατηρέω
     -ροῦσιν 9.2

παραχρῆμα   7.2

*πάρεργος   35.5
     * -γως 4.1

παρέρχομαι
    -έλθῃς 9.1

παρίστημι
    παρεστηκώς 10.3   -εστώς 2.1

*Παρμενίδειος 2.2

πᾶς 3.4; 5.2,3; 6.1,3; 9.4(quinquies); 10.4; 14.4(bis);
    16.5; 17.3; 19.4,5; 21.2; 22.1,2; 23.2; 24.3;
    26.1(quater),3(bis); 28.1(bis); 30.2; 31.3;
    34.2,3; 40.1

πάσχω
    -χετε 2.1   -χουσι 24.3; 40.2
    πάθῃ 26.2
    παθεῖν 18.4   πεπονθέναι 31.4
    πάσχοντες 26.1

πείθω
    ἐπείθετο 19.3
    πεισθῇ 9.3   -θῶσιν 35.4

Πειθώ 18.2

πειράω
    -ῶ 36.2

*Πενία   -ας 26.2

πέρας 34.3

περί prep. c. gen. 2.1(bis),3; 8.4; 33.1; 34.2; 35.5;
    36.2; 38.4; 39.1
    prep. c. acc. 2.2; 8.1,4

περιάγω
    -ονται 6.3

*περίβολος 1.2   -λου 1.2,[3]; 9.1; 12.2; 13.1; 19.1;
    35.2,4   -λῳ 1.3; 14.2; 19.5; 35.1,3[bis]
    -λον 4.2; 9.1; 12.1; 17.2; 28.1; 35.2   -λων 21.2
    -λους 1.2

περιπατέω
    -τοῦντες 1.1

*περιπατητικός 13.2

περιποιέω
    -ποιήσησθε 20.4

*περιπορεύομαι
    -εται 7.2

περισπάω
  -σπῶνται 33.3

*περίστασις 38.4

περιτρέχω
  -ειν 14.1

πέτρα   -ας 16.1   -αν 15.4; 16.4

πετρώδης 15.2

*πιθανός 5.1

πικρός 3.1

πίναξ titulum ; 1.1   πίνακι 33.1

πίνω
  -ουσι 5.3; 6.1   ἔπιον 14.3   πεπώκασι 6.3
    ἐπεπώκει 19.5; 25.2
  πίωσι 14.3
  πιόντες 5.3

πιστεύω
  -εύσῃ 7.3
  -ειν 31.1; 32.3

πλανάω
  -νᾶται 11.2   -νῶνται 6.3; 24.2; 27.3
  -νῶσα 5.2

πλάνος 5.3   -νον 5.3; 6.3; 19.5; 25.2
  Πλάνος   -νον 23.1

πλάττω
  πεπλασμένη 5.1

*Πλάτων 33.3

πλέκω
  -κονται 6.2

πλῆθος 1.3; 6.1

πλουτέω
  -τεῖν 36.1; 39.1,4

πλοῦτος 8.4; 39.2,3(bis); 41.1   -τῳ 39.4,5   -τον 39.1;
    40.3; 41.1,3

ποῦ 24.1

πράττω
   -τει 5.2   πράσσουσιν 25.3
   -τη 31.3
   -τειν 40.1

πρεσβύτης 2.1

πρό 15.2

*προαίρεσις -σεως 10.4

προβάλλω
   προεβάλλετο 3.2

προδίδωμι
   -διδόναι 9.4; 40.3

προδότης -την 34.3

προέχω
   -ουσιν 34.1,4; 35.2
   -ειν 34.2

πρόθυμος
   -μως 16.1,2

*προπύλαιος -ου 21.3

πρός prep. c. gen. 3.1
   prep. c. dat. 1.2
   prep. c. acc. 2.1; 4.2; 6.2; 15.3; 16.4,5; 18.3;
     19.1,2,4; 20.1(bis); 21.1; 24.2; 27.2,3; 28.1;
     29.2(bis),3(bis); 31.2,5,6; 32.3(ter),4; 33.4(ter),
     5; 34.1; 35.1,2,3(bis),4

προσδέχομαι
   -δέξηται 11.2

προσέχω
   -έξομεν 20.4   -έξετε 3.1
   -ετε 3.4
   -εξόντων 4.1

*προσκαταβαίνω
   -νουσι 16.4

*προσοράω
   -ιδεῖν 15.4

προσποιέω
   -οῦνται 35.3

*προσπυνθάνομαι
   -πυθέσθαι 33.1

πρόσταγμα   24.3

προστάττω
   -τει 4.3; 30.1; 32.5
   -των 1.3

πρόσωπον   18.1

πρότερος 6.3; 8.2; 19.2; 22.2(bis); 23.2; 25.1; 26.3;
      31.3; 32.3

προϋπάρχω
   -χοντα 31.5

πρῶτος 1.2,[3]; 3.1; 4.2; 12.3; 14.1,2; 19.4,5; 20.3;
      23.1; 24.2; 28.1; 35.2,3,4

*Πυθαγόρειος   2.2

πύλη 1.2   -λης 6.1; 20.2   -λη 1.2   -λην 4.2; 5.1;
      9.1; 17.2; 18.1

πυλών   -λῶνος 1.3

πῶς 5.1; 8.1,4; 16.4; 19.2; 34.2,4; 35.2,3; 36.1,2,3;
      37.2; 38.1; 39.4

ῥάβδος   -δον 4.2

ῥάκος   -κη 10.1

ῥήτωρ   -τορες 13.2

ῥίπτω
   -τει 8.1   -τεται 10.4

ῥυπαρός   10.1

σημαίνω
   -νει 7.3

σημεῖον   7.2; 18.3

*σκέπτομαι
   σκεψώμεθα 39.1

σκληρός   7.3

σκοτεινός   10.1

σοφία   -αν 2.2

*σπάνιος
   * -ως 14.2

σπουδαῖος   2.3; 39.3

στενός   10.1; 15.3

στέφανος   -νου 23.3   -νῳ 21.3

στεφανόω
    -νοῖ 22.1
    στεφανωθῇ   24.1
    στεφανοῦν   23.3
    ἐστεφανωμένη   21.3   ἐστεφανωμένοι   27.1,2
        στεφανωθείς   23.4

στολή   -λήν 18.1; 20.2

στρατόπεδον   1.2

στρογγύλος   7.1,3; 18.1; 30.3

σύ
    σοί   3.1; 23.1; 37.2   σέ   36.2
    ὑμεῖς   3.4; 30.2; 35.5   ὑμῖν   30.3; 31.3; 33.1; 35.5
        ὑμᾶς   3.1; 4.2

συκοφαντέω
    -τεῖν 40.3

συμβαίνω
    -νει 38.1; 41.1

συμβάλλω
    -λομεν 33.6   -λεται 33.4
    συμβαλεῖν 1.1

*συμβιόω
    -βιοῖ 10.4

*συμπλέκω
    -κονται 9.2

συμφέρω
    -ρει 38.4; 39.4(bis)
    -ρόντων 25.3; 32.2

συναντάω
    -τήσῃ 11.1
    -τήσασα 10.4

σύνειμι
    συνῇ 35.4
    συνεῖναι 10.1

συνίημι
    -ίημι 19.2,3   -ίει 3.2(bis)   συνήσεις 19.2
        -ήσετε 3.1   -ήκαμεν 33.6
    συνιῇ 3.3   συνῆτε 20.4

συνίστημι
    -τησιν 11.1

*σύνολος 40.1

συνομιλέω
    -λεῖν 13.1

σύντομος
    -μως 31.6; 32.3(bis),4   -μωτέρως 33.4

*Σφίγξ 3.2   Σφιγγός 3.2(bis),3

σῴζω
    -εται 3.4; 11.2   ἐσώζετο 3.2   σωθήσεσθε 20.4
       -ονται 14.4
    σωθεῖεν 35.5
    σῴζεσθαι 4.3; 6.2   σωθῆναι 24.3
    σῳζόμενοι 12.3   σεσωσμένοι 27.2

σῶμα   -ματι 16.1

Σωφροσύνη 20.3

ταλαίπωρος 28.2

ταράττω
    -τονται 24.3
    -τον 40.1

ταραχή   -χῆς 27.1

ταχύς
    -έως 31.5

τέ
    τε καί 2.2; 9.2; 16.5; 18.1,3; 29.1
    τε...καί 2.2; 17.1; 20.2; 22.1; 25.3

τέκνον   -να 8.4; 36.1

*τέμνω
    -νειν 38.1(bis)

τετράγωνος 18.1,3

τίθημι
    θέμενον 31.4

τίλλω
    -λουσα 10.2

τιμάω
    -μῶσιν 40.1
    -μᾶν 40.1

τιμωρέω
    -ρούμενος 10.4

τιμωρία
    -ρίᾳ 3.3
    Τιμωρία 10.2   -ρίᾳ 9.4

τίς   5.2; 7.1; 10.3; 17.2; 21.1; 23.3; 32.1   τί (nom./
        acc.) 2.1; 3.1(bis),3(ter); 4.3; 5.2,3(bis); 7.2,3;
        8.1; 9.2(bis); 11.1,2; 16.2; 18.3; 22.1; 24.1;
        25.1; 26.1; 30.1; 33.2; 35.1,2   τίνος 19.1
        τίνες 1.1; 8.1; 13.1(bis); 14.1; 16.1; 20.3;
        27.1,4; 29.1   τίνα 8.3(bis); 18.4(bis); 33.2

τις   1.1(bis),3; 2.1,2; 3.1,2,3,4; 7.1,3; 9.3; 10.3(bis);
        12.2; 15.3; 18.1; 19.2,4; 21.3; 22.1; 28.3; 30.3;
        31.1; 33.4; 36.3; 39.4,5   τι (nom./acc.) 1.3(bis);
        3.1; 4.3; 5.1; 6.1; 8.2; 9.2; 10.1; 26.2; 32.5;
        33.1,6; 37.2(bis)   τινός 7.1; 9.3; 15.2; 27.1;
        33.3   τινί 39.1; 41.3   τινά 2.2; 4.1,2,3; 5.1;
        10.1; 15.1,2(bis),4; 17.1; 32.4   τινές 18.2
        τινῶν 27.2; 29.4

τοί   12.3

τοιγαροῦν 20.4

τοίνυν   3.1; 4.1; 6.2; 9.1; 10.2; 12.3; 15.3; 18.2;
        19.4; 21.3; 31.5; 32.5; 35.5; 36.2; 37.3; 38.1,2;
        41.1

τοιοῦτος   4.1; 31.5; 33.1; 34.4; 38.4

τόπος   4.2; 17.2   -πον 5.1; 10.1; 15.1; 16.3; 17.1,3;
        24.2; 25.1

τότε   2.3; 14.4; 29.2

τραπεζίτης   -ταις 31.3

τραχύς   15.2

*τρίβω
    τετρῖφθαι   27.1

τρίτος   35.2

τρόπος
    τρόπον (used adverbially) 19.4; 28.3

τυγχάνω
    -νει 3.1   ἐτύγχανε 19.2   ἐτυγχάνομεν 1.1
        ἔτυχε 31.3
    τύχῃ 6.3
    τετυχηκότες 27.2

τυραννίς
    -νίδες 8.4

τυφλός   7.1(bis); 30.3

Τύχη   7.1; 30.3; 31.5   -χης 9.2,4; 36.1   -χην 8.2(bis)

ὑβρίζω
    -ζετο 9.3

ὑγεία   -αν 19.2

ὑγιαίνω
    -νειν 36.1; 38.4(bis)

*ὑγιεινός   38.1

ὑπάρχω
    -χει 37.2(ter)   ὑπῆρχεν 37.3(bis)
    -χη 37.2
    -χειν 39.4; 41.2,3
    -χοντα 7.2; 39.1

ὑπερηφάνεια   -αν 23.2 apparatus

ὑπό   prep. c. gen. 3.2,3(bis); 9.3(bis); 11.2(bis); 19.3;
      24.2(sexies); 26.2(septies); 27.2,3; 34.2

ὑποδέχομαι
    -δέξονται 26.1

ὑπολαμβάνω
    -λαβοῦσαι 24.2

ὑπομένω
    -ουσι 40.1 cj.
    -ειν 9.4

ὑψηλός   15.3,4; 21.2,3

φαίνω
    -νεται 35.1; 37.2; 39.2,3
    -νωνται 34.2
    -νομένη 5.1   -νόμενον 36.2

φαῦλος   39.2

φέρω
    -ουσα 15.1   -ουσαν 16.4; 21.2

φεύγω
    -γειν 32.3

*φευκτός   37.1

φημί
    φησί   5.2; 11.2; 33.3   ἔφην   2.3; 3.1(bis); 5.1,2;
        7.1,3; 12.1,2; 14.2; 15.[1],2,4; 16.1; 17.3; 19.1,
        2,3; 20.3,4(bis); 22.1; 23.1,3; 29.3; 30.1,2;
        32.1; 33.2,5; 35.1,3; 36.3(bis); 41.4   ἔφης 14.1;
        23.3; 26.2   ἔφη 2.1,3; 3.1(bis); 4.1,2; 5.3;
        6.1,2,3; 7.1,2; 8.2,3,4; 9.2; 10.1,2,3; 12.3(bis);
        13.1,2; 14.1; 15.1,3; 16.2,3; 17.1,3; 18.1,3,4(bis);
        19.1,2,4; 20.1,2,3,4(bis); 21.1(bis),3; 22.1,2;
        23.1; 25.2; 26.1; 27.4; 28.1; 29.2,[3]; 30.2,3;
        31.1; 32.2; 33.3,4; 34.4; 35.2,5; 36.2,3; 37.2

φθάνω
    -νοις 4.1

φθόνος   3.1; 33.1

φιλαργυρία   -αν 19.5
    Φιλαργυρία   -ας 24.2; 26.2   -αν 23.2

φιλάργυρος   34.3

*φιλότιμος   19.2 apparatus
    * -μως 19.2

φοβέομαι
    φοβεῖται   26.2

φορτίον   -ία 29.4

φράζω
    -σω 33.1

φρονέω
    -νεῖν 41.2,3

φρόνιμος   3.1

φύσις   -σιν 7.2; 31.5

φωνή   -νήν 33.6

φῶς   φωτί 17.1

χαίρω
    -ρουσι 8.3; 31.4
    -ρειν 8.1,2; 31.2

χαλεπός   6.2; 15.4

χαλινός   -νοῦ 33.3

χάρτης   -την 4.3

χείρ   -ρα 30.3   -ρί 4.3; 5.1   -ρας 8.1; 16.1,2

χορός   -ρόν 20.2

χράομαι
   χρῆσθαι   39.4,5

χρήσιμος   33.4,5

χρόνος   -νον 2.1; 32.4

*ψέγω
   -γειν 31.2

*Ψευδοδοξία   -ας 11.2

*ψευδοπαιδεία   -αν 35.4
   Ψευδοπαιδεία   12.1,3   -ας 13.1; 14.3; 33.2   -ᾳ 14.4
   -αν 11.1; 32.3

ὦ   2.1; 3.1; 4.1; 6.2; 12.1; 19.1; 20.4; 23.3,4; 33.1;
    35.5

ὧδε   9.2; 10.4; 12.3; 14.2(bis),4; 17.3; 22.1; 24.3

ὡς   1.3; 4.1(bis),3; 6.2,3(bis); 9.1; 12.1; 16.1,5;
    17.3; 19.1,2; 20.2(bis),4(bis); 24.1,2(bis);
    25.3; 28.2,3; 31.1,3; 33.6; 39.1; 40.1(bis)

*ὡσανεί   33.3

ὡσαύτως   3.2; 31.5; 41.2

ὥσπερ   3.3; 4.3; 6.3; 7.1; 9.1; 10.1; 14.2; 15.2; 16.5;
    22.1; 23.2; 24.2; 25.3; 26.1; 29.4; 31.3; 32.4;
    34.2; 35.1; 38.1; 41.1

ὥστε   22.2; 24.3; 31.5; 35.2,4; 41.3

ὠφελέω
   -λεῖ   35.2

ὠφέλιμος   37.1